Volozhin; the Book of the City and of the Etz Chaim Yeshiva

(Valozhyn, Belarus)

Translation of
Wolozyn; sefer shel ha-ir-shel yeshivat "Etz Chaim"

Original Book Edited by: E. Leoni

Originally published in Tel Aviv 1970

Volume II

A Publication of JewishGen
Edmond J. Safra Plaza, 36 Battery Place, New York, NY 10280
646.494.2972 | info@JewishGen.org | www.jewishgen.org

©JewishGen 2024. All Rights Reserved.
JewishGen is the Genealogical Research Division of the
Museum of Jewish Heritage – A Living Memorial to the Holocaust

Volohzin; the Book of the City and of the Etz Chaim Yeshiva Volume II

Translation of *Wolozyn; sefer shel ha-ir-shel yeshivat "Etz Chaim"*

Copyright © 2024 by JewishGen. All rights reserved.
First Printing: November 2024, Cheshvan, 5785
Editor of Original Yizkor Book: E. Leoni
Project Coordinator: Anita Frishman-Gabbay
Emeritus Coordinator: Moshe Porat (Perlman) z"l
Cover Design: Rachel Kolokoff Hopper
Translator: Jerrold Landau
Layout and Formatting: Jonathan Wind
Name Indexing: Stefanie Holzman

This book may not be reproduced, in whole or in part, including illustrations in any form (beyond that copying permitted by Sections 107 and 108 of the U.S. Copyright Law and except by reviewers for public press), without written permission from the publisher.

JewishGen Press is not responsible for inaccuracies or omissions in the original work and makes no representations regarding the accuracy of this translation. Digital images of the original book's contents can be seen online at the New York Public Library website or the Yiddish Book Center website.

Library of Congress Control Number (LCCN): 2022948329

ISBN: 978-1-962054-08-9 (hard cover: 350 pages, alk. paper)

About JewishGen.org

JewishGen, is a Genealogical Research Division of the Museum of Jewish Heritage - A Living Memorial to the Holocaust, serves as the global home for Jewish genealogy.

Featuring unparalleled access to 30+ million records, it offers unique search tools, along with opportunities for researchers to connect with others who share similar interests. Award winning resources such as the Family Finder, Discussion Groups, and ViewMate, are relied upon by thousands each day.

In addition, JewishGen's extensive informational, educational and historical offerings, such as the Jewish Communities Database, Yizkor Book translations, InfoFiles, Family Tree of the Jewish People, and KehilaLinks, provide critical insights, first-hand accounts, and context about Jewish communal and familial life throughout the world.

Offered as a free resource, JewishGen.org has facilitated thousands of family connections and success stories, and is currently engaged in an intensive expansion effort that will bring many more records, tools, and resources to its collections.

Please visit https://www.jewishgen.org/ to learn more.

Vice President for JewishGen: Avraham Groll

About the JewishGen Yizkor Book Project

Yizkor Books (Memorial Books) were traditionally written to memorialize the names of departed family and martyrs during holiday services in the synagogue (a practice that still exists in many synagogues today).

Over the centuries, as a result of countless persecutions and horrific atrocities committed against the Jews, Yizkor Books (Sefer Zikaron in Hebrew) were expanded to include more historical information, such as biographical sketches of famous personalities and descriptions of daily town life.

Following the Holocaust, the idea of remembrance and learning took on an urgent and crucial importance. Survivors of the Holocaust sought out other surviving residents of their former towns to memorialize and document the names and way of life of those who were ruthlessly murdered by the Nazis. These remembrances were documented in Yizkor Books, hundreds of which were published in the first decades after the Holocaust.

Most of these books were published privately, or through *Landsmanshaftn* (social organizations comprised of members originating from the same European town or region) that still existed, and were often distributed free of charge. The languages used to document these crucial histories and links to our past were mostly Yiddish and Hebrew. JewishGen has undertaken the sacred responsibility of translating these books into English so that the culture and way of life of these communities will be preserved and transmitted to future generations.

In 1986, a group of farsighted JewishGenners started a project to pool their efforts together in groups based upon their ancestors' towns and donate funds to translate the Yizkor books of their ancestral towns into English. As the translated material became available, it was made accessible for free at https://www.JewishGen.org/Yizkor . Hardcover copies can be purchased by visiting https://www.jewishgen.org/Yizkor/ybip.html (see below).

It is our hope that the translation of these books into English (and other languages) will assist the countless Jewish family researchers who are so desperately seeking to forge a connection with their heritage.

Director of JewishGen Yizkor Book Project: Lance Ackerfeld

About JewishGen Press

JewishGen Press (formerly the Yizkor Books-in-Print Project) is the publishing division of JewishGen.org, and provides a venue for the publication of non-fiction books pertaining to Jewish genealogy, history, culture, and heritage.

In addition to the Yizkor Book category, publications in the Other Non-Fiction category include Shoah memoirs and research, genealogical research, collections of genealogical and historical materials, biographies, diaries and letters, studies of Jewish experience and cultural life in the past, academic theses, and other books of interest to the Jewish community.

Please visit https://www.jewishgen.org/Yizkor/ybip.html to learn more.

Director of JewishGen Press: Joel Alpert
Managing Editor - Jessica Feinstein
Publications Manager - Susan Rosin

Notes to the Reader

The original book can be seen online at the Yiddish Book Center website:

https://www.yiddishbookcenter.org/collections/yizkor-books/yzk-nybc314103/leoni-eliezer-voloz-in-sifrah-shel-ha-ir-ve-shel-yeshivat-ets-hayim

OR

at the New York Public Library Digital Collections website:

https://digitalcollections.nypl.org/items/ade5e2b0-2ff3-0133-6e56-58d385a7b928

To obtain a list of Shoah victims from **Volozhin (Valozhyn, Belarus),** the reader should access the Yad Vashem web site listed below; one can also search for specific family names using family name option. These lists are continually updated by Yad Vashem, so it is worthwhile to periodically search them.

There is more valuable information (including the Pages of Testimony, etc.) available on this website: https://yvng.yadvashem.org/

A list of all books available from JewishGen Press along with prices is available at: https://www.jewishgen.org/Yizkor/ybip.html

Additional Resources:

https://kehilalinks.jewishgen.org/Valozhyn/Volozhin.html

Cover Photo Credits

Cover Design by: Rachel Kolokoff Hopper

Front Cover:

Volozhin Yeshiva. Photo courtesy of Alexey Eremenko, Research Architect.

Front and Back Cover Background Photo: *Dried Winter Grass*, Rachel Kolokoff Hopper.

Back Cover Photos

    Top Left: *Shif, Avraham Moshe and Shif, Leah.* [Page 39].

    Top Right: *Chayale and Shoshanale Lipshitz.* [Page 16].

    Middle Right: *Reizel (Shoshana), her husband Yitzchak Gelman, and their children.* [Page 7].

    Bottom Left: *Right to left: a) Mina Berman, b) Aryeh Leib Berman, c) Esther Berman (on his lap), d) Elka Berman, e) Tzipora Berman, f) Shmuel Berman, g) Chaya Sara Berman, h) Chana Berman.* [Page 3].

    Bottom Right: *Shapira, Rabbi Aryeh.* [Page 40].

Poem on Back Cover: A prayer in poetic form. *Shlomo Ibn Gabirol.* [Page 605-616].

Geopolitical Information

Map of Belarus showing the location of **Valozhyn**

Volozhin

Valozhyn, Belarus is located at 54°05' N 26°32' E and 44 miles WNW of Minsk

	Town	District	Province	Country
Before WWI (c. 1900):	Volozhin	Oshmyany	Vilna	Russian Empire
Between the wars (c. 1930):	Wołożyn	Wołożyn	Nowogródek	Poland
After WWII (c. 1950):	Volozhin			Soviet Union
Today (c. 2000):	Valozhyn			Belarus

Alternate Names for the Town:

Valozhyn [Bel], Volozhin [Rus, Yid], Wołożyn [Pol], Volozhyn, Vałožyn, Volozin

Nearby Jewish Communities:

Vishneva 13 miles WNW
Kamen' 16 miles SSE
Haradok 16 miles ENE
Ivyanets 16 miles SSE
Liebiedzieva 17 miles NNE
Bakshty 18 miles SW
Krevo 19 miles NNW
Maladzyechna 21 miles NE
Zaskevichi 22 miles N

Rakov 22 miles ESE
Naliboki 23 miles S
Halshany 24 miles WNW
Krasnae 25 miles ENE
Traby 25 miles W
Derevna 27 miles S
Smarhon 28 miles NNW
Radashkovichy 29 miles E
Lyubcha 30 miles SW

Jewish Population (1897): 2,452

INTRODUCTION TO TRANSLATION OF THE VOLOZHIN YIZKOR BOOK

As one of several translators who contributed to the English translation of the Volozhin Yizkor Book, it is an honor to have been asked by the current coordinator, Anita Gabbay, to write a few words of introduction.

Volozhin – for those familiar with the world of Eastern European Torah learning, the name implies far more than a remote city somewhere in Belarus. The term 'Volozhin' is sanctified in the Torah world as the location and namesake of the flagship Yeshiva of the Lithuanian style, *Misnagdic* houses of Torah learning that used to dot the landscape of Eastern Europe, and continue on to this day in Israel and North America. The rabbinic dynasty of Volozhin, known as 'Beit Harav' [The household of the rabbi], with names such as Berlin, Bar-Ilan, Soloveitchik, continues to be prominent in the Yeshiva world of today. Many of the leaders of what is today known as religious Zionism, as exemplified by the Mizrachi movement, went through the Volozhin Yeshiva, including Rav Kook, Rabbi Mohilever, and Rabbi Reines. Rabbi Isser Zalman Meltzer, whose son-in-law Rabbi Aaron Kotler, founded the prominent Lakewood Yeshiva of New Jersey, is a product of Volozhin. The Soloveitchik family of Yeshiva University fame, are direct descendants of the Volozhin dynasty. It is no understatement to say that Volozhin, its Yeshiva, and the students who were educated there have shaped the landscape of Jewish Orthodoxy, and guaranteed the continuation of serious Torah study in the world today and into the future. The famous Yiddish writer Chaim Nachman Bialik, the renowned businessman and tea-magnate Wissotzky, as well as many other influential people in the general Jewish world were also alumnae of the Volozhin Yeshiva.

This book has two sections. The first section deals with the Yeshiva and rabbinic personalities. The second section deals with Volozhin as any other city in Eastern Europe, with its culture, factions, education. Like any other Eastern European city, the Shoah did not skip over Volozhin. Everything that once was, the Jewish community and the communal infrastructure, was destroyed during the Holocaust period. Whatever small remnants might have remained were then subject to the brutal rule of the former U.S.S.R.

Several translators have been involved in this translation and each had their own style. Therefore, the reader will find that some names and terms are spelled differently in different chapters. Out of deference to the late coordinator and translator of large parts of this book, Moshe Porat of blessed memory his stylistic form and modes of spelling have often been preserved. Most of Mr. Porat's translations were written in summary form. I personally edited and enhanced many of his translations, ensuring that all quoted sources and original detailed footnotes were included. On the other hand, Mr. Porat, himself a scion of Beit Harav, often enhanced his translations with his own original material and personal photos. In order to remain true to the integrity of the original text, while simultaneously showing respect for Mr. Porat's legacy, I moved such enhancements to the footnotes, unusually in an unedited fashion.

The translation effort, and subsequent editing and reorganization of prior translations, was a momentous task that took far longer than originally anticipated. The translation coordinator for this project, Anita Frishman Gabbay, deserves a hearty Yasher Koach for persevering, dealing with unanticipated delays, and ultimately seeing this project to conclusion. We owe a debt of gratitude to Lance Ackerfeld and his team of volunteers from JewishGen tireless work and sage advice in order to bring this project to completion.

It has truly been an honor to participate in the task of translating the Volozhin Yizkor Book. I hope that my translations, and those of my colleagues, do justice to the city and its significant legacy within the Jewish world. May the Yizkor Book and its translation serve as a memorial to the victims of the Shoah, and as a testament to the ongoing vitality of the Jewish people and its Torah.

Jerrold Landau
Toronto Canada
July 15, 2024, 9 Tammuz, 5754

Table of Contents

Holocaust

"The German Thunder"	The Editor	3
The Destruction of Volozhin	Mendl Volkovitsh	3
Atrocities at the Extermination of the Jews of Volozhin	Hessel Perski	4
The Big Slaughter	Mendel Volkovitch	5
What My Eyes Have Seen	Pnina Hayat (Potashnik)	8
Pages About the Volozhin Holocaust	Fruma Lifshits (Gapanovitsh)	12
From a Girl's Memoirs of the Holocaust	Sonia Puter (Perski)	21
A Ballad About Shneur Kivelevitch	Mendl Volkovitch	22
In the Ghetto and in the Forced Labor Camps	Lyuba Volkovich (Girkus)	27
Franz Karl Hess - The Volozhin Hangman	From Soviet trial-Minsk 1946	33
In the Volozhin Ghetto and in Revenge Actions	Yaakov Kagan	38
Nissan Perski's Death	Simcha Rogovin of Kiryat-Haim	41
On the Path of Suffering	Mendel Volkovich	42
Wandering and Struggling	Rachel & Reuven Rogovin	44
My Life As a Partisan	Hessel Perski	47
Partisans from Volozhin Who Died in the Course of Duty	Hessel Perski	48
A Visit to Volozhin After the War	Rachel & Reuven Rogovin	52
Volozhin As I Saw it in 1945	Moshe Eliyashkevitsh	54
"Yizkor" to the Flames	Sara Sholomovitz (Rappaport)	56
Calendar Dates of the Second World War and the Holocaust in Volozhin	E. Leoni	57
In Conclusion	Binyamin Shapir	60

Yizkor - Remember

And These are the names of the Pure Holy Martyrs of Volozhin	Eliezer Leoni	63
Dear Mother!	Yehuda Khaim Kotler	64
Volozhin - Martyrs (1275 names)	Editorial team	66

From One Generation to Another and to Eternity

Bar-Ilan University & it's President Professor Pinchas Churgin	Eliezer Leoni	85
Kibbutz "Ein HaNatziv"	Eli Avisar	89
Israel Rogozin	Yitzhak Yaakobi	93
The Association of the Descendants of Volozhin in Israel	Eliezer Leoni	95
Fallen Sons of Volozhin in Israel's War of Independence	Editorial team	129
Benyamin Perah - Ind. War	Editorial team	129
Chaim Perski - Ind. War	Editorial team	130

Eliezer Rogovin - partisan, decorated as USSR Hero-Ind. War	Editorial team	131
To Leyzer Rogovin's Memory	Yaffa Abramovitsh	133
Expressions of Gratitude	Binyamin Shapir (Shishku)	135

English

Sefer Volozhin, the Book of Volozhin	Eliezer Leoni	136
Volozhiners in America	Dr. Avraham Yoblons	141
I remember Volozhin	Irving Bunim	150
The Destruction of Volozhin	Mendel Volkovitsh	153

Supplement to the Book of Volozhin

Volozhin Natives Who Perished in the Holocaust	158
Volozhin Natives who Died in the State of Israel, in Volozhin, and in the United States.	197

Supplementary material
(Not included the Yizkor book)

Volozhin & Volozhiners after World War Two	
Volozhin 2000 - Map, legend, description	234
Etz Chaim Yeshiva - Kulinaria, Memorial plaque. Photos, description	237
First mass slaughter Memorial (Sport Stadium) - Photos, description	241
Second mass slaughter Memorial (2000 victims) - Photos, description	242
Third mass slaughter Memorial (Volozhinka Stream Bed) - Photos, description	244
The Ancient Cemetery - Schema, Legend (Yr. 2000)	245
The Ancient Cemetery - Sheep Pasture field Photo's (Yr. 1988)	247
Volozhiners at the tombstones, photos (Yr. 1998)	248
Old tombstones-Gitl Bunimovitsh, Tsart, Sonia Perski -(1988 & 1998 photos)	249
Victims mass graves on the cemetery (1988 & 1998 photos)	251
Cemetery Memorials to the Volozhin congregation and to Rabbi Chaim Volozhiner	253
Red Cross activity	254
Our Parents' Saw & Grist Mills - By M. Perlman	256
Volozhin Memorial inauguration, 1980	261
Babushka Khaya's letter	265
How did I survive - By Leyzer Meltser	270
A look at the country's history	273
Childhood In Volozhin	276
List of martyrs in Cyrillic [From Volozhin - Martyrs (1275 names)]	290

Memory to Volozhin Region   309

Name Index - Volume II

VOLUME II
Volozhin; the Book of the City and of the Etz Chaim Yeshiva
(Valozhyn, Belarus)

54°05' / 26°32'

Translation of
Wolozyn; sefer shel ha-ir-shel yeshivat "Etz Chaim"

Edited by: E. Leoni

Published in Tel-Aviv, 1970

Acknowledgments:

Coordinator

Anita Frishman Gabbay

Emeritus Coordinator: Moshe Porat (Perlman) z"l

This is a translation from: *Wolozyn; sefer shel ha-ir-shel yeshivat "Etz Chaim"*;
Wolozin; the book of the city and of the Etz Chaim Yeshiva.
Ed. E. Leoni. Tel-Aviv, former residents of Wolozin in Israel and the USA, 1970 (H,Y,E)

This material is made available by JewishGen, Inc. and the Yizkor Book Project for the purpose of fulfilling our mission of disseminating information about the Holocaust and destroyed Jewish communities.
This material may not be copied, sold or bartered without JewishGen, Inc.'s permission. Rights may be reserved by the copyright holder.

JewishGen, Inc. makes no representations regarding the accuracy of the translation. The reader may wish to refer to the original material for verification.
JewishGen is not responsible for inaccuracies or omissions in the original work and cannot rewrite or edit the text to correct inaccuracies and/or omissions.
Our mission is to produce a translation of the original work and we cannot verify the accuracy of statements or alter facts cited.

[Page 539]

Holocaust

[Page 540] Blank [Page 541]

"The German Thunder"

by The editor

Translated by Naomi Gal

We hereby bring you, as a forward to Volozhin's Holocaust, the prophesy of Heinrich Heine who in 1834 spoke about the German People. Heine warned that the German philosophy is a deceiving disguise, that because of the sublime philosophical systems of the German People "Revolutionary forces are developing and they are just waiting for the day when they can outburst and fill the world with horror and wonder".

And this is what Heine predicted:

"and if one day you will hear a huge thunder blasting, the kind of explosion that was never heard before in the history of the world, you would know: the German People arrived at their destination. To this sound and fury eagles will fall dead to the ground, and the lions that are at the edge of the Africa–desert, will fold their tails and come to be buried in their royal lairs, and the hour would arrive."

(Henrich Heine, "The History of Religion and Philosophy in Germany", page 283 "Legevulam" Publishing House, with the cooperation of Mossad Bialik, editor Dr. S. Perlman, "Masada" company, Tel Aviv, 1952)

And the hour indeed arrived as Heine had forecasted, and even worse. Now, more than thirty years after the break of World War Two, which historians call "The Ovens Period" – we have to remember even better, Heine's predication. Because there is no certainty that this Holocaust would not happen again, God Forbid, one way or another. We have to understand Heine's wise words. We should never lose sight of these sage words. "Impress them on your children. Talk about them when you sit at home and when you walk along the road, when you lie down and when you get up". (The book of Deuteronomy 6:7).

[Page 542]

This section is equivalent with the English section pages 30-34

Hebrew preamble translated by Jerrold Landau

"The sounds of Torah are no longer heard from the Yeshiva buildings, from the Beis Midrash, and from the tender lads, their pale faces are hidden, as they are immersed in their Talmudic studies, delving deeply into Gemara, from their thoughts… No, it is not pale, it is only splendor, it is only brightness… These have already been extinguished… Rabbis, Yeshiva heads, Gaonim, weakened, thin, and full of Talmud and rabbinic literature… Jews, small bodies with a large head, high foreheads and bright eyes – they are no more and will never be again.

(Yitzchak Katznelson, "The Song of the Murdered Jewish Nation" page 65, translated by M. Z. Wolfowsky.)

[Page 546]

Atrocities at the Extermination of the Jews of Volozhin

by Hessl Perski

Translated by Jerrold Landau **based on an earlier translation by** M. Porat z"l
that was edited by Judy Feinsilver Montel

"Every Jewish person has a hold on one letter of the holy Torah" (Sermons of the Mahara"ch)

When the Germans entered Volozhin, they attacked Alter Shimshilevich, the brother-in-law of Lunil (husband of Chaya Leah) and murdered him. The Jews were ordered to leave his body on the road, so that they would see and hear. Similarly, they murdered Chaim Eliyahu Perski and burnt him and his house. They captured Zalman Kagan from Aroptzu (they called him Zalman Sheive's) and began to torture him. They forced him to shout, "Death to the Jews!" Then they murdered him before the eyes of the Christians, to prove that the band was untied, and the life of the Jews was open for all.

The German murderers and the local *shkotzim* once noticed Freydke, Yehuda Avraham Dubinski's daughter, taking a bottle of milk from a gentile woman. For this "transgression" they hauled her to the foot of the hill. They threw potatoes onto the hilltop and forced her to crawl on all fours uphill and fetch the potatoes. The tortures continued uninterrupted for several hours. Her arms and legs were flowing with blood. When her strength ran out, they put an end to her life.

The murderers led Dvora (Esther Rashe Dvoshe's daughter) and the granddaughter of Shimon der Dzik to the "Mountain of the Priest" ["Dem Galechs Barg"]. They were accompanied by two dogs. On the mountain they shot the girls and beheaded the dogs, so as to mix Jewish with animal blood. Those who passed away naturally were considered lucky. This "privilege" was earned by Asna (Asnat) Chaya Paretski and her son Yosef; Yehudit (the butcher's daughter) and Chaya Elishkevich (The Shochet's wife).

There was a smith named Yosef Zarin in the ghetto. Once a police officer entered his shop and requested money. At this time, I was there with my brother-in-law Leybe Lavit. I took advantage of the fact that nobody else was present. I picked up a heavy hammer, bashed his skull and hid his dead body in the soil. The Germans searched for the police officer.

[Page 547]

We told them that he had run away to the partisans. They went to his home, killed his wife and children, and then burnt them up.

As Mendel Volkovich recounted in his testimony, all the Jews were enclosed in the ghetto. The teacher Gliker served as the commandant of the ghetto. The ghetto had two gates which were guarded by armed police officers. The gates opened only when people were guided to work or back from work.

The Judenrat was composed of twelve men. Among them were Gliker, Shneur Kivilevich, Getsel Perski, Ele Malot, Shaye Kaganovich, Aron Kamenetski, Yaakov Kovalski, Israel Lunin, and Yaakov (Yanie) Garber. At Passover 5702 (1942) the Gestapo came to the Judenrat and requested fifty strong, healthy Jews. When it became known in the ghetto that the Germans were interested only in strong men, they interpreted this as a bad thing, and refused to report. The Germans did not let up from their demand and declared that if the men do not report, one hundred Jews will be taken to be killed. Having no choice, the men reported. I was among the fifty. We were placed in lines of five, and ordered to take axes and saws with us. They took us to the barracks where we worked until late night. Then we each were given a large loaf of bread and ordered to return to the ghetto. The ghetto Jews, seeing us safe and sound and carrying food, were very happy. The trusting Jews interpreted it as a change in the German's policy. Regrettably, the later events did not confirm this interpretation.

I survived the mass slaughter of 23 Iyar 5702 (May 10, 1942) miraculously. When the Jews began to enter Bulava's house, they brought them in group by group, and forced them to lie face down. At the moment when the murderers approached the line in which I stood, Kushke from Aroptzu issued an order for the people standing in line to fill their pockets with sand. As we approached the entrance to the house, we threw the sand in the eyes of the Germans, calling out "Hurrah!" The eyes of the Germans were temporarily blinded. We were saved at the appropriate time, and we escaped.

When we were about a kilometer from the vale of killing, we saw that the house had gone up in flames. We understood from this that our dear ones were no longer alive.

I escaped to the Zabzheza [Zabrezye] Ghetto, and from there to the Krasno Ghetto. After a short time, I escaped from the Krasno Ghetto and returned to Volozhin. I found a hiding place in Gelbovich's house. Even though he and his family were living in hunger, they provided me with food every day.

Gelbovich told me that my sister Esther and her two children had been hiding in the cellar of our house, but the Germans had discovered them and killed them. My sister-in-law Bashke (my brother's wife) had twins. The Germans entered the house and murdered them while they were asleep. Leizer Golubenchich lived in the house of Janke Bielonovich in the ghetto. When they began to bring the Jews to slaughter, Leizer succeeded in escaping, and he hid along with Beila in a pit for several days. After the slaughter, Janka showed the Germans the hiding place. Leizer succeeded in escaping, but a police officer shot him near the bridge and killed him. The Germans killed Beila, Frumale and Nachumke in the pit.

[Page 548]

The Big Slaughter

by Mendl Volkovitch

Translated by Janie Respitz

Donated by Anita Gabbay

Edited by Jerrold Landau

It was 27 years ago.
More than a quarter century has passed.
However my wound is fresh and new,
Because I was there.

It is etched deep in my memory,
Because on this sad day
We lost our dear Volozhin Jews.

My heart is crying, tears are pouring from my eyes,
This will never be forgotten.

I remember the day, the hour.
It was Sunday morning, 5:00.
It was the 10th of May 1942,
The 23rd day of Iyar, 5702 years since the creation of the world.

I hear the steps of Nazi boots.
The murderers shout: Juden heraus!
The ghetto is encircled by barbed wire
They shoot, they kill.

The Jews are running here and there,
In the streets in the courtyards – there is nowhere to run,
The streets are sowed with the wounded and dead.
The Angel of death, in all his fervour: Your death will be soon.

Later we gathered,
Children, brothers, sisters, mothers and fathers,
Bruised, and bitten,
Skin torn from our bones,
And they were sent into the Soviet smithy.

[Page 549]

Whisky and wine on the table of our murderers,
They gorge, drink and get drunk,
As they shoot into the smithy
From there and from everywhere.
Jewish blood spurts
As from a fountain.

There is turmoil in the smithy,
Two brothers are arguing,
The Olshan rabbi, Rabbi Ruven Khadash,
And the Volozhin rabbi, Reb Yisroel Lunin.

Rabbi Ruven Khadash with his wounded hand,
Stands leaning against the wall,

He is bleeding,
There isn't even anything to wrap the wound
To make a bandage.

Rabbi Ruven Khadash says: we must attack the murderers,
Take their weapons, kill them and run away.
But Reb Yisroel Lunin says: No!
We are bruised, tortured, we have no strength,
We are weak and small.
You will lead us to our extermination.

Rabbi Khadash replies: you can see for yourself,
They want to annihilate all of us.

They both had the same intention:
They wanted to save us.

The remnants of the smithy were collected,
The Jews from the hide outs and holes, chased away –
To the pyre!

[Page 550]

Grandfathers and fathers in prayer shawls and phylacteries,
Mothers held babies from their cradles in their arms.

The murderers grab children from their mother's arms
Smashing their little hands and feet into the walls.

The mothers are crying and screaming: give us back our children!
We cannot live without them!

The murderers mock them and laugh.

Those martyrs who were killed are taken away,
Beaten, bruised, some without feet, some without hands
And everyone burned in the fire.

Who can comfort us, who can calm us.
We must remember this for generations:
Remember what the Nazi German Amalek did to us.

[Page 550]

What My Eyes Have Seen

by Pnina Chayat nee Potashnik of Holon

Translated Jerrold Landau based on an earlier translation by M. Porat z"l

"It is appropriate to shed tears for them like a torrential river without stopping, for the victims of the Children of Israel and the nation of G-d."

(A sermon from Mahara'ch)

The Germans met no resistance when they entered Volozhin, because the Soviets left the city while there was still time. The Germans parachuted in not far from our house. They were followed by the armed forces, which shook up the city. Airplanes dropped firebombs, and fires broke out.

We were immediately forced to engage in forced labor. The Judenrat was in charge of carrying out that decree. The principal workplaces were the sawmills of Rappaport and Polak. The women worked at cleaning the Gestapo residences. We walked to work in groups, equipped with a special permit. During work, they would start thrashing us with whips.

[Page 551]

After that, the edict was issues that every Jew must wear the yellow patch on their sleeves. With time, the patched changed to a yellow Star of David, with the word Jude printed on it. We were forbidden from walking on the sidewalks. An edict of confinement was also issued, through which the Jews were confined to their dwellings.

The tribulations increased after the Jews were confined in the ghetto. After about two months, they suddenly brought the Jews of the Olshan Ghetto to us along with their rabbi, Rabbi Reuven Chadash. The crowding increased greatly after they came, and the sources of food grew scarcer. We looked for various ways to bring food to the starving Jews in the ghetto, even though this was fraught with mortal danger.

From time to time, the murderers attacked the ghetto. On *Kol Nidre* night, the Gestapo men appeared in our house and demanded money and valuables. This demand was accompanied by cruel blows. From our house they went to the Weisbord and Brodna families.

I worked with my friend Batya Rogovin. Once, as we were walking along the length of the road, Polish police officers and Gestapo men attacked us, and thrashed us with whips. A great deal of blood flowed from Batya's nose from the beating. Her face became pale from the beating.

On 7 Cheshvan 5702 (October 28th 1841), Gestapo men appeared in the ghetto and ordered the Judenrat to assemble all the Jews on the main street of the ghetto. The Jewish police officers went from house to house to ask the Jews to fulfil the edict. Since I was working in the police, I was exempt from the duty to appear. They chose two hundred people from among those gathered, including Yaakov (Yani) Garber, the head of the Judenrat, and the Jewish police officers. We knew that a day previously, they had dug pits. Those being taken to death were locked in barracks, and were taken out in groups of ten to be killed. The Jews were surprised and asked the murderers: Why are you not taking them all out at once? They responded in innocence that they are taking the belongings from the Jews, since they are commanded to do a "precise registration." Therefore the "activity" is being carried out slowly.

My school friend Tzvia Lunin was among those being taken to death. She survived because of the German "precision." They worked by "quotas," and since Tzvia was beyond the "quota," they returned her to the ghetto.

The area of the ghetto was reduced after this aktion. Shneur Kivilevich was chosen as the head of the Judenrat. Worrying rumors reached us that the Germans were preparing a new slaughter. Rivka Drotvitski played a significant role in transmitting this news, since her Christian husband was friendly to the Jews. He would come and go among the Germans, and knew their plans. Many people were saved thanks to this information.

Early in the morning of Sunday, 23 Iyar 5702 (May 10ᵗ, 1942), Shneur Kivilevich came to our house and informed us that the situation was very serious. The ghetto was surrounded, and we had to go immediately to our hiding places. The Germans began a siege of the ghetto. They searched for Jews even in hiding places, and paid attention to any rustle or whisper. They found a woman from Olshan in a certain cellar. They promised her that if she reveals the hiding places

[Page 552]

of the Jews, they would keep her alive. However, she refused this degrading offer out of disgust, and died a martyr's death.

Danger awaited us with every step. My brother Yehuda Yosef, Asher Perski, his son, and I, decided to escape from the ghetto. There was a river near the ghetto. We crossed it under a volley of bullets, and continued to run. We hid in a grove. The gentiles chased after us, and we heard their voices. I went to the Horodok Ghetto. My brother went to Lebedovo, and Asher Perski and his son when the Zabrezhe. When I arrived there, I found the Jews shaken up and frightened, for they had heard that a slaughter had taken place in Volozhin.

I remained in the Horodok Ghetto for several days. I received encouraging news that they were setting up the Volozhin ghetto once again. The Germans promised the surviving Jews that no evil would befall them. I saw that the ghetto had been made significantly smaller, for only a few had survived. I worked in the "guild" of carpenters. My supervisor was a Pole named Jezierski. Several Jewish girls worked along with me, among them Miriam Kagan and Rachel from Miejiki.

Once, before we returned to the ghetto, we saw that the Germans were surrounding the ghetto. The Jews broke through the gate and began to escape. When we saw this atrocity, we removed our Magen Davids and searched for a place to save ourselves. The Germans shot at us, and ten girls were killed. Only Miriam Kagan and I succeeded in reaching the field. We hid among the paths. At night, we set out in the direction of the village of Miejiki.

After much wandering and meandering, we reached the village of Kolodiki. We entered one house and requested mercy from a gentile, to give us a morsel of bread, for we were swollen from starvation. This was a family of poor people. Nevertheless, they filled us to satiety. We wound our way to the village, and approached a house. I told Miriam that we were in any case doomed, and there is nothing to lose – let us knock on the door, and what will happen will happen. A gentile answered. He brought us into the barn and closed us in.

After two hours of strong heart palpitations and nervous waiting – the gentile came to us and invited us into his house. There entire house was only one room. It had two large beds, a broken table, and an oven. A righteous gentile lived there, Ivan Kowalski and his wife, three daughters, and two sons. This impoverished family received us with a pleasant face and unusual warmth when they saw our unfortunate appearance. They all burst out in bitter weeping. We warmed our frozen bodies and ate warm food. After that, Kowalski returned us othe barn, and provide us with a warm blanket. This was on Saturday night, 5 Kislev, 5702 (December 14, 1942). In the morning, one of Kowalski's daughters brought us food.

We were happy, and we also saved some food for the journey, for we were sure that Kowalski would send us away. He came to us in the afternoon. When he saw the left-over food, he asked us the reason. We answered him: "We are sure that you will not want to hide Jewish girls with you, for you are endangering your life. Therefore, we have decided to continue along our way." Kowalski was saddened by our response and said to us: "Dear girls

[Page 553]

my family and I have decided to keep you with us. Your fate is our fate, and our house is your house."

The winter was in full force. It was extremely cold in the barn. Kowalski, the good benefactor, brought us into his house and hid us on top of the oven, where there was stifling heat, so we could "get some air." Kowalski would bring us down to the potato pit for several hours. His children also concerned themselves with us. At times of danger, they would gesture to us with special signs.

Once, the Germans surrounded the village of Krazhina, which was about four hundred meters from us. They brought all the residents into a barn, poured kerosine on it, and burnt it along with everyone inside. It seemed that partisans were ambushing Germans near that village, and they had killed some of them. The partisans retreated through the village of Krazhina. Therefore, the residents of the village received their "punishment." Even though Kowalski knew that he was liable to such a bitter fate, he nevertheless did not turn us away. On the contrary, he calmed us as a good, merciful father.

However, it was a prophesy of the heart that it was dangerous to remain in that house. The partisans were operating in the area, and battles broke out between the Germans and them from time to time. Kowalski and his wife pleaded with us to not leave their house. Nevertheless, we decided to set out on the way. Kowalski, who concerned himself with our lives, scouted out several villages in order to discover the paths of the partisans. Indeed, he brought us to them.

Ivan Kowalski, his wife, daughter, and son

[Page 554]

However, they behaved in a hostile fashion to us, because they suspected that we had come on a mission from the German scouting corps. Thy conducted a quick field trial and sentenced us to death. When the verdict was about to be carried out, a partisan from the village of Krazhina approached us and asked us who we were and from where we came. When I told him my name, he told me that my brother Yehuda Yosef was in a group of partisans. The partisan informed the commander that I am the sister of a very active partisan. Thus, the verdict was nullified.

The partisans transferred Mariasha Kagan and me to Baksht, where there was a large concentration of partisans. My brother took me to the Lidioyev Otriad, which was located west of Nolibok. After a few days, the Germans surrounded the entire area. We hid in pits and other hiding places. When the Germans left the area, we gathered in a remote area in the wilderness of Nolibok. We set up a winter camp, where we remained until the liberation of Volozhin.

After the liberation, we returned to the city. I immediately set out to visit Kowalski. Our connection was once again forged. He visited me daily. His son and daughter, who worked in Volozhin, lived with me.

In the year 5705 (1945), I left Volozhin and moved to Poland. In the year 5707 (1947), I made *aliya* to the Land. I constantly wrote letters to Kowalski, but did not receive a response. In the year 5625 (1966), I received his address. It became clear that he and his family were living in Ural. I immediately sent him a package of clothing. He confirmed receipt of the package with thanks and enthusiasm.

From that time, I have remained in constant correspondence with him, and I continue to send gifts to him and his family, as a token of thanks for saving us from death.

Note by M. Porat about the preceding chapter:

Pnina Hayat, Born in Volozhin (as Peshka Potashnik), deceased in Israel 1974, VIB photo: p. 588, (seated, 1st, on right). Potashnik Menahem Mendl, Rabbi, Pnina's brother, born in Volozhin, Volozhin Yizkor Book committee member in USA., VIB Picture: p. 661. Potashnik Yehuda Yosef, Pnina's brother, born in Volozhin 1905, deceased in Israel 1965. - VIB Photo: p. 36 counted from left. I remember: Peshka and Mendl Potashnik were employed at our family business (Grind & sawmill) in Volozhin before the war.

[Page 554]

Pages About the Volozhin Holocaust

Fruma Lifshits (Gafanovich) United States

Translated by Jerrold Landau **incorporating extracts originally translated by** M. Porat z"l

Before the entry of the Soviets, I served as principal of the religious Chorev School in Ivenets, near Volozhin. After the entry of the Soviets, I returned to Volozhin, where I had lived with my husband Yaakov Lifshits from the year 5691 (1931), in order to teach at the Hebrew school that had turned into a Yiddish school, so to speak according to the "demands" of the parents at a general meeting.

In the year 1940-41, that school turned into Russian School Number 1; the Polish school turned into a Byelorussian School; and the Polish Gymnasja into a Russian Gymnasium [high school]. All the students who had previously studied at the Jewish school remained there. The teachers who taught previously continued in their work, among them Rachel Kivilevich, Rachel Lop, Avraham Yafa, and Shlomo Biekalski. Several teachers from Russia were added,

[Page 555]

as well as a Communist principal, a Jewess named Sara Azbel. (Noach Perski left teaching, as he refused to teach under the Communist regime.)

The Jewish teachers were treated with lack of trust. They were hired because there was no choice, either because of their high pedagogic level or because of a dearth of teachers. A teachers' seminary was also founded, in which Yaakov taught mathematics and physics.

We did lack food. Aside from the stockpiles that everyone prepared before and after the entry of the Soviets, it was possible to obtain everything from the "black market." Our tribulations were primarily spiritual tribulations. We were afraid to utter a word within the walls of the school. We were forced to conduct publicity that was foreign to our spirit, foreign to the Zionist spirit and to the Hebrew language in which we had been educated. I recall a celebration in honor of the civil New Year. We gathered in the home of Shneur and Rachel Kivilevich, to celebrate, so to speak, the advent of the new year. However, due to our custom through the year, the *Hatikvah* song and other Hebrew songs emanated from our mouths.

Each of us prepared sacks in case the N.K.V.D. would come to exile us to Siberia – so that we would be able to quickly place necessities into them. We were listed in the "blacklist" of those designated for exile.

People were exiled in accordance with an order. First, they exiled the factory owners (they were slandered for having helped the Poles).

I sent my daughters Chayale and Shoshanale, who were born in Volozhin, to a summer vacation with my parents in Radoshkovich, while my husband and I prepared for our entrance exams to the university that the Soviets had set up in Grodno – I in languages and my husband in mathematics and physics. However, our plans were for naught, for the Germans attacked the Soviets. As they invaded the Russian area, a panicked escape by vehicle or on foot of the Soviet citizens from the areas of Poland that had been occupied by the Soviets ensued.

We lived with Leibe Berman. We left everything at home. We took only two bags, in which was packed diplomas and permits of the oversight office of the schools, as well as some flour and water for our daughters. We escaped to Radoshkovich on foot. We walked all night. My husband became completely exhausted and remained near the town. I entered the town myself and met my father. My mother, sister, brother, and daughters had escaped to the village of Udranka, which had served as a recuperation center during normal times. The town was crowded with an influx of refugees from Lithuania and Poland. Fires broke out. I succeeded in removing some clothes from our burning house.

In the meantime, my husband regained his strength and came to Radoshkovich. We went together to my family members in Udranka. Along the way, we encountered many German paratroopers, but they did not treat us badly. We returned with my family to Radoshkovich, which for the most part had turned into a heap of ruins. We decided to move to Horodok where my eldest sister Cheina lived.

As I have stated, we went out on the journey with empty hands. We required clothes to be used as barter for necessary food provisions. A certain Christian agreed to travel with me to the Volozhin Ghetto, on the condition

[Page 556]

that I pay him for his effort with furniture, clothing, and other belongings. I lay down in the wagon, dressed in gentle woman's clothing (according to my husband, I was to be taken to the hospital in Volozhin). I reached the village of Miejiki in peace. I went to a Jewish woman who was married to a gentile in order to obtain directions as to how to get to Volozhin, and how I could enter the ghetto, which was under heavy guard. In accordance with her directives, I went to Pinchas the smith, whose smithy was located outside the ghetto. Through his good advice, I succeeded in sneaking into the ghetto without anyone knowing.

The family of my aunt (the Berkovich family[11]) lived in the house of their daughter-in-law Sonia Dubinski, the wife of their son Yaakov. When they saw me, they were astonished, because a rumor spread that they had killed my husband and me. I quickly took what I could and left the ghetto. It was necessary for me to return to Horodok before dark. The bag that I had brought with me was small. In exchange for it, I received bread and potatoes. We also salvaged the potato peels and fried them into "meatballs."

Winter was approaching and I had to concern myself with warm clothing for my family. The Christian who brought me to the ghetto offered his services once again. However, he preferred to travel himself, due to the danger of travelling with a Jewish woman, even if she was dressed as a gentile, He entered the ghetto and took several belongings. The guards chased after him, but he succeeded in escaping from them.

The survivors of Maladechno and Volozhin reached us. The Germans did not liquidate the ghettoes immediately. There was a railroad junction from Poland to Russia in Krasno, and the Germans required workers. They drafted the Jews of the ghetto for work. There was also a small concentration camp in Krasno, in which the Jews imprisoned there worked for *Tod Organizatzion* (a brigade of German soldiers and captains whose job was to supervise the building of bridges and the laying of railway tracks), and in repairing roads and railway tracks. Jews from Volozhin, Lida, Mir, Novogrudek, Horodok, and other places were sent there. Several groups were sent from Horodok, including my husband. I parted from him with the following words: "My fate and the fate of our daughters is already sealed, but you will survive since you are a useful Jew." (That is what the Jews believed in their naivete).

Every Sunday, several of the workers from Horodok were permitted to come and obtain food. In that manner, we also sent food from Volozhin for the Volozhiners in the camp. My six-year-old daughter became ill with scurvy, a serious gum disease. Mr. Ratzkin, the chairman of the Judenrat, with whose family I lived in the ghetto, had mercy and sent a different "number" instead of my husband (every worker was considered to be a number and not a person). He came to me on the Sabbath, and he had to return on Sunday. However, the bitter end came on that Sabbath, 26 Tammuz 5702 (July 11, 1942). The ghetto was surrounded all night by the Germans. The Jews did not sense the impending danger, and they slept their last sleep, as the sleep of the just.

The Gestapo men accompanied by police officered entered early in the morning to remove the Jews from their houses. Five people lived in our house. It had three hiding places. The hiding place in which I hid with

[Page 557]

my daughters was discovered by the local police after the aktion. Mr. Ratzkin, who was elderly, could not bear the stifling air in the hiding place and was forced to leave it. This led to a search for all those hiding in it. They shot and killed my husband. The murderers brought all the Jews to a yard and conducted a selection. Those fit for work were transferred to Krasno, whereas the elderly, handicapped, and children were sent to death. Fruma, the mother of Tzvia Tzart, was among those taken to death. The Germans beat her until she bled, for she could barely stand up and was unable to walk. They brought them all into a threshing floor behind the town and shot them.[2]

As I noted above, there was a ghetto and concentration camp in Krasno. My older sister Chenya with her brother-in-law and oldest son lived in the camp. My younger sister and I lived in the ghetto. I met Volozhiners there, including Yosef Tabachovich (he served as a work supervisor) with his wife Beilka (nee Shaker). The Volozhiners lived with them in the barn. I took Tzvia Tzart with me on the plank. I took care of her along with my sister. There was no possibility at all to take care of minimal hygienic conditions, so a typhus epidemic broke out. My sister, Tzvia, and I were placed in the hospital that opened in one of the houses outside the ghetto. We "merited" the visit of a doctor. He was a Gestapo man, and with the wave of his baton, he determined that so-and-so was already fit to be sent to the "bathhouse." I was very weak due to malnutrition. My father risked his life, making his way from the ghetto through fields to the camp, to bring me a bit of grain to strengthen my weak body a bit. We were brought to the "bathhouse." The Germans looked at our emaciated bodies, but we somehow maintained our stand, and our fate was not sealed. From time to time, the Gestapo captain visited the camp. He did not leave the place without seeing Jewish blood. On one of his visits, a Jew who had been returned to the hospital appeared before him. When he saw this Jew, he did not hesitate at all – he shot him. If my memory is correct, Yosef Mordchovich was shot to death on one of those visits.

Thanks to the "special status" I earned in the Krasno Ghetto, I was freed from work, and I dedicated my free time to search for food for those who were starving. My strength of spirit urged me to leave the ghetto without any fear. The first time I went out, I went with my brother-in-law and Esther Rogovin from Horodok (she and her brother live in Israel). We reached a village, collected several loaves of bread, and returned in peace. The three of us left a second time as well. That night, group of partisans attacked a police unit, and a battle broke out between them. All of the police officers were killed in that battle except for one who was injured and succeeded in reaching the village.

Even though my brother-in-law knew all the paths, we still got lost and ended up in a grove. From afar, we saw guards who were wearing the clothes of the killed police officers. We did not notice the red band on their sleeves, and thought that they were German guards. To our pleasant surprise, this was a group of partisans. They asked us to remain, but we preferred to return to the ghetto. I told the Volozhiners that there is a partisan unit in the vicinity who are willing to accept Jews. We searched for ways to obtain weapons, for it was impossible to be accepted to the partisans without weapons.

[Page 558]

With unusual dedication, many people removed ammunition parts from the ammunition storage depot and hid them in secret places while they waited for hour zero – the hour of escape to the partisans.

One night, the Volozhiners decided to cross the railway tracks and join the partisans. Even before that, Hershel Lunin, and Chaim Perski (Nisan's son) left the camp. The typhus illness that sapped my strength prevented me from joining them. But I got a bit stronger, and we – my brother-in-law, I, and several other Jews – decided to escape and search for contact with the partisans. It was not easy to remove the two hunting guns that I had hidden near the camp. Risking my life, I went to the camp from the ghetto, and I helped three men leave the camp at night with weapons in their hands. They reached the nearby village in peace, and immediately informed me of their wellbeing via a farmer. Without wasting time, I left the camp the next day after work with two other Jews. We walked with Christians who also worked with Germans – for a fee of course. We equipped ourselves with various work tools, as if we were leaving work along with the Christians. Suddenly, shots were heard. We thought that they were directed at us. However, it became clear that the Germans were shooting Soviet prisoners who had escaped to the forests.

During the shooting, we approached the farmer's towing wagon. He loaded us aboard, took us away from the danger, and gave us directions to the partisans. We arrived at a village where we met the three Jews who had gone out previously. The partisans had not been seen on the horizon for ten days. News came that the Germans were about to arrive at the village in their pursuit of the partisans. We escaped to a nearby grove and waited until evening. At night, we left and came to another village, but there too we did not meet partisans. We finally succeeded in reaching them. We already had a horse, some clothing, some weapons, and some food. This made it easier for us to join the partisans. They brought us to a village that was full of partisans, including the *Nakem Veshilem* [Revenge and Payback] Brigade, whose aim was to cross to the side of Minsk. A difficult battle had taken place with the Germans on the evening before our arrival. They were very vigilant since they suspected a new attack by the Germans.

There was a strong guard of partisans surrounding the forest. They refused to accept us and ordered us to leave the area. They agreed to accept us thanks to the intervention of Eliezer Rogovin who served as a scout. We met several Volozhiners in the forest, including Feigele Perski, Hershel Rogovin, and Yeshayahu Liberman. All of them made efforts on our behalf, even though it took great energy.

At night, Pasha (Pesia), Simcha Perski's wife, arrived. She worked in the next village, disguised as a Christian. A new group was formed from us and several Soviet prisoners. It was named for the commander Staritski, and was part of the Tshkalov Brigade. After a few months, I moved from the Staritski group to the workshop for repair of weapons. I worked there until the liberation in July 1944. At times, there were battles between the partisans and the Germans. The fiercest attack of the Germans against the partisans took place in July 1943. At that time, there were already large brigades of partisans, from which the Germans suffered significant blows. To fight against the partisans, the Germans organized the Vlasovs,

[Page 559]

an army of hooligans named for their commander Vlasov – a Russian traitor. There were Russians, Byelorussians, Lithuanians, Ukrainians, Cossacks, and other murderers in that army. Their first deed was to liquidate the villages near the forests. The fate of those villagers was no different than the fate of the Jews. Many of them escaped to the forests. The Germans rained heavy fire upon the partisans to annihilate them. The partisans were forced to disperse and wander from place to place. My brother-in-law, Pesia Potashnik, Kopel Kagan, and I succeeded – literally in front of the eyes of the Germans – in arriving at a refuge next to the Staritski camp. We hid there. Fate was good to us, and we obtained a bit of flour, beans, dishes, and clothes. We squeezed water out of the mud near the refuge. We mixed it with the flour and consumed "the food of kings."

The memorial ceremony in the Heinering Camp

Every day, we awaited a major attack from the Vlasov troops. However, to our good fortune, they attacked at the front and not at the rear. They liquidated many partisan groups near the city of Smolensk. The time of the major attack of the Soviets arrived. The Germans escaped to the forests and fell into our hands. However, in accordance with the command of Stalin, we were forced to keep them as prisoners, rather than to liquidate them. I participated in a march in Minsk, and then I separated from my group and returned to Volozhin via Krasno and Horodok. I lived together with Pesia Potashnik and her brothers Yehuda and Yosef.

I decided to escape from Volozhin, for every stone there was saturated with the blood of our dear ones. I was recommended

[Page 560]

to teach in the Byelorussian school, but I refused to teach children who assisted the Germans in their murderous deeds. I decided to move to Poland. I wandered through various cities and towns for a period of time until they permitted me to cross the border. I reached Białystok, but I could not remain there because the A.K. (Armja Krajowa) ambushed Jews. We (four people) set out from Białystok in the direction of the city of Lublin. A group began to form, through the means of which we arrived in Czechoslovakia, Hungary, and Romania.

The first memorial ceremony in memory of the martyrs of Volozhin. It was arranged by Yosef Schwartzberg in the Heinering camp in Germany on 23 Iyar 5707 (May 13, 1947)

Sitting (from right to left): a) Michael Polak, b) Binyamin Polak, c) Kopel Kagan, d) Yosef Schwartzberg (reading from the paper about the Holocaust), e) Shmuel Kagan

The Second World War ended in May 1945. We did not want to remain under Soviet occupation. We arrived in Austria in groups. Some went in the direction of the city of Graz, and others went to Vienna. After a few days, we moved on to Italy, which was under British-American occupation. They transferred us to *Hachshara* in a village near Bari. We prepared for *aliya* to the Land of Israel. However, the Mandate government refused to give certificates. The illegal immigration began. We met with soldiers of the Jewish Brigade and Jews who served in British units. They sent a boat to the shores of the Land of Israel. I arrived in the Land of Israel in September 1945 with a group of 170 survivors of the sword.[3]

Translator's Footnotes:

1. M. Porat indicates the aunt was Keile Berkovich.
2. Mr. Porat added the following note and pictures at this point. (I did not edit: JL):

Translator's note: (as Fruma told me the evening I wrote it) In this barn together with the 900 (nine hundred) Jews of Horodok, Fruma Lifshits's mother surrounded by her five grand children also found their tragic fate, among them Shoshanele and Hayele Lifshits.

Yakov had been shot by one of their gentile neighbors in Horodok. Fruma witnessed her husband's death and saw the bestial murderers throwing away his body.

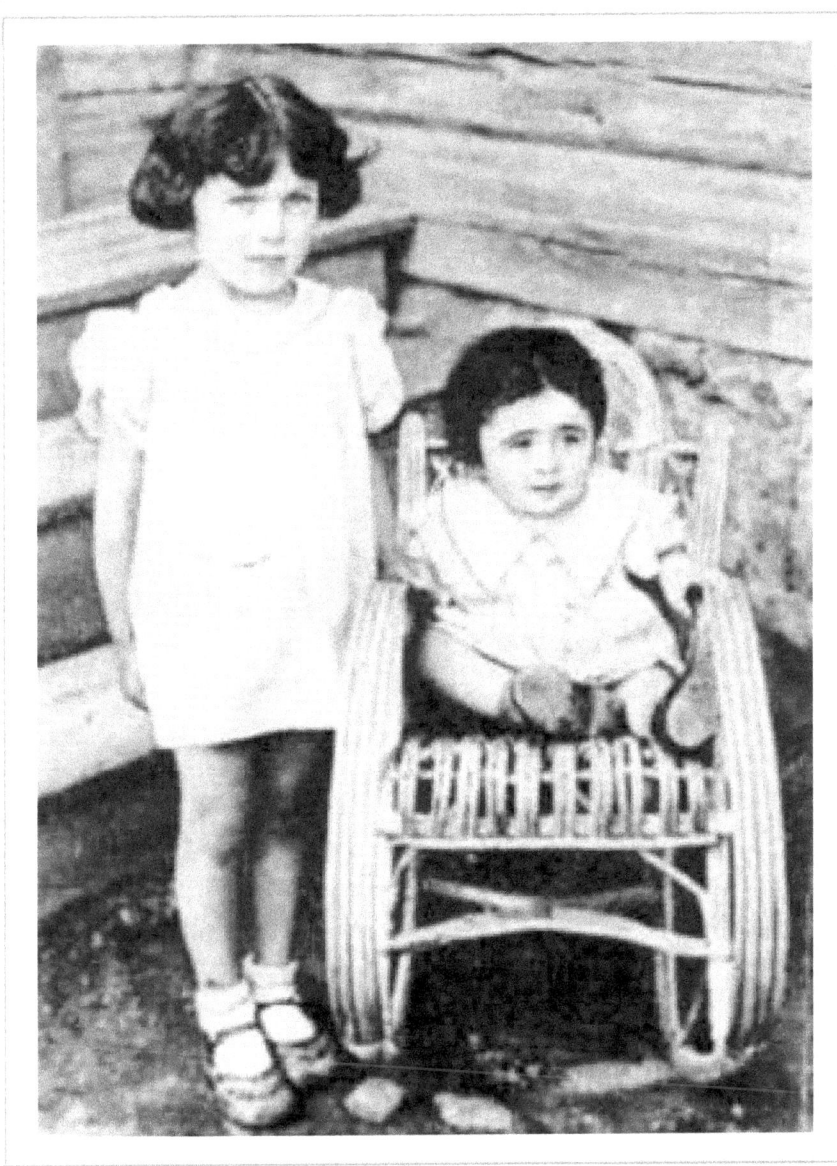

Lifshits children: Both were born in Volozhin, Shoshanele on July 7, 1933; Hayele on April 24, 1936. Both of them were shot and burned in Horodok on July 9, 1942.

This memorial tombstone was erected in the nineteen nineties near the site where 900 Horodok Jews were slaughtered. The plate on the left side (written in Hebrew) is dedicated to Yakov Lifshits and to his daughters Shoshanele and Hayele.

3. Mr. Porat added the following note:

We found in "PAMYAT' "– "MEMORY" (published by the Volozhin Region Authorities, 1996), page 272, a German-SS officer reporting to his headquarters:

General Commissar Office of the Minsk City
Department No 1 – Politics

Translated from German to Russian language.
The City of Minsk, May 31st 1943.

To the head of Department No 1:

I'm reporting to your knowledge about the events as follows. Dr. Valkovitsh, head of the Belarus Self-Help Organization notified me that on May 27th 14:00 Ukrainian units of the SS gathered all the inhabitants of Krivsk hamlet into two houses. They set fire the houses. The gathered people were burned to death. A similar event took place in Krazhino on May 21st. Both hamlets are positioned in the Volozhin region of the Vileyka district.

Signed: Langer

[Page 561]

From a Girl's Memoirs of the Holocaust

by Sonia Puter (Perski)

Translated by Jerrold Landau

The Germans entered Volozhin suddenly. Several German airplanes appeared in the sky. Their appearance aroused a tumult, and everyone dispersed to their homes. During the first weeks after their entry, the Germans took several Jews, including my aunt Chasia (Chasha) Leahke Gordon, imprisoned them in barracks, and killed them.

At first the murders were "small." The Germans were not interested in taking the Jews out immediately to be killed, because they wished to use them for work. The Soviets had burnt the marketplace during their retreat, and heaps of debris were piled up. We had to seal the pits and cellars in these ruins. Similarly, we had to uproot the weeds that grew among the clumps of rock. We worked from morning until night under the supervision of cruel guards who whipped us with the whips in their hands. The Germans imposed a strict blackout. At nightfall, they imprisoned us in the houses, and we were forbidden to go out. It was terribly suffocating inside because we covered the windows with thick blankets so that the light would not be seen from the outside.

I lived in the ghetto with my aunt Chaya Gita and uncle Hertzl Dubinski, my aunt Liba and uncle Dolgov, my grandmother Etl Perski, and the family of Avraham Berkowitz. My uncle Shalom Gordon and his children lived in the adjacent house. A shoemaker lived with us, who sewed boots for the gendarmerie. He was busy with his work until late at night. He regarded his toil as an advantage to protect him from trouble, for he was a "useful" Jew.

After the first aktion, the Jews began to build bunkers. There was a cellar in our house. We built a double wall in it. We went down to the bunker whenever we heard shots, and sat there cramped and oppressed. The only one who remained in his place was the shoemaker, for he was "useful."

When they attacked out house, my father and Avraham Berkowitz did not succeed in going down to the bunker, so they went up to the attic. They were found and taken to be killed. Even the shoemaker was liquidated in that attack despite his "usefulness."

Since we realized that our life was in constant danger, my mother, two sisters and I fled to Horodock. We returned to Volozhin when news reached us that the Germans were announcing that they would not hurt those that survived. I worked in the bathhouse. Once when I returned from work, I saw that the Germans were surrounding the ghetto and shooting. My niece Rachel Gordon and I looked for a hiding place. Along the way, we saw Shlomo Shuster running like a madman. A woman and her young daughter were running after him. We also ran behind them. My niece suddenly fell. A bullet hit her. I could not save her, and I left her to her bitter fate. I met Shlomo Skliot along the way. We hid in the forest. Jews from Volozhin joined us a few days later.

We decided to divide into small groups for security reasons. A woman named "Sara the

[Page 562]

Volozhiner" and I walked to Zabrezye, where my uncle Feivel Perski lived. We reached there towards morning. We entered the house of a gentile woman. She told us that the Germans had killed a Jewish woman yesterday (she was referring to my niece, who succeeded in reaching Zabrezye, where she died). We went to the workplace of my uncle. He was even afraid to talk to me. He gave me his breakfast and a fur coat, and advised us to immediately escape to Krevo for the police were liable to kill us.

We walked for an entire day over fields of stubble. My feet were bare and swollen. When I arrived in Krevo, I entered the first house in the ghetto, and immediately collapsed. My energy departed. I could not stand on my feet, for they were swollen.

I remained in Krevo for several weeks. From there, I wandered from camp to camp. I was in many camps, and my soul was sated with much difficulty, until the awaited liberation finally came.

A Ballad About Shneur Kivelevitch

by Mendl Volkovitch (Natanya)

Translated by Janie Respitz

Donated by Anita Gabbay

The 21st of June 1941
Hitler declared war on Russia.
They beat, kill and spill
Human blood for no reason.
The murderer's army marches into Volozhin
They shoot and slaughter.
People fall like flies,
They even drag babies from cradles.
There is a commotion and noise,
People are running and screaming,
But there is no one to shout at.

The Germans demand the creation of a Judenrat
The Judenrat will be chosen together with Shneur,
It will be a link between Germans and Jews.
Shneur is proud, not afraid,

[Page 563]

Even when they speak to him with their murderous "melody".

Approximately two months later,
They make a ghetto for the Jews.
They take everything from the houses,
They drive them out quickly, and shout,
"There is no room for you Jews"!
Shneur works auspiciously,
He delivers secrets in the ghetto.
This is how some time passes.
Everyone thinks his own fate
Is not far away.

Within a short time
Jews are taken out to the sports field
They are placed ten in a row
They shoot them to death.

Shneur is stunned,
But does not lose his courage.
"Jews", he shouts to us, "it's not good! We must dig holes, hide outs,
We must hide,
Maybe some of our brothers will survive".

In between there are horrific moments.
The police run into the ghetto,
They rob, beat us up and take what they want.

I saw with my own eyes
How two policemen snuck into the ghetto,

[Page 564]

Into a house
And began to rob a beat the Jews.

They ran to the Judenrat
And brought Shneur at night.
He entered the house
And shouted to the murderers with courage and pride: "Get out already!
You are not permitted to be in the ghetto"!

They began to laugh at him.
He shouted: "I am going straight to your commander"!
They left immediately.

Shneur always walked with courage, pride and confidence
And with devotion to victory.

I would like to mention another terrifying moment,
As I write my hands are shaking:
Shmuel Berman (Leybe Zekharia's son)
Escaped to Zabzhevi ghetto after the slaughter.
Once as he was walking to work
He bumped into two Zabzhevi police.
They asked him: what are you doing here?
Did you run away form Volozhin?
Then they said to him: You are a partisan.

They immediately took him to Volozhin
And he was sentenced to death.
They commanded him to climb the priest's hill
So all the Jews could witness the punishment
Which awaits a Jewish partisan.
And deliberately, in the middle of the day,

[Page 565]

So all the gentiles could watch and be pleased
To see what they do to the Jew.

Shmuel's sister ran to Shneur
So he can save him
He ran there as quickly as possible.
Unfortunately, it was too late.
Shmuel was lying shot in a pool of blood.
Shneur stood there dejected. He lost his courage.

This is how the chain
Of horrible deaths continued.
Until the arrival of the frightful day,
The 19th of May 1942.

The ghetto is surrounded,
They run in, beat us, kill and shoot.
The murderers are drunk.
They are laughing and rejoicing
As the ground is soaked
With Jewish blood.

Jews run into holes
Shneur also jumps in.
Everyone thinks and says:
Perhaps the Almighty will
Help us survive.

Unfortunately: nothing helped.
Our towns' bandits, the Christians,
Worked together with the German murderers.
They discovered everyone and pulled them out
Also from Shneur's hiding place.

[Page 566]

Shneur began to beg and argue
For them to let everyone go.
He defended the misfortunate with his coattails
Like an eagle with its wings,
When you come to steal his children.

This did not help,
His asking and cries.
They stood everyone together,
The sick, weak – the children separate.

They are thrown in heat and cold,
Everyone feels and thinks,
He will soon be leaving this world.

Hitler's murderers shout: "annihilate all the Jews"!
They take them away to the Soviet smithy,
They beat, wound and slaughter.
They choose a few Jews, professionals,
Together with Shneur,
And place them on the side,
The rest they take to the sergeant's house
And burned everyone.

The angel of death in the likeness of
A Hitler slaughterer,
Walks around with a big knife in his hand
However not yet pleased.
He says: there must be a few more Jews,
We must finish our "work".

Shneur lifts his eyes toward the sky
With a complaint to the Creator:

[Page 567]

You, who sits above
In the high heavens,
Do not want to see or hear
The Jewish tears and prayer?

For this you chose us as a nation?
"You chose us from among all other nations"?
So our blood will pour over all seas?
Are the gates of compassion closed?

The Hitlerites are bathing in our blood,
They have annihilated almost everyone,
However the last Jews with Shneour
Are still being left alone.

The Jews are happy,
They are of a variety of professionals,
Perhaps they will let them live?

However the murderers mock in their murderous hearts.
They promise them, ostensibly, they fool them as always,
Saying they will not kill them, they won't lay a hand on them.
"You may rejoice, sing,
Dance and jump".

Shneur is with them, but he is not who he was.
He has lost his confidence.
Observing their issues,
He was already broken:
Physically and spiritually,
No courage, a changed man
With his head down.

[Page 568]

He can no longer fight, defend, comfort.
Shneur could have escaped
As he was free to move around in the ghetto, and out,
But his pure conscious does not allow him to and says: No!
I will not leave the Jews here alone!

And when their turn came like all the others,
They gathered them all together and persuaded them
They are allegedly being taken to work in Vilayke.

But this is a lie,
They are thrown into a truck
And brought to the death place,
And when they approach their and his
Last moments of life, they hear a voice:
"The blood of your brothers and sisters

Mothers and fathers, small and big children
Is crying from the earth, from the graves, revenge!

He shudders and looks,
He stands and thinks
What should he do?
I lost the battle:
I fought, defended, blocked with my coattails,
Wanting to see comfort, solace.

I go to you, with you,
With everyone, with the martyrs,
To the pure souls, large and small,
Over there, very far, high above in heaven
Together with the six million.

[Page 569]

You have disappeared from us,
Far, far away.
Never to return!

Gone and not here.
However your good deeds,
Your spirit and soul are here.
They soar around us and with us,
And on Memorial Day
We announce we will
Never forget you.

You left us when you were young
But you will remain eternally in our memory.

In the Ghetto and in the Forced Labor Camps

by Lyuba Volkovich (Girkus), Netanya

Translated by Jerrold Landau

The second slaughter, in which most of the Jews of Volozhin were murdered, took place on 23 Iyar 5702 (May 10, 1942). When I saw that the slaughter was approaching, I went up to the attic with my husband Shmuel Berman, my brother-in-law Yaakov, my sisters-in-law Feigel and Chana, my nephew Avraham Eliyahu Baran, Hertzl Gurvich, and a lad from Krewo. I lay down next to one of the windows and saw what was happening to our dear ones.

We descended from the attic when night fell. Human voices rose up from the sewers. These were the voices of my nephews Eliyahu and Yona Kleinbord. We lifted them out of the sewer and fled to the forest. The conditions in the forest were exceedingly difficult, so we decided to return to the Volozhin Ghetto. There were approximately four hundred Jews in the ghetto who had gathered from the forests and other secret places. The Germans promised the Jews that from that day on, they would live in quiet, and no harm would befall them. However, this was a false promise. Next to this festive proclamation, Germans came from the Krasne labor camp to draft workers for the camp. They took approximately eighty people with them,

[Page 570]

including my brother-in-law Yaakov Berman (the son of Leibe Zecharia's). My husband Shmuel and I accompanied his brother, and we went out together to the Krasne camp. Our situation was unbearable.

During the month of Tammuz 5702 (June 1942), we escaped from there to Zabzhez [Zabyeraz]. Once, my husband and Asher Perski returned from work. On the way, the guards arrested them. They freed Perski because the recognized him from the Zabzhez ghetto. But they suspected that Shmuel was a partisan, so they led him to the Zabzhez police station. The guards informed the Volozhin police that they had a partisan in their hands. The police chief sentenced Shmuel to death, and he was taken out to be killed at "The Mountain of the Priest."

I toyed with the hope that Shmuel was alive, and that he was in prison. I disguised myself as a gentile woman and went to Volozhin to save him from death. When I arrived in the ghetto, they informed me that Shmuel had been taken out to be killed.

The third slaughter took place on one of the Sabbaths of the month of Elul 5702 (August 1942). The Jews went to the *Mincha* service. Suddenly, Gestapo men appeared from the road to Minsk, and started shooting at the ghetto. The prisoners broke through the barbed wire fence and began to run. I ran with Netanel (Saneh) Lavit to the village of Rudnik.

Suddenly, we heard a voice: "Saneh, I'm wounded!" This was the voice of Rachel Lavit, Shlomo's wife. A dum-dum bullet had had hit her hand, causing her a severe injury. She fell down in pain, and we did not have the means of calming her pain.

Only isolated people had mercy upon us. They threw pieces of bread from the window, as one throws to dogs, and ordered us to go away immediately. In the forests of Rudnik, we met several Jews of Volozhin, including Shmuel Berman, my sister-in-law Sara and her two children Rachel Tzart (sister-in-law of Avraham Tzart) and her daughter, and the young daughter of Leibe Skliot. We went to the village of Manegurje near Volozhin, and approached the house of a gentile. He refused to let us enter his house unless we would give him gold and valuables. I gave him ten gold rubles and he opened the door of his house.

We requested that he go to Volozhin to find out if any Jews survived there. When he returned from the city, he told us that not one Jew could be found there. The rest of the Jews had been murdered, and their bodies had been incinerated in the lime pit of Avraham the Vafelnik. (The pit was on Poloczani Street on the way to Shapowel). The farmers had extracted the gold teeth of the corpses and stripped their clothes. He also visited Krewo and Vyshnieva. We learned from his reports that the most secure place was Krewo, for the commandant of the ghetto was lenient toward the Jews.

The situation with Rachel's hand became very serious. She pleaded with us to return to Volozhin. We did not accept her request, for we still believed that a miracle would occur, and we would survive. Rachel did not believe in miracles, so she got up and went herself.

We decided to go to the forests of Volozhin with the hope of connecting with partisans. We reached the village of Bielokorets. As soon as we sat down to rest, we heard human footsteps. These were

[Page 571]

Jews who had escaped from the Volozhin ghetto. Among them were Gavriel Brudna (his father's name was Kushke), Leizer Meltzer, and Yaakov Shuster (son-in-law of Shlomo Raphael).

After we despaired of connecting with the partisans, we decided to go to Krewo. Saneh refused to join us because he was afraid of going in large groups. Rachel Tzart preferred to go to Zabzhez, and others agreed with her opinion. Having no choice, I joined them, even though my heart prophesied terrible things.

We arrived in Zabzhez. Skliot's daughter and I went to the Judenrat to request that they accept us into the ghetto. They responded to our request with a definitive refusal. The Judenrat claimed that if the police discovered that they were giving shelter to refugees, they would kill all the Jews of the ghetto. When I turned to leave, "Yosef the Expeditor" of Zabzhez approached me and brought me to the *Beis Midrash*. He bent down behind the oven. He moved several bricks and told me to go down. As soon as I lowered my leg, I ran into Shlomo Shuster.

I found out that the Judenrat understood my situation, for indeed the police had entered the ghetto to search for refugees. They had captured Merke Rudnitzki, the daughter of Chasha Lea Perski, several other girls, and Saneh Lavit, and brought them to the village of Dajnowka. There, they murdered them and covered their bodies with a thin layer of earth. (When we returned to Volozhin in the month of Av 5704, July 1944, my husband Mendel and Saneh's son Leibe carried them to a burial place. They found several bones there, and brought them to eternal life in the Volozhin cemetery.)

I decided to go to Krewo on my own. There, I found Lea Paretzki and Freidel, the daughter of Yosef Yekutiel. After some time, Mendel Wolkowitz, Yehuda Yosef Putshnik, Tovia Slyovski, and Yaakov Kagan arrived.

From Krewo, they transferred me to a labor camp in Zazmaria [Žiežmariai], Lithuania. There, I worked on paving the Vilna-Kovno Road. This work was even difficult for men, and especially so for women. My first workday in that camp was on Yom Kippur. I fasted and worked. Gestapo men guarded us. One of them (his name was Gyorgy), a veteran murderer, beat us with a belt made of thick, hard hide.

The autumn of that year was very difficult. Torrential rains fell incessantly. Later the harsh winter arrived. Snowstorms broke out in fury. The murderers did not pay attention to the weather, and chased us out to work daily. We were covered in worn-out rags, and we wore torn shoes. In truth, we were barefoot. Thus, did we work for a certain time until all the people of the camp became ill with abdominal typhus. Approximately four hundred ill people lay in several small rooms, men and women separately. Most of the sick people died since there were no doctors or medicines. Very few survived, and they did so because of the camp director (who was a Volksdeutsche). He traveled to Vilna, incidentally at the risk of his life, and brought us medications, which set us back on our feet.

The epidemic lasted for about three weeks. Those who survived went about for about two weeks.

[Page 572]

deaf and blind. However, we slowly recovered, and they chased us once again to work. They brought surviving Jews from the towns close to Vilna to us and the crowding in the camp continually increased. We felt that tribulations were approaching. The frequent visits of the Gestapo men forewarned us to this. A command was received that a portion of us should be transferred to a different place. The people whispered amongst themselves, and a tall mound of theories were proposed. Some believed that they were taking us to be killed, and others believed that they were hauling us to work.

I refused to go. I was together with Mendel Wolkowitz, Shmuel Berman, and Shlomo Rozen. Gyorgy the murderer broke into the bunk, dragged me out, and placed me together with the rest. They hauled us to the railway station. Wagons were waiting there. It seems that they had brought three more Jews there than the number that had been requested by the Gestapo men. Shmuel Berman approached the camp director and asked them to leave me behind since I was sick and weak, and there was no benefit in me. They freed me and I returned to the camp.

One day, a German from the Koshedar [Kaišiadorys] camp (eight kilometers from Zazmaria) came and asked that eight tradesmen along with one woman for cleaning services be given to him. They chose me for this task. Christian workers, including a Soviet citizen, also worked in this camp. I started a conversation with him. I told him that the fear of slaughter was upon the Jews, and therefore we have decided to escape to the forest. He was prepared to help us. However, the escape plan did not take place, because they returned us to Zazmaria.

One Sabbath during the spring of 5703 (1943) two Jewish Kapos from Vilna arrived in the camp. (They had assisted the Germans in liquidating the Ashmina camp). They informed us that they had come on a mission from the Gestapo to take three hundred Jews to an aktion. The matter immediately became known to Dr. Yitzchak Elchanan Rabinovitch (the grandson of Rabbi Yitzchak Elchanan, the famous rabbi of Kovno), the representative of the ghetto to the Arbeitsamt (work office) in Kovno. He hastened to the Gestapo and informed them that the Zazmaria camp, there are young Jews who are effective workers. He requested that we be brought to work in Kovno, thereby thwarting the Satanic efforts of the Germans and their Jewish Kapo assistants.

The next day, many trucks with Jewish police officers and Gestapo men arrived from Kovno. They listed the tradesman. Each of them was permitted to take his family members along. Since most of the Jews of the camp were widows and widowers – the men listed other women along with their names. Mendel Wolkowitz listed me with his name.

They brought us to Slobodka Street in Kovno. They gave us several slices of bread and coffee, and we lay down to rest. Later, they announced that in the Koshedar they required workers to dig peat. I went there with Mendel Wolkowitz. The Koshedar camp was comprised of several bunks surrounded by barbed wire. They gave us spades, and we did our work in the place of bogs. The chief work director was a Dutch Christian. The guards consisted of Germans and Ukrainians who had given themselves over to the Germans willingly. There were also Jewish supervisors who treated us well.

We received one hundred grams of bread and coffee for breakfast. In the afternoon, we were served horsemeat and soup.

[Page 573]

Once, I watched how they prepared the food. They brought a leprous horse, killed it, skinned it, chopped it up, and placed the chunks into a large cauldron. They cooked the meat for a few minutes, and it was already "ready" to be eaten. Mendel and I did not sully ourselves with this disgusting meat, so the hunger afflicted us greatly.

Once, a great tragedy took place in the camp. Two young Jewish lads came to the camp and asked us to escape to the forest with them. The purpose of their arrival became known to the police. The police killed them, and left their bodies at the entrance gate of the camp. A general of the S.S. gathered us together and commanded us to make two circuits around the corpses. He delivered a hateful lecture in which he emphasized that if we would dare to escape from the camp, our end would be like theirs. We were commanded to bury the killed people at the entrance to the camp, so that their graves will remind us at all times of the bitter end that awaits us.

After some time, a reinforcement of Ukrainian police was brought to the camp. All of them were young and healthy, and they instilled fear and dread upon us. These police conducted an exacting search in our bunks to discover whether we have hidden weapons in them. At the end of the search, they commanded us to take our bundles of rags with us and go outside. We sat from morning to night. To our surprise, the police officer tossed pieces of bread at us with great caution.

When it got dark, we were commanded to return to the bunks. After a few hours, when we were fast asleep, a large number of shots woke us up. We crowded around the window, and saw people running around, raising a great tumult. A Jew approached us and calmed us. The time of revenge had begun: The young Ukrainian police who had been brought as reinforcements killed the Dutch camp director and all the guards. They took all the weapons and food, and opened the camp gate wide so that we too could escape. They all escaped to the forest.

In the morning, S.S. men arrived in the camp with transport trucks. They called the men and commanded them to place the bodies of those murdered on the trucks. The corpse of the camp director was cut into pieces. His head had been severed from his body. They piled up his body parts into a single heap and loaded them on the truck.

Our situation improved after this act of revenge. The Jewish workers whispered among themselves that they should escape to the forests. Working with us was a Soviet prisoner who also was preparing to escape to the forest. The Jews of the camp asked me to negotiate with him. He told me that the conditions for escape was receiving weapons. We obtained weapons in various manners. The prisoner hid and guarded them.

In the meantime, a frightful thing happened that thwarted our plan of escape. One day during the month of Nisan 5704 (March 1944), German troops and Gestapo men came from the direction of Kovno. They were armed with automatic guns and machine guns. The Gestapo chief entered the camp with several soldiers. They commanded us to go outside and line up in rows – women and children separately and men separately. The children stood next to their mothers. The children, who understood what was taking place, sobbed quietly, and cleaved to their mothers. The Gestapo men attacked the children and separated them

[Page 574]

forcefully from their mothers. The mothers fainted. The murderers dragged them to the bunks, but they jumped through the windows, ran to their children, held them close to their hearts, and shouted in a loud voice: "Our dear children, we will not leave you alone. We will go to the grave together with you!"

A woman from Olshan named Itka Rabinovitch was among these mothers. She had three lads. The oldest of them was aged twelve. She approached the chief and requested that he leave at least one of her children alive. As a response to her request, he beat her cruelly and pushed her to the side.

They imprisoned us in bunks and warned us to not dare to go outside. We placed ourselves next to the windows to find out what would happen to the children. A wagon hitched to two horses entered the camp. They placed the children on the wagon and took them to an unknown place.

The next day, they took us out to work as usual. The women whose children had been stolen from them were permitted to rest for several days. When we came to work at the railway station, the gentiles from the nearby villages told us that the children had been brought to the railway station. They were kept hungry and thirsty for the entire day. At night, they were placed on a railway wagon and transported to the German border.

After the Gestapo men had killed the children, we felt that we ourselves were in great danger. We decided to immediately escape from the camp. One group of Jews of the camp worked in the forest. Once they saw three men coming out from among the trees, dressed in Soviet army uniforms and armed with automatic weapons. The Gestapo men, who guarded the workers were certain that not one of their people would escape, turned aside, sat on the ground, and began to stuff themselves and smoke. At this unusual opportune time, two people from the groups of Jews rose up and walked along the surrounding paths to meet the partisans. They were asked to identify themselves. They responded, "We are Jews." The partisans asked, "What are you doing here?" The two responded, "We are at a work camp close to here in the city of Koshedar." "How many are you?" The Jews responded, "About four hundred individuals."

After the questioning, the partisans identified themselves. They said that they were part of a group of four people: two Russian commanders and two Jews. They continued to inquire about the number of Jews working in the forests and the number of Germans guarding them. The Jews responded that their group consisted of fifteen people, guarded by four Germans.

Then the partisans replied, "We will kill the German guards and you can go with us." "But," they continued to ask with great worry, "What will be with the rest of the Jews in the camp? When the Gestapo men find out that your group escaped to the partisans, they will take out all the Jews to be killed." Therefore, they advised us to wait until the proper time for this. They promised that they would come soon to free all the Jews. The sign of the action of liberation would be: A farmer will enter the camp riding on a white horse, and will throw a white note upon which will be written the time that we must all prepare for escape.

[Page 575]

The partisans went on their way, and we continued with our work. This took place approximately two weeks before the Passover festival of 5704 (1944).

On the eve of Passover, a farmer riding on a white horse appeared in the camp. (He was really a disguised partisan.) He threw the note of redemption on the ground, upon which was written that the time of escape had arrived.

The next day, approximately forty partisans went to the forest in which our forestry group worked. They surrounded the workers and removed the weapons from the German guards. They sent two Jews to inform all the Jews in the camp that they must escape immediately.

I worked in the railway station loading lumber. I saw that two Jews among the heaps of lumber sticking out, and telling us from mouth to ear that we must escape. We stopped our work, and we all began to advance slowly and cautiously toward the route lading to the forests. However, as soon as we began to run, the guards noticed and began to shoot. I ran together with Leizer Dniszewdski from Krewo. We heard the shots, but we continued to run on a long route until we arrived in the forest. There, we found four men and one woman. We looked for contact with the partisans. Along the way we met several Jews who told us that many of the Jews of the camp had been killed, and the rest had returned to the camp.

To our dismay, we did not find the partisans. We found out that they had taken a group of Jewish workers with them, as well as the Germans who were guarding them. In the meantime, the number of escapees increased, and the group reached about twenty individuals. A few of them were almost naked, for when they escaped from the camp, they took off their clothes to make the running easier. Our situation was hopeless One of our group, Yitzchak Ziskind, said that he knew the guard of the forest. He intended to approach him, and perhaps we could be saved through him. He took one of us with him and set out on the journey. The guard told him that a group of forty partisans had visited him a few days earlier, with a group of Jews and four Germans. They left notice with the forest guard that they would return in a few days, and if there were any Jews with him, they would take them with them.

And thus it was: The partisans kept their promise, and took us into the forest. We hid there until the time of liberation.

[Page 576]

Frantz Karl Hess - Volozhin Hangman

Translated by Dr. Yosef Porat

Number one murderer, who was the head of the extermination of the Volozhin ghetto on May 1942. Summary of the stenographic protocol, which was published as a book by the title " The trial of the natzy invaders who committed acts of horror in Belarus"

The trial started on January 15th 1946 and was finished on the 29th. In these days the martial court of the Minsk County was weighing the accusations against eighteen nazi officials who served in the German police and army; Among them – four S.S. and S.D. commanders, two chiefs of battalions, a Major, two Captains, two Uberlieutenants and the rest of lower ranks. Frantz Karl Hess, second lieutenant of the thirty second " Zondercommando" stationed near the police and S.S. in Minsk was one of the eighteen convicts.

The following judges held the trial:

>Chairman of court: General Kadrov.
>Judge: Chief of Battalion Sacharov.
>Judge: Chief of Battalion Vinogradov.
>The prosecutors: Lieutenant Colonel Yatzanin and the Battalion Head Palachin.

Lawyers nominated by the state represented all convicts, except Frantz Karl Hess who renounced the lawyer and preferred to represent himself. After some formalities, the hearings began.

The hearings on the 19th of January 1946 were dedicated to the investigation concerning the prosecution that was held against Frantz Karl Hess.

Given here is a briefing of the hearings and the verdict.

Chairman (addressing accused Hess):	Are you confirming your testimony given in the early investigation?
Hess:	Yes I confirm it.
The chairman to the prosecutor:	Comrade prosecutor, do you have questions to the accused?
Prosecutor:	Yes. Addressing Hess asks: Tell me Hess; on what year did you enter the ranks of the fascist party?
Hess:	In 1939.
Prosecutor:	What was your military rank and in any what regiment were you serving your duty?

[Page 577]

Hess:	I was a simple private in the S.S. army.
Prosecutor:	What is your family origin?
Hess:	I come from a working family. My father worked in a factory.
Prosecutor:	What office did your father hold in the factory?
Hess:	He worked as a simple worker.
Prosecutor:	Your father was a Nazi?
Hess:	No. He was apolitical and died in 1916.
Prosecutor:	How come that you, as a son of a working family, finds yourself in the ranks of the Nazi party?

Hess:	Because I am German.
Prosecutor:	Just because you are German?
Hess:	Yes.
Prosecutor:	What did you do in the army?
Hess:	I worked in a factory producing weights.
Prosecutor:	When did you come to the Zondercommando in Minsk?
Hess:	I came in the beginning of December 1941.
Prosecutor:	What duties were put upon you?
Hess:	I had to guard the offices and establishments of the army and the SS.
Prosecutor:	This is not true! You were trained in courses for commanders of the border police, in managers courses and in handling trained dogs – all these were done for house guarding only? Tell the court all of the truth!
Hess:	All right, I shall tell! Our work as house guards was only for deception. Our main mission was the extinction of Jews. The orders were given from above and we were forced to commit them.
Prosecutor:	To where did you go on the first half of May 1942 with a shooting squad?
Hess:	We drove to Volozhin.
Prosecutor:	To which county does Volozhin belong?
Hess:	To Molodechna County I think. I am not sure.
Prosecutor:	What did you do in Volozhin?
Hess:	We exterminated the Jews there.
Prosecutor:	How many Jews did you kill there?
Hess:	Approximately two thousand.
Prosecutor:	Who was in charge of this 'actsia'?

[Page 578]

Hess:	Untersturmführer Grabe.

Prosecutor:	How did you gather the Jewish community in order to commit the horror acts?
Hess:	We took the people from their houses, they were locked in the cowshed, and there we shot them to death.
Prosecutor:	What have you done with the property and valuable objects of the dead?
Hess:	We sent the valuables to Villieka.
Prosecutor:	From whom were the two thousand dead, in the town of Volozhin of Molodechna County, composed?
Hess:	From men, women and children.
Prosecutor:	Why did you kill the people? Just because they were Jews?
Hess:	Yes. Just because they were Jews.
Prosecutor:	Were within the two thousand dead also other nationalities members?
Hess:	No. Jews only.
Prosecutor:	In what way did you execute them?
Hess:	We divided the Jews to groups of eighty – hundred people. Every group was entered into the cow shed, and there they killed them one by one- till the last one of them.
Prosecutor:	Within the two thousand were also people from Volozhin vicinity, or from Volozhin only?
Hess:	I do not know.
Prosecutor:	You took out all of the Jews from the ghetto?
Hess:	Yes, we took out all of them.
Prosecutor:	Who were the shooters?
Hess:	All were ordered to shoot, including me.
Prosecutor:	How many Jews did you kill with your own hands in Volozhin?
Hess:	I personally killed about one hundred and twenty Jews. (Noise in the courtroom).
Prosecutor:	In what part of the body did the bullet hit? Did you shoot the back of the neck?

Hess:	Yes, we shot the head. The Jews were kneeling on their knees and we shot the head, which means – the back of the neck.
Prosecutor:	Did the children also were kneeling on their knees and shot in the back of their necks?
Hess:	Yes, all of them – children, men, women, old and young.
Prosecutor:	From what weapon did you shoot?
Hess:	From a pistol.

[Page 579]

Prosecutor:	What kind of gun was it?
Hess:	It was a 0.8-mm army gun.
Prosecutor:	What have you done with the bodies? Buried them?
Hess:	No. We soaked most of the bodies with gasoline and burned them.

The last words of Hess were that he regrets his actions in Belarus, but that he is innocent because he was forced to do it by his superiors.

He declared before the judges and the people whose sons have judged him, that fascism was the greatest curse that the world has ever known.

These ended the hearings on the 29th of January. In the late hours of the night, the court published its verdict.

The verdict

The court martial concluded, that Frantz Karl Hess, as an inferior rank officer of the eighth Zondercommando' by the security police of the SS and SD, took an active part.

In the December 1941 'aktion'. In this 'aktion' a hundred patients that were hospitalized in the Minsks' mental hospital were shot, as well as two hundred and fifty civilians that were temporarily arrested in Minsks' prison.

Many times, Hess took part in the killings of soviet citizens from Jewish origin, among them old, women and children.

In December 1941, he took part in the killings of two thousand people in Minsk.

In 1942 he took part in the killing of the peaceful Jewish community in the city of Vileycky. In the small town of Ivia, Molodechna County, Hess killed sixty people with his own hands. In the cities Dolginova and Vishnieva, Hess participated in murdering three thousand five hundred soviet citizens of Jewish origin.

In the town of Volozhin, he took part in the execution of two thousand Jews, of which he himself killed one hundred and twenty. In the town of Trastenitz-Zutta he was a part of a company that executed in shooting and strangling eighteen thousand Soviet citizens of Jewish origin.

As a whole Hess participated in killing and strangling of thirty thousand people, most of them Jewish. He himself killed several hundreds of them.

According to a section of the order submitted by the superior court of the SSSR, on the day of 19.4.43, the German Frantz Karl Hess born in 1909 in the village of Kastill of Louatmaritz County in the Sudeten region, was charged to death by hanging.

On the 30.1.1946, on 1430 in the afternoon by Moscow time, the verdict was executed. Hess was hanged on the hippodrome of Minsk.

Over one hundred thousand people attended the hanging of the convicts.

[Page 580]

In the Volozhin Ghetto and in Revenge Actions
By Yaakov Kagan of Tel Aviv

Translated by Jerrold Landau **based on an earlier translation by** M. Porat z"l
that was edited by Judy Feinsilver Montel

I went to Vilna immediately after the outbreak of the German-Polish war with the goal of making *aliya* from there. I lived in Vilna for two years but did not succeed in accomplishing my heart's desire. I decided to return home after the Germans invaded the Soviet Union. I wanted to be together with my family during the time of trouble. From afar I saw Volozhin in flames. I found many Volozhiners near Mount Bialik escaping the flames. I went to our house. Many Germans were walking about the streets. They did not stop me, and they let me go.

The Germans sent us to different sorts of hard labor. I worked as the steam engine stoker at the Rapoport grist mill. I became friends there with the chief machinist Kadirko. Polish policemen with Gestapo men entered the mill one day, gathered all the Jewish workers, and told them that they were being taken to a general meeting. I continued working because Kadirko was stubborn, and said that if they take me, he would be forced to stop the mill. This reason convinced the Gestapo men, and they let me work. However, my heart was not quiet. I felt that something was being plotted against us. I returned to the ghetto in the afternoon and saw that many Jews had been concentrated in one place. They were waiting impatiently for the "speaker." I understood that this was not going to be a lecture, so I left the line and returned to work.

I decided to at least save the Jews who were involved in paving the road to the village of Kapustino. My brother Nachum was among them (useful people were exempt from listening to the "lecture"). I warned them to not return to the ghetto. My brother and I immediately set out on a journey, and reached the village of Solony. At night, we entered a building where they were drying flax. We were chased out of there. Having no choice, we returned to Volozhin.

When we returned, we heard that an aktion had taken place. After that life returned to its "normal" order. The Jews continued to work, and I returned to work at the mill. After some time, they took about 100 Jews to work in the forest near Bielokorets. My brother Nachum and I were among them. We lived in a shack in the woods. Yoda, previously the police commander in Yatskovo, was now the forest works supervisor.

In the woods we met Soviet prisoners of war. They conveyed wood logs to the sawmills in Volozhin. Once they told us that in the near future "flowers" would grow in the forest. (That was a euphemism for partisans.) They suddenly disappeared, and after some time they appeared anew. This time they were armed. They suggested that we join them. We refused their proposition, for it was difficult for us to leave our families in the ghetto. They did not insist. Thus, I continued my work in the forest until the second slaughter, which took place on 23 Iyar 5702 (May 10, 1942).

On my way to Volozhin one day before the slaughter, I stopped in the village of Kapustino to take a bottle

[Page 581]

of milk from there. I encountered a gentile from the area of Volozhin. He told me that partisans killed three Germans on their way to Horod'ki railway station. He advised me to not return to the ghetto, for the police were blaming the Jews for the act of murder. I did not heed him, and I continued on my way. There was an astonishing calm in the city. Lone Gestapo men were seen on the streets. The Jews walked about in the ghetto and outside of it without being disturbed. Nobody stopped them or paid attention to them. The Judenrat was ordered to prepare three garlands. Gestapo men calmed the Jewish representatives telling them not to fear, because Jews were not suspected in killing the three Wehrmacht soldier. The Jews sensed there was no truth in their calming words, because they saw clearly that something very serious was about to happen. Shneur Kivilevich sat with the Jewish policemen in the Judenrat office until late in the night. He returned home at 2:00 a.m. after they did not find any signs of anything to arouse concern.

Miriam Weisbord knocked on our window at 4:00 a.m. She said: "Get up quickly, something not good is happening in the ghetto!" We immediately jumped out of bed and got dressed. We heard shooting. The Germans approached our house and broke our neighbor's door. Kopel and I exited through the back door and turned toward our garden where there was a secret door through which we smuggled food into the ghetto. We crossed the bridge on Pilsudski Street. A German armed with a machine gun stood on the bridge. When the German bent down to light his pipe, I escaped in the direction of Novogrudski Street (it was called Ponizha). I heard a voice from afar. I stopped. Kopel reached me after a brief time. He was injured. The German who was guarding the bridge shot him in his shoulder. We walked together and reached the Islach River. The waves had brought a boat to the shore. We entered it and crossed the river.

We reached a forest near Bielokorets, and met Jews from Olshan who had escaped from the Volozhin Ghetto. The conditions in the forest were very serious. Having no choice, I returned to Volozhin. From there, I was taken to work in Krasno. Later, I reached the Oshmiany Ghetto together with Yehuda Yosef Potashnik.

There were Jewish police officers from the Vilna Ghetto in the Oshmiany Ghetto. I contacted them and made a proposal to set up a self-defence in the ghetto. One of them, a man of the underground, promised to send me weapons. We would stand up for our lives when they come to liquidate the ghetto.

News arrived that they would soon be transferring the Jews of the Oshmiany Ghetto to a labor camp near Vilna. The Judenrat appointed Ganz, the head of the Jewish police in Vilna, asking him to clarify whether the news was true, that indeed they were going to liquidate the Oshmiany Ghetto. Ganz hurried and went immediately to Oshmiany. He gathered the Jews and calmed them that all the rumors of the liquidation of the ghetto were baseless. Every attempt of escape to the forest and joining the partisans endangered the existence of the Jews in the Oshmiany Ghetto.

Many among us had already had experience with such assurances and did not believe Ganz' promises. In the ghetto, a group of Jewish doctors, nurses, and police officers were preparing to go out

[Page 582]

to the forest. Kopel and I joined that group. We contacted the partisans who were operating in the area. They told us that they were prepared to accept us on the condition that we bring a portable infirmary with us. We sent emissaries to Vilna who brought back all the necessary medical equipment Prior to the liquidation of the ghetto, a German captain came to the carpentry shop where I worked and said that he had to tell me something. He got to the point immediately and told me, "I know that a group of Jews is about to go to the forest. I have decided to keep a Jewish brother and sister alive. Take them with you. If not, I will be forced to kill them. Since I know that the partisans do not accept people with empty hands, I will give them two rifles and two grenades." The German kept his promise, and the brother and sister joined us.

We decided to prepare to take out the medication and surgical equipment. We had to go to the Sol railway station. We decided to send the medication to the town of Barun. We planned to place down the weapons on the way, and to disappear into the forest. This plan seemed to be practical, because the Germans appointed members of our group as caravan accompaniers. Thanks to this, the medication reached its destination successfully. However, we could not disappear with the weapons, because the camp director appeared suddenly. We reached the Sol railway station. A German approached me and asked, "What does the luggage contain?" I told him that it cannot be sent, and the package should be returned to the Oshmiany Ghetto.

We returned to the ghetto with the package of weapons. At night we made the decision to go to the forest, be what may. We went to Barun, and from there to Bukotovo near Vishnievo. There, we met scouts of the partisan brigades, who received us nicely. In time, Jews from other partisan groups joined us. I met Hessel Perski and Eliezer Rogovin.

Our first assignment was to obtain weapons. We found out that in Baksht, one could obtain weapons from the gentiles in exchange for tobacco and salt. We went there, and we indeed obtained some weapons. In Bakst, we made contact with the Staritzki Otriad. Eliezer Rogovin served in that camp as the commander of a group of miners. I also found there Mottel Malot, Yosef Girkes, and other Jews from Volozhin. After some time, we amassed a significant stockpile of weapons. We went through difficult training, and set out for actions. I was appointed as a scout thanks to my expertise in battle. Our field of operation was in the region of Volozhin. I made contact with a gentile from Volozhin who helped me enter the city to see if there were any Jews left.

I visited Volozhin in the year 5703 (1943). I found the Weisbord family, Eli the Locksmith, his son Hatzkel, and his daughter Rashel. The sisters Rivka (Ipta), and Rachel Perski lived with them. There was also a Jewish smith who had a smithy in Aroptzu. I asked them to come to the forest with me, for they had no hope in surviving. They refused my request. I went to Volozhin several times, and continued to urge them to come to the forest. Finally, when I succeeded in convincing them and promised to take them to the forest – there was already nobody to take. I was told that they were taken to Vileyka. That was the final liquidation of the Volozhin Ghetto.

[Page 583]

During one of the patrols in the area of Volozhin, I received an order from the commander to help a group of partisans destroy a German camp in Shapoval. I was injured in my leg during that battle. They brought me to a camp in the forest, and then they flew me to a hospital in Homel.

When I recovered, I was sent to the draft division of Homel. From there, I was transferred to the central command of the partisans in the village of Shevroki (near Homel). In that village, I met Eliezer Rogovin, who had been seriously wounded in one of the battles.

When Volozhin was liberated, I returned there from Shevroki. There, I encountered the survivors from our city: Pnina Potashnik, Yehuda Yosef Potashnik, Shayke Lavit with his brother-in-law, Leibe Lavit, the Skliot brothers, Leibke Liberman, Mariashe Kagan (Zukerkopf) with her husband, Areh and Zelig Rogovin, Mottel Malot, Zelig Meltser, Tsofen with his wife, Mendel Goldshmid with his wife, Shmuel Perski, and Mintzer with his wife (in his time, he was in the Hashomer Hatzair kibbutz in Volozhin, and worked as a mechanic for Polak).

After working for several months at the grist mill in Pershay (twelve kilometers south from Volozhin) I was sent to Ivianiets. Kopel worked there at the draft office. I was appointed as a director at the flourmill in Rubyazavich. After some time, Koppel and I moved to Poland together. Finally, I made *aliya* from Germany to the land of Israel in 5707 (1947).

Note by M. Porat:

Yankele Kagan was member in the Irgun Tzvai Leumi the rightist underground organization commanded by Menachem Begin. He was seriously wounded preparing ammunition in the Irgun's undercover laboratory. Yankele the partisan lost an eye and burnt his face. The scar was with him all his life. In Israel he was happily welcomed by the Tel Aviv Volozhiners especially by Bela Saliternik (Kramnik). She arranged his marriage to Rivka, a girl who survived the Shoah in Poland. The wedding ceremony was led by Rabbi Langbord the last Volozhin town Rabbi. Bela told me that for Yankele Kagan's marriage she baked 10 (ten) cakes. He was very active at the committee of the Organization of Volozhin Natives. Yakov Kagan passed away after Rivka was deceased, leaving a daughter with grand children in Ness Tziona in 1998.

[Page 583]

Nissan Perski's Death

by Simcha Rogovin of Kiryat-Haim

Translated by Jerrold Landau

I will tell about the death of Nissan Perski in these few lines. Seemingly, what is the reason to tell about the death of an individual when the entire community of Volozhin was destroyed. However, this death was one of a kind.

I escaped with my family to Horodok one day before the entry of the Germans. We could not continue our escape because the Germans ruled over the entire area. I was imprisoned in the Horodok Ghetto. After time, they took about fifty lads from there, I among them, and transferred us to Molodeczno. The work was very difficult and backbreaking. When the situation became unbearable, and I realized I could not continue to hold out any longer in that torture camp, I escaped from there with three other Jews. To our good fortune, we did not meet a Polish or German police officer along the way. We entered an isolated house in a grove. The gentile who lived there treated us mercifully and showed us the way to the partisans.

We walked on foot to the village of Rudki on the Islach River. There, we met two Jews from the Krasno Ghetto. The villagers related to us in a humane fashion and employed us with different jobs. At first, the partisans refused to accept us because rumors were spreading that the Jew were involved in spying for the Germans. However, after much urging, they agreed to accept us to their unit.

[Page 584]

Even after we were accepted, the partisans warned us that if any trace of duplicity would be found among us, our blood would be upon us. After a week, we were commanded to obtain arms and to be prepared for action.

On one of the actions of bombing a train, we found out that Nissan Perski was hiding in an isolated house next to the city of Rakow. After the successful execution of the action, I took bread, salt and butter with me. I went out with my unit late at night to save Nissan. I reached the hiding place and knocked on the window. Since I spoke Yiddish, the door opened, and I entered. When I entered, a man was groaning under the oven. This was Nissan. He was downtrodden, and his entire body was trembling. I told him that I had come to save him. He should come with me to the forest, join the partisans, and remain alive. However, he asked me to leave him, since he had become accustomed to the place and decided to remain there until the salvation would come. He regarded this house as a protection from tribulations. I did not succeed in convincing Nissan to join me, so I left full of worry and fear for his life. About a half a year later, I found out that the Germans set the house on fire and Nissan Perski went up in flames.

On the Path of Suffering

by Mendel Volkovich, Netanya

Translated by Jerrold Landau

I was one of the survivors of the third slaughter. I was taken to work the Krasno camp. They made me work at the building of bunks and in porterage at the railway station. After some time, they transferred me to work in the sawmill. Tovia Slyowski, Yehuda Yosef Pucznik, Yaakov Kagan, Eli Yaakov Rogovin, Leizer Nul from Horodok, and a barber from Vishnyeva worked there.

On the Sabbath of Elul 9, 5702 (August 22, 1942), we found out that the Germans were planning to liquidate the Krasno Ghetto and the labor camp, and to take out all the Jews to be killed. We decided to escape from the camp beforehand. The escape was fraught with great difficulties. We crawled among the heaps of lumber that were in the sawmill. We climbed from heap to heap until we approached the road. We crossed it quickly and entered the grove.

We removed our Magen David [patches] and set out for the forests of Horodok. We sat down to rest in the forest. Suddenly, we heard Yiddish being spoken. We saw before us a group of Jews who had fled from the Krasno Ghetto and Camp, the majority from Horodok and the minority of Volozhin. Among the Volozhiners were the brothers Hershel and Moshel Skliot and the brothers Areh and Zelig Rogovin.

Our food supplies ran out. It was difficult to obtain food because the gentiles of the area were anti-Semitic. So as not to die from hunger, we carved forms of guns from branches. We threatened the gentiles with these "weapons" that if they do not give us food, their blood will be upon them. The gentiles were frightened of the sticks that resembled guns and gave us an abundance of food.

[Page 585]

Through the energy of this eating, we reached Pershai, (a large farm between Volozhin and Ivaniec, from where the routes between the Nlibok steppes and the forests of Volozhin cross). We could not go on the highway, for it was guarded by the Gestapo men. Therefore, we went on tortuous routes. We reached a pond that was about forty meters long. We measured the depths of the water with a stick. The beach was shallow. However, as we advanced, the water got deeper until it reached our necks. We were concerned about going further out of fear of drowning. However, Hershel Skliot urged us on, telling us that we were casting away our lives, for death was pursuing us from behind. We crossed the pond in peace.

Dawn had already broken when we arrived in Pershai. We were wary of resting there because flights were splitting the air. We went to the Volozhin forests. We saw traces of tanks, humans, horses, and dogs in the forest. Many corpses were wallowing between the trees. Yaakov Kagan and I felt the hand of one victim, and it was still warm, proving that the person had only recently been killed.

I had a friend in this area, a gentile named Yoda. I went to him and asked him to explain the killings. He told me that three days earlier, the Germans had surrounded the forests and started shooting. They conducted a search for partisans and Jews. He advised me to escape from the area. I returned to the forests and told my friends about the bitter fate about which Yoda had told me.

Hershel and Moshe Skliot, and Zelig Rogovin decided to return to the Krasno camp. This decision was like suicide. Therefore, we accompanied them with sadness and agony. Tovia Slyowski told me that he intended to go to Krewo[Kreva]. He had formerly served there as a teacher, and was much loved by the householders, especially by the rabbi of the city. He advised me to join him. I agreed. Yaakov Kagan and Yehuda Yosef Pucznik also accompanied us. We arrived in peace to the Krewo Ghetto. This was on the first night of Rosh Hashanah 5703 (September 12, 1942). Tovia and I entered the house of the rabbi. Yaakov Kagan and Yosef Pucznik went to a different house.

The rabbi lifted his eyes and was very astonished, for he could not identify me at all. He was astonished at Tovia's appearance, which had changed due to the troubles and tribulations. The rabbi invited us to eat the "festive meal" which was nothing more than "the bread of affliction.," for the Jews were starving due to a lack of food. However, the warm reception of the rabbi satiated us. We recited the blessing on the food and lay down to sleep on the ground. The next day, we went to worship in the synagogue. We prayed with broken, trembling hearts. The *Unetaneh Tokef* prayer expressed the situation. We knew that we were all awaiting, "Who by fire, and who by water, who by sword, and who by beast."

After lunch, we consulted with the rabbi about what to do. The rabbi said that Tovia could remain in his house because everyone knew him as a resident of Krewo. But I must leave, for the police was conducting searches in the houses for Jewish refugees who escaped from other camps.

The Judenrat also demanded that I leave the ghetto, for my presence endangered the lives of the Jews.

[Page 586]

I parted from my good friend Tovia with great agony. (He was later taken out to be killed by the partisans, with no iniquity on his side.) I went to Smargon, where they registered me in the name of someone who had been killed. After a few days, a truck arrived from the Zizmiria [Žiežmariai] camp in Lithuania to get workers. The Smargon Judenrat announced that anyone who wishes to travel to Zizmiria was permitted to do so. I decided to travel there, for my heart told me that life in a labor camp was more secure. I arrived in the evening. The camp was surrounded by a tall, barbed wire fence. The imprisoned Jews looked at me with surprise.

After a brief conversation with several of them, we walked together to the Kol Nidre service. We worshiped silently out of fear of the Gestapo. The next day, Yom Kippur, each of us was given one hundred grams of bread and coffee. They removed us from the bunks, lined us up in lines, conducted a roll call, and we were sent to work. During the work, we succeeded in making contact with the outside world. Thanks to those contacts, I remained alive.

[Page 586]

Wandering and Struggling

By Rachel & Reuven Rogovin

Translated by Jerrold Landau **based on an earlier translation by** M. Porat z"l
that was edited by Judy Montel

Note: this photo and introduction are not in the original. They were added by M. Porat:

The Rogovins (the authors) were born in Volozhin, Rachel in 1906, Reuven in 1904. They married there, worked and lived there and fled the town with their two children to escape the Nazis, going to Tadzhikistan. At the end of the war the family came to Riga, and went to Israel in the early fifties. Reuven Rogovin was devoted to Volozhin. He expressed his love in many stories about the shtetl's colorful folksy types. Some of them he described and offered his articles to the Volozhin Yizkor Book. See: Reb Itshe der Balegole (coachman), Reb Chaim der Shnayder (the tailor), Reb Eyzer Der Raznoshtshik (postman) etc.

We fled Volozhin at night, four days after the Germans invaded the Soviet Union. The day before we packed our valuables and brought them to the cellar of our neighbor, Sholom Leib Rubinstein's. We left the town empty handed. Our son Grisha took his bicycle. Reuven left wearing slippers, because good friends persuaded him walking would be easier in slippers. After walking some kilometers on roads paved with building stones, his slippers tore, and his feet were exposed.

Rachel and Reuven Rogovin - 1950

We felt better when we arrived at Miejiki. We saw about thirty large wagons hitched to horses. Our acquaintances with their families were in almost every wagon: all the Simernitski brothers, Berl Spektor, Avraham Molot, Chatzkel der Olshaner, Hershel Sheyniuk with his wife, and others. They were happy to see us, and asked about how things were in Volozhin, for they had left the city the day before. We told them that although it seemed quiet now, it was not a portent for the future. We asked if we could join them in order to cross the border to Russia, but Avraham Molot responded, "We are not going eastward, but rather westward. That is, we are returning to Volozhin. We escaped to here because they told us that they would be bombing Volozhin. But if it is now quiet in the city, we are returning." They went back to the mouth of the lion – To Volozhin, where they all perished at the hands of the Nazis.

Having no choice, we continued to walk and arrived in the city of Rakov. There we met acquaintances, who received us cordially. The mistress of the house, Chaika Rubinchik (sister of Getzl Perski), asked us to leave our children with her. She would protect them, and no harm would befall them, for the Germans are not doing any harm,

[Page 587]

neither to Jews nor Jewish children, but rather only to Communists and Communist collaborators... We did not rely on her "expertise" in matters of Nazi Germany, and we told her that our children would go wherever we went.

At night we arrived at border (the border as it was until 1939). There we found a large crowd. However, the border guard closed us off and did not permit us to proceed. Having no choice, we returned to Rakov. On the way we met Leibke, Meir the Slovensker's son, wearing a military coat. He told us that he brought wives of captains to the border on his wagon, with their belongings, but they disappeared in the morning and had not returned. We decided to go to Volma, fifteen kilometers away, to try to cross the border from there. However, that was also a sealed crossing. In the afternoon, we suddenly heard a shot, and saw that many people were advancing to the border crossing on wagons. Leibke hitched the horse, and we crossed the border. We reached the town of Dzherzhinsk-Yehomen. Leibke told us that he was returning to Volozhin. Our protestation that he was returning to the mouth of the lion had no effect. He left the horse and wagon for us, got up, and left. (He perished in Volozhin.) After a few days of travel, the horse's energy was depleted, and it was unable to move from its place. As we were standing there waiting from whence our help would come, a Christian lad approached us riding on a horse. Grisha offered him his bicycle in exchange for the horse, and he agreed. We hitched the new horse and quickly reached the city of Mohilev. From there, we reached the town of Mstislaw. There was a draft office there, which announced that all men up to the age of fifty were required to report for army service. I (Reuven) reported, and was sent from there to the forest. I was appointed as Politruk (guide) of the third battalion. I obtained two hours of leave to bid my family farewell. I did not know where our fate would take us. We agreed that if we survive, we should search for one other at my aunt's home in Stalinabad [Dushanbe] in Tadzhikistan. My family finally reached Stalinabad after much difficult physical suffering. Rachel set herself up with a dwelling and work, and the children were sent to school.

I went out with two other battalions, and we reached the city of Mchensk, not from Uriol. From there, I travelled to Crimea. I fought on Perekop, Simferopol, Feodosia, and Sevastopol. I was injured in my left hand in that city, and was sent to a hospital in Uzbekistan. A wounded captain was hospitalized next to me. He asked me to write a letter to his friend, Major Dyumin in Stalinabad. I asked him if he would permit me to include a letter to my aunt in the envelope. The major instructed the entire N.K.V.D. to find my aunt. They indeed found her and my family.

About two weeks after I sent my letter, I received a telegram from Dyumin that my family was healthy and whole, and they were coming to visit me. They arrived two days later. They remained with me for a week, and returned. I spent another two weeks in the hospital. After I recuperated, they gave me a six month furlough. During that time, our fifteen-year-old son volunteered for the army. He was badly wounded in 1942 in the battles near Stalingrad.

[Page 588]

My Life As a Partisan

By Hessel Perski of Bnai Brak

Translated Jerrold Landau based on an earlier translation by M. Porat z"l that was edited by Judy Feinsilver Montel

The first of the Volozhiners to escape to the forest and join the partisans were Etele and Yosef Rogovin. (Their father was called Hershl Der Bunier). They appealed to Jews imprisoned in the ghetto to escape to the forests. I responded to their call and joined the Otriad in which Etele was the wife of the commander. I was knowledgeable in the area of Volozhin. Therefore, the commander put five partisans under my command, we went out to take down trains from the railway tracks on the Volozhin-Bogdanovo line.

We succeeded in bringing down seven wagons laden with planks for the front. Thus began my life as a partisan. My second mission also resulted in taking a train down from the rails. I arrived with my people to the vicinity of Molodchina. We planted a mine under the railway tracks about four kilometers from the city. Two wagons overflowing with German soldiers flew up in the air. The number of dead and wounded was large. I received information about that from a gentile who was among those drafted to dig a grave for the victims.

A group of Volozhin partisans and fighters

From left: Mendel Volkovich, Lyuba Volkovich, Yaakov Kagan, Hessel Perski, Pnina Potashnik

[Page 589]

Thanks to my excellence, I was granted the rank of commander. I went out to Yurashchok near Lida with a group of partisans. We reached the Neman River, where we blew up a large bridge. Many Germans drowned in the river. The Germans worked hard for several days to repair the bridge. In the meantime, several trains were backed up, waiting for the bridge to be fixed. We "took care" of them successfully. For that deed, I received a citation of praise from the commander of the Kuznetzov-Klobaski Otriad, to which I belonged.

After these successful actions, the Otriad decided to conduct a face-to-face fight with the Germans. Our plan was to conquer the town of Horodok. It was a bloody battle. We conquered the town and held it for four hours. We lost twenty-five men during that battle.

On the way back we were ordered to destroy some buildings of a large farm near Horodok, in which Germans lived. I entered the yard with people from my unit, and we set the buildings on fire. The action was crowned with success, and we did not suffer any losses.

I went to the front and joined the artillery battalion, whose motto was "Death to the Germans!" I crossed through Poland and reached East Prussia. There, I was wounded for the first time. I recovered after a month and returned to the front. On 19 Iyar 5705 (May 2, 1945), I was wounded again, and I remained handicapped for life. I was hospitalized in the hospital in Baku. I spent three years there lying on the sickbed – most of the time unconscious. When I left the hospital, I went to the command in Minsk and received awards of excellence.

Partisans from Volozhin Who Died in the Course of Duty

by Hessel Perski (Genadi) of Bnei Brak

Translated by Jerrold Landau **based on an earlier translation by** M. Porat z"l
that was edited by Judy Feinsilver Montel

Yeshayahu Bernstein, may G-d avenge his blood

He was the son of Avraham and Rivka, born in Volozhin in the year 5680 (1920). His parents lived from the work of their hands, as did he. He was locked in the ghetto, but he sought a way to escape from it.

When the Nazis and their assistants took the Jews of Volozhin to be killed, Yeshayahu succeeded in escaping from them. However, he was caught after a few days, and brought to the Krasno Ghetto. There too, he did not sit idly. He began to amass weapons along with Tzvi Lunin, Eliezer Rogovin, and Mordechai Kaganovich. There were a great deal of weapons in the Krasno labor camp. The Germans tasked Yeshayahu and his comrades from Volozhin to sort the weapons and transport them to a specific place. They seized the opportunity, and hid weapon parts in the sand as they were working. They discussed among themselves about leaving the camp in the darkness of the night, with

[Page 590]

the weapons in their hands. They succeeded in escaping, and sought contact with the partisans, who refused to accept them into their Otriad and tried to take their weapons from them. However, the lads displayed fierce opposition, and did not part from their weapons. The organized an independent Otriad named for Staritski, composed entirely of Jews.

Yeshayahu was brave. One sole thought filled his heart: to take revenge from our enemies for the innocent blood that they spilled. I met him often. He was involved in ambush, planting mines on the roads that the Germans traversed, and wreaking havoc upon them. He fell during the blowing up of a bridge. There was a German post not far from the bridge, about which Yeshayahu did not know. The Germans opened fire upon him. He defended himself bravely and fired at the Germans. When he ran out of bullets, he drowned himself in the river on 11 Kislev 5704 (December 8, 1943).

Miriam Golobenchich, may G-d avenge her blood

Miriam Golobenchich

Miriam was born in 5685 (1925) in Volozhin to Leizer and Bayla. When the Germans entered Volozhin, Miriam escaped with her parents to the village of Bialokorets. When groups of partisans were organized in the village, Miriam was accepted as a partisan in the Stalin Otriad.

She was tasked with mobilizing additional partisans to the Otriad. She was sent to the Volozhin Ghetto for that purpose. When she arrived, she was caught by the Germans and forced to work at various jobs in the kitchen. There was a woman there who reported to a German that Miriam was sent to draft Jewish partisans. Miriam sat in the next room and heard the words of the woman. Since she realized what awaited her, she took a large meat cleaver and smashed the skull of the German whose ears had heard the bad report. The next day, they found the body of Miriam next to the church.

Note from M. Porat:

The Golobenchich house with their haberdashery store was located on the other side of the Minsker Street, the street where we lived. The Golobenchich girls learned in the same school in which I learned, Frumke a class lower, Mirele a class higher. Miriam Golobenchich was a real beauty and a very talented girl. She certainly was one of the most beautiful young ladies of Volozhin.

Miriam Golobenchich, may G-d avenge her blood

Miriam Golobenchich

Tzvi – Hirshle Lunin with his sisters Tsviya and Nekhama
[Not in the original book but was added by M. Porat z"l]

He was born in Volozhin in the year 5681 (1921), the son of Yisroel and Shaina. He succeeded in escaping from the Volozhin ghetto, but was captured and brought to the Krasno camp, where he worked for a certain period. In time, he obtained a gun. He escaped to the partisans, and joined the Staritski Otriad. He was tasked with following the movement of the Germans and placing booby traps in their vehicles.

Tzvi penetrated the town of Ivanets with a partisan unit. They conducted a bloody battle with the Germans and expelled them from the town. Once, he was sent with a group of partisans to sabotage activities in the Nalibok forest near Volozhin. The unit encountered a German ambush. A battle broke out in which all the partisans fell except for Tzvi. He defended himself with extreme bravery until

[Page 591]

the final bullet. He was seriously injured in that battle and died on 1 Adar II, 5703 (March 8, 1943).

Yosef Skliot

Yosef was born in 5675 (1915) in the village of Mijeiki, where he lived until the war. He was transferred to the Krasno camp from the Volozhin Ghetto. He amassed weapons in the camp and escaped too the forest, where he was accepted to the Chkalov Brigade. To our sorrow, Yosef did not have the opportunity to earn acclaim through acts of bravery, for he was taken out to be killed after a short time, despite his innocence.

This is what happened: Yosef went to the village of Mijeiki to get his personal belongings from a gentile with whom he had hidden them. The gentile reported to the commander that Yosef stole his clothes from him, and he has nothing to wear. All of Yosef's protestations that he had taken his own personal belongings were to no avail. The commander hardened his heart and refused to accept Yosef's claims. He shot him before the eyes of all the partisans.

Mordechai Kaganovich, may G-d avenge his blood

Mordechai was born in Volozhin to Zalman and Lea in 5670 (1910). He was one of the first Volozhin partisans. He mobilized many Jews to the ranks of the partisans. He belonged to the Stalin Otriad, which was active in the Nalibok forest. He fell in battle in the village of Bialobereg near Baksht on 15 Adar I, 5703 (February 20, 1943), as he was going to conduct a mission with a group of partisans.

[Page 592]

A Visit to Volozhin After the War

By Rachel & Reuven Rogovin

Translated by Jerrold Landau **based on an earlier translation by** M. Porat z"l
that was edited by Judy Montel

After I received my discharge, I traveled with Rachel in 1946 to Riga, and from there we went to Volozhin. When we arrived in the city, it became clear that there was not much to see. We went to see the destroyed city. "The entire city is weeping." Jewish Volozhin was no more. As if from itself, I recalled a stanza from Bialik's poem, "Look around, and in my heart – ruins. Ruins, my friend." ("Starts Twinkling and Extinguishing").

On our first day in Volozhin, our friend Roman Horbatchevki visited us. He told us everything that he had seen. Tears were in his eyes the entire time. He told us that when the large "shipment" of Jews was sent out to be murdered, he hid behind the gate and saw everyone going on their final journey. They walked silently, as if they were ignorant of where they were going. "Tell me, Mr. Rogovin, why did they accept the verdict so quietly, why did they not resist?"

I left the question without an answer, for my heart was not given over to debates of that nature. After two days, we met an old friend, the Pravoslavic priest Katovitz from the village of Lusk. He was a very cultured man who liked Jews. He did not hide his joy that we had survived and that he was privileged to see us. He invited our mutual friend the priest Salizh. At noon, the "Holy father Katovitz" repeated the question that Horbatchevki had asked me. Members of his congregation told him that in every place, Jews were going calmly to their death, and did not display any resistance. How can this be understood? They take a person to his death, and he does not resist!
This time I could not restrain myself and answered his question by asking other questions: You do not understand why the Jews did not resist? And the fact that of four million Red Army captives only 100,000 returned home, and the rest perished without resistance – that you do understand? Why did the Soviet commissars who were taken prisoner by the Nazis not display any resistance, even though they knew that

they face certain death – that you do understand? Why did the 9,000 Polish captains taken to be killed in the Katyn forest not display any resistance – that you do understand?

The answer to your question, Holy Father, you can only get from the mouths of the martyrs, from the mouths of those who were taken to slaughter. It is not for us to judge their deeds. After my questions, my interlocuters sat silently without saying anything, for they realized that my agony was very great.

That conversation greatly vexed our spirits, which were already gloomy. We went to the cemetery where the remnants of our dear ones were buried. We saw the large mass grave, two meters high. The grave looked like a hill covered by weeds.

During our visit, a committee arrived to investigate the crimes of the Nazis. They opened the grave. Woe to the eyes who saw what we saw. We looked at the corpses, even though the flesh had already separated from bodies –

[Page 593]

nevertheless, we recognized several of our neighbors and friends. There are no words to describe this, therefore, it is best to not scratch such wounds, so as not to add pain to our pain, and so that we do not go crazy, Heaven forbid. Each person should go to their beds with the pain in their hearts, without adding to it. We can tell about what we saw through innuendoes, and leave the rest to imagination. In such a case, the imagination is far less frightening than the reality. No imagination has the power to describe what we and other survivors of Volozhin saw.

We visited Volozhin again prior to our *aliya* to Israel in 1958. We went again to see the common grave. Time had taken its toll. The teeth of time had destroyed this remnant. The communal grave had sunk, had been swallowed up, and was as if it never was. Their blood had been absorbed into the abyss of the dark grave. However, to our sorrow, it had not consumed or destroyed the institutions on the ground, and the world ran as usual. Pigs were burrowing in the grave that had taken in the remains of our dear ones, the remnants of the community of Volozhin that had existed for five hundred years; the Volozhin about which we shall lament all the days of our lives, until the end of time.

[Page 593]

Volozhin As I Saw it in 1945

by Moshe Eliyashkevitsh

Translated by Jerrold Landau **based on an earlier translation by** M. Porat z"l **that was edited by** Judy Feinsilver Montel

Moshe Yoodl Eliyashkevitsh - 1965
[Not in the original book but was added by M. Porat z"l]

I returned to Volozhin on Tammuz 14, 5705 (June 25, 1945). The first night I spent under the open sky. I did not know who had survived and in which house I could find a Jew. The town was ruined. The destruction was frightful. The fear rose at night. It seemed to me that each stone screamed to the heart of the heavens. In the morning I went to the cemetery. I will never forget my visit in this holy place, where Yeshiva heads and prodigious leaders were buried to rest in peace. The burial canopies of the greats of Volozhin were in the center of the cemetery. All was turned into ruined mounds. The mounds of stones appeared as if after a heavy bombardment. The tombs of the victims of the First World War, which occupied a prominent place in the cemetery, were also destroyed and broken to pieces. It was a rainy day. Drops of water fell upon me and drenched me to my bones. I did not sense this, for it was as if I was outside of time and place. My spirit transported me far away to the splendid past. I wept over the glory that had disappeared and over the Jews of Volozhin that were no more. On the second day I went again to the graveyard. I saw goats and cows grazing upon the grave of Rabbi Chaim of Volozhin and other graves. I encountered some survivors of the magnificent community of Volozhin: Shayke Lavit, Motl Molot, Mendel Volkovitch, Mendl Bakshter, Kopl Kagan, Zelig Dunie's and the Skliot brothers.

[Page 594]

I went to see what remained of the ruined town. The Yeshiva building stood in its place, however its roof was slightly damaged. No trace remained of the *Beis Midrash*. I did not find a synagogue in which I could pour out my soul. There was not a sign of a Hebrew letter. I went to Vilna to obtain a Siddur and Tefillin. (I guard the Book with me till now).

Some of the survivors of Volozhin

Standing from right to left: a) Miriam Leviatan b) Moshe Eliaskevitch c) Dina Lechi (Feigenbaum) d) Meir Shiff e) Ethel Shiff f) g) Binyamin Klenbord h) Yosef Gelman i) Zimel Chadash j) Yona Rogovin k) The wife of Chatzkel Glik
Sitting: a) Avraham Yaakov Shneider b) Pnina Pomashnik (Chayat) c) Hasel Perski d) e) Yaakov Kagan f) Dodman g) Lyuba Volokovitch h) Yechezkel Glik i) Mendel Volkovitch j) Pnina Hochman

I encountered gentiles my schoolmate "friends". They did not show any signs of penitence. On the contrary, they asked me: "What? You survived? How can that be?" I seemed to be superfluous in their eyes, as a creature without a place in this world.

All the days that I walked in the Volozhin streets I was in fear. I was not afraid of the Gentiles, of the local robbers and murderers, for I had been forged as a soldier during my battles with the Nazis. It was a secret fear for the holy souls of our martyrs. I wanted to see the common grave, but as I was about 100 meters away, I fainted. When I came to, I saw a gentile standing over me. He asked what I was doing there and chased me away.

[Page 595]

I was not bear any more of the heart-breaking places of atrocity. Everywhere I stepped I heard voices of crying and lamenting piercing the space. I waited and am still waiting to this day for another voice – and it will surely come. I am waiting for the voice of G-d who will avenge His enemies. I left my destroyed nest and went to my cousin in Olshin.

"Yizkor" to the Flames

by Sara Sholomovitz (Rappaport), Givatayim

Translated by Jerrold Landau

I remember you, my city
An important city in Israel.
I remember you
In you, vibrant Jewish life existed
A life of the simple folk
And of Gaonim who were mighty in spirit.

*

I remember the vibrant Jewish youth
Their actions to redeem and be redeemed

*

Where are you, my city?
How, o how, my house?
You went up in flames
You were strangled and burnt
By the Nazi enemy.

*

Yizkor to my city
Yizkor to my house
Yizkor to the dust and flames!

*

Our Father in Heaven!
Let us take revenge for the flames
In which your dear Jews ascended to on high –
The Jews of Volozhin.

[Page 596]

Calendar Dates of the Second World War and the Holocaust in Volozhin

by E. Leoni

Translated by Jerrold Landau

The outbreak of the Second World war – 17 Elul, 5699 (September 1, 1939). The Germans invaded Poland at daybreak on September 1.

Britain and France declare war on Germany – 19 Elul, 5699 (September 3, 1938)

The conquest of Poland by Hitler's forces – 4 Tishrei, 5700 (September 17, 1939). The German losses in Poland included 10,572 dead, 5,029 missing, and 30,322 wounded.

The invasion of Poland by the Red Army – 5 Tishrei, 5700 (September 17, 1939). On September 18, 1939, the Soviets conquered Vilna.

The Molotov Ribbentrop agreement – 15 Tishrei, 5700 (September 28, 1939). On this date, the foreign ministers of Germany and the Soviet Union met and divided Poland between themselves. They signed the agreement that was called "The German-Soviet Border of Friendship Agreement."

Designation of Auschwitz as a place of annihilation – 12 Adar I, 5700 (February 21, 1940). On this date, the Uberfuehrer Richard Glücks, head of the inspectorate of Concentration Camps, who toured the area of Krakow, informed Hitler that he found an "appropriate place" for the new concentration camp in Auschwitz, a remote city surrounded by marshy lands.

Churchill elected as Prime Minister – 2 Iyar, 5700 (May 10, 1940).

Mussolini declares war on the Allies – 4 Sivan, 5700 (June 10, 1940).

Auschwitz officially opened as a Concentration Camp – 8 Sivan, 5700. At first, the town of Auschwitz served as a concentration camp for Polish political prisoners. However, this place quickly turned into the worst place of atrocities in the entire world. Rudolf Höss testified at the Nuremberg trial that he oversaw the deaths of 2.5 million people in Auschwitz.

Hitler issues a secret order to attack Russia – 6 Tevet, 5700 (December 18, 1940). Hitler issued a secret command that the German armed forces must be prepared to crush the Soviet Union in a quick military operation.

The flight of Rudolf Hess to Scotland – 13 Iyar, 5701 (May 10, 1941). Hess landed in Scotland alone to see the Duke of Hamilton. Hess explained to the duke that he had come on a "humanitarian mission," that the Fuehrer does not want to vex England, and that he desires to put an end to the battles.

[Page 597]

German invasion of Russia – 27 Sivan, 5701 (June 22, 1941).

Beginning of the "Final Solution" – 7 Av, 5701 (July 31, 1941). On this date, Göring sent a directive to Heydrich, the head of the SD [Sicherheitsdienst]: "I hereby empower you to carry out all preparations related to the total solution of the Jewish question in the areas of Europe under German influence." Heydrich stated at a meeting of high German officials that this final solution of the Jewish problem would affect approximately eleven million Jews.[1]

The Formulation of the Atlantic Charter – 16 Av, 5701 (August 9, 1941). On that date, Churchill and Roosevelt met in Placentia Bay, Newfoundland, where they formulated the "Atlantic Charter." Roosevelt agreed with Churchill that American warships and airplanes will patrol the western side of the Atlantic Ocean and will inform the British about any German submarines.

The Germans retreat from the approaches to Moscow – 24 Kislev, 5702 (December 14, 1941).

Heydrich, the head of the SD, dies from his wounds – 19 Sivan, 5702 (June 4, 1942). On May 29, 1942, when Heydrich was traveling in his sports car from his country villa to Prague, he was attacked by two Czechs, Jan Kubiš and Jozef Gabčík of the free Czech Army of England, who parachuted from a R.A.F airplane. A British manufactured bomb crushed the car and crushed Heydrich's spinal cord. Heydrich died of his wounds on June 4, 1942. The Germans retaliated for this by destroying the small village of Lidice, not far from Prague.

Rommel stopped at El Agheila [Al Uqaylah] – 15 Kislev, 5703 (November 24, 1942). With this, the war turned in favour of the allies, and the Jews of the Land of Israel were saved from the Holocaust.

The German defeat in Stalingrad – 25 Shvat 5703 (January 31, 1943).

The Allied attack on Sicily – 7 Tammuz, 5703 (July 19, 1943).

The deposing of Mussolini – 22 Tammuz, 5703 (July 25, 1943). Mussolini was summoned to the palace by the king, and effectively dismissed from his position. He was transported to the police station in an ambulance as a prisoner. General Badoglio was appointed in his place.

The Allied invasion of Italy – 3 Elul, 5703 (September 3, 1943). The ceasefire between Italy and the Allies took effect on 8 Elul 5703 – September 8, 1943.

The plot against Hitler's life – 29 Tammuz, 5704 (July 20, 1944). Hitler convened a meeting somewhere in East Prussia. Colonel Graf Schenk von Stauffenberg, a captain who had been seriously injured in Tunisia, smuggled a bomb into the meeting room in his briefcase. The bomb exploded. Von Stauffenberg returned to Berlin, convinced that Hitler had died. However, to our sorrow, only four Nazis

[Page 598]

of the more than twenty that were present were killed. Hitler's left ear became deaf, his legs were injured, and his left arm was temporarily paralyzed.

The Allied invasion of Normandy – 15 Sivan, 5704 (June 6, 1944).

The Soviets enter Vilna – 22 Tammuz, 5704 (July 13, 1944).

The Soviets enter Warsaw – 3 Shvat, 5705 (January 17, 1945).

Mussolini and his mistress were taken to be killed – 13 Iyar, 5704 (April 25, 1945). On that date, Mussolini and his mistress Clara Petacci were captured by Italian partisans as they were attempting to escape to Switzerland. On Saturday night, April 18, their bodies were brought by truck to Milan and hanged in the city square. The next day, they were hanged by their heels on lampposts, and then tossed into the sewers.

Suicide of Hitler and his mistress Eva Braun [2] – 18 Iyar 5705 (May 1, 1945).

The surrender of Germany and the end of the war – 24 Iyar, 5705 (May 7, 1945). In a small school in Reims, the place of Eisenhower's headquarters, Germany surrendered unconditionally on the morning of May 7, 1945, at 2:41 a.m. Signing the surrender for the Allies were General Walter Bedell Smith, General Ivan Susloparov for the Soviet Union, and General François Sevez in the name of France. Admiral Friedeburg and General Jodl signed in the name of Germany. The war had lasted for five years, eight months and seven days.

The Nazi war criminals ascend the gallows – 21 Tishrei, 5707 (October 16, 1946) [3]. Ribbentrop was first to ascend the gallows in the death cell of the Nuremberg prison. Following him were Keitel, Kaltenbrenner Rosenberg, Frank, Frick, Streicher, Seyss-Inquart, Sauckel, and Jodl. Göring swallowed poison vial that had been smuggled into his cell. Heinrich Himmler, the head of the Gestapo, also hid a capsule of potassium cyanide that he hid in a space in his mouth. When his fate was certain, he bit the vial and was dead within twelve minutes.

Hess, Raeder, and Funk were sentenced to life imprisonment. Speer and Baldur von Schirach were sentenced to twenty years; Neurath to fifteen years, and Dönitz to ten years.

[Page 599]

Dates of the Holocaust in Volozhin

Entrance of Germans to Volozhin – 1 Av, 5701 (July 25, 1941).

Establishment of the Ghetto – Elul 5701 (August 1941).

First slaughter – 7 Cheshvan, 5702 (October 28, 1941).

Second slaughter – 23 Iyar, 5702 (May 10, 1942).

Third slaughter – 16 Elul 5702 (August 29, 1942).

Hanging of Franz Karl Hess – 28 Shvat 5706 (January 30, 1945).

About Germany

"We cannot deny that German culture hovers between two diametrically opposite worlds. It hovers between the abstract sublime world, and the world that reveres blood and power, between the heights and the depths, between godliness and Satanity. The role of each of them is great in defining and forging its image. Both of them are part of its body.

The success of Hitler and his gangs demonstrates that excellent tactics in education and guidance, including broad-ranging publicity material, both written and oral, along with means of coercion for both the classroom and the country – all within a short period of time, of ten years – can thoroughly uproot the old traits and manners, and to lead "a nation of poets and thinkers" to the service of cruelty and deeds of atrocity of which even wild beasts are incapable of. It led to a situation where they practiced and became experts in the trade of slaughter and murder of large populations at one time, and especially perfected the art of suffocating myriads upon myriads of men, women, and children -- without any feelings of conscience during or after the deeds.

There is no nation and no country that is immune from such changes and revolutions. They are not restricted to any place or time. They remain within the range of possibility, even to the extent of Hitler and his gangs. In any case, we must not become complacent with the idea that this was only the plague of a unique country in the world, and that we must not be concerned that this may be repeated in other countries of culture. This idea misleads the masses and is extremely dangerous for all generations."

Dr. Yaakov Kletzkin, Writings, published by Ha'am Haoved, Tel Aviv, 5713 [1953], pp 40-46.

Translator's footnotes:

1. This date is two days prior to Tisha B'Av. See https://en.wikipedia.org/wiki/Tisha_B%27Av where it notes that the directive was actually received two days later, on Tisha B'Av – a date known for a coincidence of Jewish tragedies over the centuries.
2. The word used is "mistress" although Hitler and Braun were married the night before their suicide.
3. The day was Hoshana Rabba in the Jewish calendar, the seventh day of the Sukkot festival, and a day associated with the final judgment of the High Holy Day period.

[Page 600]

In Conclusion

by Binyamin Shapir

Translated by Jerrold Landau

Jewish Volozhin had many merits. The eyes of all Lithuanian Jewry, Russian Jewry, and Polish Jewry were raised toward it.

As we come to erect a memorial to it, we are in the category of "Here I am, poor in worthy deeds"[1]. A heavy responsibility has fallen upon us – to ascribe greatness to those who were great in Torah, wisdom, and good deeds; and to present a faithful description of the city and its residents.

The survivors tell of the greatness of the souls of the people of our city. At nightfall toward the end of the holy Sabbath in the month of Elul 5720 [1960], the survivors of the sword gathered for the *Mincha* service, and upon their lips were the words "You and one and Your Name is one, and who is like Your nation of Israel, a singular nation in the world. Greatness of glory, and a crown of salvation, a day of rest and holiness You gave to Your nation."[2]

This time, the rest was proper under the wings of the Divine Presence. The Jews, the final ones of the community of Volozhin, had been brought to the vale of killing, with "*Ani Maamim*" on their lips, testifying to the unity of the Creator and His unity with Israel, in accordance with "The Holy One Blessed be he and the Community of Israel are called One" (Zohar, Emor 93).

We do dare to state that this book has provided a complete description of the material and spiritual life of Volozhin. We, the survivors of the exalted city, did everything that we could. Nevertheless, as the book draws to a close, our hearts are full of trepidation lest we have hurt ourselves, and lest we have hurt anyone. We testify on high that everything that we have done was not done for our own honor, but rather for the holy, pure memory of the dear Jews of Volozhin. May their names be magnified and sanctified[3].

Translator's footnotes:

1. The opening words of the cantor's petition prior to Musaf on the High Holy Days: *Hineni Heani Mimaas*.
2. The opening statement of the middle blessing of the *Mincha Amida* for Sabbaths.
3. A paraphrase of the opening words of *Kaddish*.

[Page 601]

Yizkor - Remember

[Page 602] Blank [Page 603]

And These are the names of the Pure Holy Martyrs of Volozhin

by Eliezer Leoni

Translated by Jerrold Landau

Every name is a living soul, an entire world. This is the cemetery of Volozhin. Here is buried all the splendor of Volozhin. Here, the bastion of strength of Volozhin was brought to eternal rest. Here rests "until the ends of the world" (for eternity).

"And Absalom took and set up a monument for himself in the vale of the king, for he said, I have no son to remember my name; and he called the monument after his name, that is Yad Avshalom, to this day." (II Samuel 18:18). Absalom did not have a surviving son, so he concerned himself with setting up a memorial monument for himself during his lifetime.

G-d did a benevolent deed for the martyrs of Volozhin, who live in their communities, in the State of Israel and in the Diaspora – with a small number of sons and daughters who concerned themselves to set up a memorial for their parents, family members, relatives, neighbors, and all the Jews of Volozhin. This memorial is the monument [*Yad*] of each and every family of Volozhin.

As long as the pathways of the water froth and bubble; as long as the trees blossom; as long as the sun and the moon stand in their heavens; as long as the starts of G-d shine their light; as long as the ocean storms; as long as the grass of the ground sprouts; as long as our eyes do not sink in their sockets and our tongues do wither in our mouths; as long as "the Spreader of the heavens and Forger of the earth" conducts His world – we will stand next to these graves and we will not cease shouting: Here are buried the martyrs of Volozhin who were cut off from the land of the living before their time; here sleep forever the martyrs of Volozhin, upon whose mouths was the Torah of truth, upon whose lips was not found perversity, and who walked along the straight path in peace all their lives. They were murdered only because of their only "sin" – that they were Jews.

We will moisten their graves with our tears, and we swear that their candle will never extinguish. "For as the rain cometh down and the snow from heaven, and returneth not thither, except it water the earth, and make it bring forth and bud, and give seed to the sower and bread to the eater;" (Isaiah 55:10).[1] – thus will our martyrs make our prayers effective, and bring our prayers before the Holy Throne, that this Holocaust will never happen again. "And He will swallow up death forever, and the L-rd G-d will wipe the tears from all faces." (Isaiah 25:8)

Translator's Footnote:

1. The translation of this verse is from Mechon Mamre: https://mechon-mamre.org/p/pt/pt1055.htm

[Page 604]

Dear Mother!

by Yehuda Khaim Kotler (New York)

Poem translated by Janie Respitz

Dedication translated by Jerrold Landau

Edited by Anita Gabbay

Dedicated to the holy memory of my mother, who was shot by the Bolsheviks on Tammuz 3, 5679 (July 1, 1919), and the holy memory of all the dear Volozhiner mothers who were murdered in the Holocaust by the Hitlerist and Polish murderers.

Why are you lying in the field, mother dear?
Why do sadness and tears rule over you?
You were always cheerful – free,
So fly home to your children.
They must wait there,
For Mother to come to them.
So fly home to your children.

"I can no longer fly, I cannot return,
Not home, not to any child".

A Bolshevik's bullet found her.
His heart was from stone,
And she fell into eternal sleep
And we were left alone.

And now I'm standing distressed, pensive,
Tears are pouring from my eyes.
For us the world is an eternal night,
Mother will never return.

[Pages 605-615]

Note from Jerrold Landau: Mr. M. Porat z"l transliterated the list of names on pages 605-615. The original was alphabetized according to the Hebrew *aleph beit*, but M. Porat alphabetized his translation in accordance with the English alphabet. We have maintained Mr. Porat's English alphabetization, so the exact pages are not matched. The original title of this section is "Yizkor" – but we kept Mr. Porat's version of the title. Mr. Porat's name transliteration style does not always match that used by the other translators of the book. Many of the pages of the original contain quotes, which were not in Mr. Porat's translation. The following table indicates which Hebrew letters are covered on each of the eleven pages, as well as the quotes included on each page.

Page	Letters on page	Quotes on page
605	Aleph Beit	Top: Hah, tear out your hearts from your closed chests, and place stones there instead of hearts. Pull out from your skulls your eyes, the wellsprings of weeping, and cover them in the groves." (Yitzchak Katznelson: "The Song of the Jewish People Who Were Killed") Bottom: Rabbi Chiya lay down on the ground, kissed the dust, wept, and said: Dust, dust how stubborn are you, how brazen are you, for all pleasant things will be broken down within you, all pillars of the lights of the world will come to an end and be broken." (*Mishnat Hazohar*, volume I, People and Deeds, page 38, published by Bialik Institute, Jerusalem, 5717 – 1957.)
606	Beit	All Jewish souls are literally like a Torah scroll. As our sages state in tractate *Moed Katan,* someone who is present when the soul departs is required to rend his garments. What is this compared to, it is like someone witnessing a Torah scroll being burnt. (Commentaries of the Mahara'ch – or teacher Rabbi Chaim of Volozhin)
607	Beit Gimel	
608	Gimel Daled Hei Vav	"Your bones shall be released" – This is the resurrection of the dead, for in the future, the Holy Blessed Be He will revive the dead and will put together the bones of a human being to be a complete body, as previously. The soul will add light through the clear lens [note: A clear lens, *Asplaklaria Hameira*, an esoteric Kabbalistic concept of a clear vision of G-d], to illuminate the body into a full being, as is appropriate. (*Mishnat Hazohar*, Volume I, page 200)
609	Vav Zayin Chet Tet Yud Kaf Lamed	
610	Lamed Mem	Go, grant what you have hidden for the righteous, and make them disappear. See him that he is good – and hide him; there will be the dwelling place for the pure souls that are bound in the bonds of life, and that will be touched and will fly, where they will exchange their power, and where the weary will rest. (Shlomo Ibn Gabirol *Keter Malchut*)
611	Mem Nun Samech Ayin Pey	Where is Torah, Talmud and those who study it: Are they not in the place which is sitting desolate. And you shall weep greatly and bitterly – for the House of Israel and the Nation of G-d who have fallen to the word" (The hymnist Kalonymus ben Yehuda)
612	Pey	

613	Pey Tzadi Kuf	How has the gold become dim, the fine gold is changed (Lamentations 4:1)
614	Kuf Reish	Rabbi Yehuda said: For all seven days [note: referring to the *Shiva* period] the soul goes from its home to its grave, and from the grave to its home, and mourns over the body, as is written "His flesh shall be pained over him, and his soul shall mourn for him" (Job 14:22). It goes and sits in its house, sees them all sad, and mourns. (*Mishnat Hazohar*, volume II, page 174)
615	Reish Shin	The cup of agony, slow down! Back off a bit! For my waist and my soul have already been sated with your bitterness. (Yehuda HaLevi, *Tzion Halo Tishali*).

Volozhin – Martyrs

Transliterated by Moshe Porat-Perelman z"l

Alperovich Mendl, his wife Tamara, their children Berl, Fruma

Alperovich Michael, his wife Sima, their children Rachel, Ioash, Moyshe

Alpert Shamay, his wife Haya

Alpert Yakov

Altman Itshok, his wife Lifsha, their children Eliezer, Yosef

Askind Naftali, his wife Eshka

Avram Rudes

Baksht Binyomin

Baksht Moyshe

Baksht Yoshua Leyb

Baskin Arye

Baskind Chaim, his wife Fruma, their children Sara, Fayvl

Basuk Yehezkel, his wife Gitel, their children Yakov, Haya, Sara

Baydes Zvi, his wife Feygl, their children Hilel, Lea, Rivka

Beker Yehuda, his wife Hana-Rochl

Berger Fayche, their children Hinda, Lea

Bergman Chaim

Berkman Dosia

Berkman Mina

Berkman Sima

Berkovich Avrom, his wife Keyle, their son Leyb

Berkovich Israel, his wife Beyle

Berkovich Yakov, his wife Sonia

Berman Alter, his wife Sara, their son Shmuel

Berman Arye-Leyb, his wife Muma, their children Zvi, Braha

Berman Arye-Leyb, his wife Elka, their children Yakov, Shmuel, Etl, Hana, Feygl

Berman Ayzik

Berman Eli-Ber, his wife Hana, their children Mira, Zev

Berman Golda, their son Meir

Berman Henie Mere, their son Haim Meir

Berman Hone, his wife Mihla, their children Henia, Israel

Berman Itsak Meir, his wife Rivka, their children Rosa, Note

Berman Itsak, his wife Malka, their children Zvi Avrom, Rachel

Berman Mordhay, his wife Sonia Sara, their children Monia, Moyshe

Berman Moyshe

Berman Shmuel

Berman Shula

Berman Yehoshua, their children

Berman Yosef, his wife Zipora, their children

Berman Zeharya, his wife Sheyne Gitl, their children Yoshua, Natan, Shraga Fayve

Berman Zlatke, their children Gershon, Yrahmiel

Bernstein Avrom, their son Yshaya

Bialovski Chaim, his wife Avigail

Bloh Yehuda, his wife

Borohovich Chaim, his wife Miryam, their children

Botvinik Chaim, their children Perla, Binyamin, Moyshe

Botvinik Herzel, his wife Masha-Lea, their children Beila, Hava, Perla

Botvinik Kalman, his wife Liba, their children Hana, Micaela, Baruh

Bren Fayve, his wife Rivka, their children AvromEle, Dvora, Rasha

Bren Fayve, his wife Dvoshe

Bren Yakov, their son Tuvia

Brudno Bashe

Brudno Eli-Meyshe, his wife Zipa

Brudno Shlomo-Chaim, his wife Pesia- Rezl, their children Michael, Wulke

Brudno Yekutiel, his wife, their children Binyamin, Gavriel

Bumrash Yaakov, his wife Hinda, their children

Bunimovich Alter, his wife Gitel

Bunimovich Avrom-Moyshe, his wife Lea

Bunimovich Hana

Bunimovich Chaim

Bunimovich Hilel, his wife Dina

Bunimovich Ishaya, his wife

Bunimovich Israel, his wife

Bunimovich Leyb, his wife Malka

Bunimovich Michael, his wife

Bunimovich Mordhay, his wife Hinda

Bunimovich Moyshe, his wife Fruma-Beyla

Bunimovich Pinhas, his wife Mirele

Bunimovich Shmuel, his wife Sheynke, their children Dvora, Miryam

Bunimovich Yosef, his wife Sara

Bunimovich Zvi

Butrimovich husband, his wife Rachel

Davidson Dov Ber, his wife

Davidson Meir, his wife Sara

Davidson Yoshua, his wife

Davidson Zirl, their children

Derechinski Haim, his wife

Derechinski Kopl

Derechinski Moyshe, his wife Sheynke

Deul Eliezer-Itshak, his wife Hana-Rochl, their children Nudel, Zviya, Rivka

Deul Leybl, his wife Bat-Sheva

Deul Yosef Iche, his wife Zlata

Dikenstein Gdalia, his wife Etl

Dikenstein Hirsh, his wife

Dikenstein Natan,

Dinerstein Natan, his wife

Dolgov Itshok, his wife Hasia

Dolgov Yakov, his wife Liba

Dolgov Zalman, his wife Hana, their children Yoheved, Reyzl

Dolgov Zvi-Hirsh, his wife Sara-Itka, their son Yakov- Itshok

Dubinski Herzel, his wife Haya-Gita, their children Alter, Yosef

Dubinski Israel-Yakov, his wife Rohl-Etl

Dudman Isroel-Zisl, his wife Feyke, their children Elisha, Hasia, Rivka, Sara-Risha

Dudman Zvi

Dvoretski Chaim-Leyb

Dvoretski Shmuel, his wife Ester-Rohl

Elyashkevits Golda, her son Shimon

Elyashkevits Hirsh, his wife Masha

Elyashkevits Israel, his wife Lifsha

Elyashkevits Shimon, his wife Rivka

Elyashkevits Yosef, his wife Haya, their daughter Pnina

Elyashkevits Zvi, his wife Rachel, their children

Epstein Eliyahu, his wife Freydl

Farber Eliyahu, his wife , their children Pola, Shimon

Faygenboym Nahum, his wife Bluma, their children Hinda, Herzl, Yosef, Shmuel

Finger Meir, his wife Hana, their children Bluma, Arye

Finger Yosef, his wife Sora, their children Yakov, Eyzer, Bentsie

Garber Moyshe

Garber Yanie, his wife Broha

Gelman Alte, their children Rohl, Elisha, Michael

Gelman Ayzik, his wife Matke, their children Hayka, Lea

Gelman Boruh, his wife Feygl

Gelman Chaim Zvi, his wife Itka

Gelman Itka

Gelman Itshok, his wife Heyna, their children Ele, Chaim, Rivka

Gelman Merke, her son Chaim

Gelman Mordhay, his wife Reyzl, their children Ele, Hana, Feygele

Gelman Yohanan, his wife Zelda

Gertsovski Zev, his wife Rivka-Miryam, their children HayaSara

Ginsberg , their children Itshak, Reuven

Ginsberg SaraRivka, their children Beyla Lea, Mina, Masha

Girkus Arye, his wife Haya Lea

Girkus Ayzik, his wife Dreyzl, their daughter Rivka

Girkus Ayzik, his wife Sara, their children

Girkus Meir, his wife Ester-Malka, their daughter Haya-Sara

Girkus Pesia

Girzon Aharon, his wife

Girzon AvromBer, his wife

Girzon ChaimEle, his wife Sara

Girzon Matityahu, his wife Hana-Ita, their daughter Rivka

Girzon Meir, his wife Yudit

Girzon Michal-Gavriel, his wife Roha

Girzon Mordhay-Ele, his wife

Girzon Shraga-Fayve, his wife Bashe

Girzon Yoshua, his wife Duba-Lova

Girzon Zvi, his wife Malka

Glas Hilel, his wife Maytke

Glik Itshok, his wife Nomi-Hana

Glob Bluma

Glob Dvora

Goldshmid Ben Zion, his wife

Goldshmid Dov Ber

Goldshmid Mordhay

Goldshmid Reuven, his wife Etl, their daughter Hana- Lea

Goldshmid Shmaya, his wife Gitl

Goldshmid Yakov, his wife lea, their children

Golovenchits Eliezer, his wife Bela, their children Naum, Miryam, Fruma

Golub Zipora

Gordin AryeLeyb, his wife Itka

Gordon Shalom, his wife Hasia-Lea their children Feigl, Rudl

Goryan Dov-Ber, his wife

Goryan Mina

Gurvich Avrom, his wife Sonia, their daughter Zipa

Gurvich Yehezkeleyla

Gurvich Yona, his wife Malka

Gurvich Yosef-Iche, his wife Asha, their children Batya, Grunia, Arye Leyb

Hadash Ita

Hadash Shmaya, his wife Fruma

Hadash Yakov, his wife Etl

Hayklin Avraham, his wife

Hayklin Idl

Hayklin Masha

Hayklin Mordhay, his wife Shosha, their children

Hayklin Zeharya

Haytin Isroel-David, his wife Rudl, their children Mina, Haim, Yoshua, Izhak, Nisn

Heler Meir, their son Arye-Leyb

Hlopski Meir, his wife Mere, their children Yakov-Itshok, Shmuel

Hohberg Note, his wife Mariasha

Horovitz Avrom, his wife Sonia, their daughter Zipa

Izkovits Mordhay, his wife Rachel

Kagan Fayvl, his wife

Kagan Haya

Kagan Hirsh, his wife Rohl their children

Kagan Malka

Kagan MoysheYona, his wife Fruma-Rohl

Kagan Nahum, his wife Batia

Kagan Noah, his wife Hinda, their children Itshok, Rohl

Kagan Yakov, his wife

Kagan Yehiel, his wife Sora

Kagan Yosef, his wife Rivka, their children Shoshana, Sora, Ezra

Kagan Yosef, his wife Mihal, their children Shoshka, Chaim, Eyzer

Kaganovich Arye-Leyb, his wife

Kaganovich Meir, his wife

Kaganovich Mordhay

Kaganovich Moyshe, his wife Dvoyre-yente

Kaganovich Yosef, his wife Dobrushka

Kaganovich Zalman, his wife Lesha, their children Hana, Lifsha

Kahanovich Ishaya, his wife Henia, their daughter Leya

Kalman Alter, his wife Reine

Kalman Hone, his wife Rohl

Kalmanovich Chaim-Yoshua, his wife

Kalmanovich Sora

Kaminietski Aron, his wife Haya-Sora

Kantorovich Dovid-Iche, his wife

Kantorovich Leybe

Kantorovich Yakov-Tsodik, his wife Nehama-Lea

Kaplan Dovid, his wife, their children Rivka, Leybl

Kaplan Eliyohu, his wife Riva-Lea

Kaplan Isroel, his wife Heyne, their children Bashe, Rohl, Itshok

Karpuchevski Yosef, his wife Mera, their children

Kats Mina

Kats Rachel

Katsin Itshok, his wife Hinie-Yohke, their children, Leybl, Motl

Kisiel Eliyahu, his wife Matke

Kisiel Chaim, his wife Rashl

Kivilevich Aron, his wife Rohl, their children Taybl, Kreyna

Kivilevich Shneur, his wife Rohl, their son Igal

Kleyn Avrom, his wife

Kleyn Hanan, his wife Rohl

Kleyn Chaim, his wife Hasia

Kleyn Hinda

Kleyn Lea

Kleyn Shimon, his wife Fayga, their children Shayna, Moyshe-Yakov

Kleyn Shlomo, his wife Fayga-Riva

Kleyn Yakov, his wife, their son Shlomo

Kleynbord Meir, his wife Rosa

Kleynbord Tsvi, his wife Rivka

Klik Malka, his wife Itka, their children Yudit, Rohl

Kohen Yakov, his wife Beyla

Kotik, Rebetsn

Kovalski Yakov, his wife Haya

Kozakevich Tsirl, his wife Hana-Sora, their daughter Tema

Kozlovski Itshok, his wife

Kozlovski Lea

Kozlovski Pinhos, his wife Rohl

Kramnik Freydl

Krasny Alter, his wife Sora

Kuchevitski Fayva, his wife

Lamleman wife

Lapidot Man, his wife, their son Haim

Lavit Alter, his wife Sara, their children Zlatka, Mina, Isroel

Lavit Eliezer, his wife Rudl

Lavit Mordhay-Yudl, his wife

Lavit Natanel

Lavit Reuven, his wife Ita

Lavit Shimon, his wife Heyna, their daughter Beyla

Lavit Shlomo, his wife Rachel

Levin (Shadal) Shmuel-Dovid, his wife Matla, their children Malka, Haym, Mordhay, Shlomo

Levin Aba, his wife Rela

Levin Avrom-Itshok, his wife

Levin Berl, his wife Hana, their children Beylka, Hasia, Miryam, Yosef

Levin Levin, his wife Shmuel, their family

Levinson Yoha-Hinda, her children Rivka, Zeev, Yaakov

Levinson Yoheved, her son Volfke

Liberman Anshl

Liberman Arye, his wife Hana-Gitl

Liberman Shabtay, his wife Ester, their son Leybke

Liberman Sloyme-Avrom, his wife Roh'l

Lidrovich, children Haykl, Mordhay

Lidrovich Eliyahu, his wife Sore-Rayze, their children Haya-Roh'l, Alter, Gdaliya, Haim

Lifshits Nahman, his wife Aydele, their son Arye-Leyb

Lifshits Yakov, their children Hayele, Shoshnale

Liker Husband, his wife

Lipovetski Berl, his wife Sore-Rashke

Lungen Moyshe, his wife Sara, their children Shmuel, Chaim, Pesia, Rohel

Lunin (rabbi) Isroel, his wife Sheynke, their children Nehoma, Zvia, Gershon, Zvi

Lurye Liba, her son Meir

Malkin Mula

Malkin Zvi-Hirsh, his wife Haya-Riva

Maretski Mordhay, his wife Ester, their children Avram, Isroel,

Maze Gdaliyahu, his wife Hinde, their children Zviya, Eliezer-Pesah, Shlomo

Meltser Alter his wife, their children

Meltser Arye-Leyb, his wife

Meltser Eliezer, his wife Gitl

Meltser Hanan, his wife Sara

Meltser Isroel, & family

Meltser Mendl-Eliezer, his wife

Meltser Moyshe, his wife Rohl, their children Sara-Rivka, Tsvi

Meltser Moyshe, his wife Mihal

Meltser Shimshn-Itshak, his wife

Meltser Shlomo, his wife Gitl, their children Shprintsa, Shimshon

Meltser Yehoshua, his wife Mania, their children Batia, Tsviya, Ester-Mina

Mendelevits Reuven, his wife Bikha

Mendes Fayvish, his wife Martsa

Meyerson Avrom

Meyerson Boruh-Mordhe

Meyerson Fayve, his wife

Meyerson Haykl, his wife

Meyerson Itshok-Yakov, his wife

Meyerson Yekutiel, his wife

Miler David, his wife Rivka

Milikovski Yehuda, his wife Lea

Mishkin Itshok, his wife

Mlot Elie, his wife Sonia

Molot Avram, his wife Feygl

Molot Roha-Matke

Morduhovich Isar-Leyb, his wife

Morduhovich Moyshe-Aron, his wife

Movshovich Moyshe, his wife Batya

Namyot Tsvi-Yehuda, his wife Sora, their children Elta, Doba, Rohl

Narushevich Avraham, his wife Hasia

Narushevich Brayna

Narushevich Eliyahu, family

Narushevich Isaak

Narushevich Itshok, his wife Sora

Nosn(1st name) his wife their daughters Zelde, Neshke, Rashke

Osherovits Asher, his wife

Paretski Asna-Haya, their son Yosef

Paretski Shahne, his wife Fruma

Peker Itshok

Perelman Malka

Perelman Yosef

Perski Alter, his wife Dvora

Perski Avrom, his wife Rivka

Perski Beyla, their children Gisha, Feygl

Perski Doba, their daughter Henia

Perski Dovid, his daughter Itke

Perski Etl

Perski Fayve, his wife

Perski Fayve, his wife Raya, their children Moyshe, Mina

Perski Getsl, his wife Haya-Raytsa, their daughter Rivka

Perski Hasia-Lea

Perski Chaim, his wife Liba

Perski Chaim-Ele

Perski Chaim-Zeev, his wife Dunia

Perski Isroel, his wife Haya, their children Itshok, Lifsha

Perski Isroel, his wife Batia, their children Avram, Shmuel

Perski Itshok, his wife

Perski Leybl

Perski Lipa, his wife Henia, their children Rivka, Lea, Rohl, Eliyahu

Perski Meir, his wife Gita, their children Elka, Hayka, Sonia, Rohl

Perski Michael, his wife , their son Tsvi

Perski Michael

Perski Mina, their daughter Rishka

Perski MoysheYona, his wife Hana-Eshke, their children Liba, Rivka

Perski Natanel, his wife

Perski Nisan, his wife Rasia, their children Golda, Chaim, Fayvl

Perski Noah

Perski Ori-Yakov, their son Aron

Perski Ori, his wife Rohl, their children Bela, Gretl

Perski Osher, his wife Bunia, their children Sonia, Reuven-Ruvele

Perski Shalom

Perski Shimshon, his wife

Perski Shlomo, his wife Freydl, their children Rivka, Dovid, Chaim, Itshok

Perski Sonia

Perski Yehuda-Chaim, his wife Merke, their children Blumke, Reyhl, YakovZeev

Perski Yosef, his wife Tsirl, their son Eli-Zalman

Perski Yudit, their daughter Beyla

Perski Zeev, his wife Gnesia

Perski Zisl, his wife Rohl, their children

Podolski Michael, his wife Reyzl, their children Hana, Shmuel

Podvarski Arye-Leyb, his wife Sora

Podvarski Arye-Yosef, his wife Luba, their daughter Batya

Podvarski Irmiyahu, his wife

Podvarski Mendl, his wife, their son Nosn

Podvarski Mordehay, his wife Rohl, family

Podvarski Nosn, his wife Dushka

Podvarski Shmuel, his wife Rashl

Polak Aron

Polak Nehama

Potashnik Akiva, his wife Etl

Potashnik Dov-Ber, his wife Hana

Potashnik Eliezer, family

Potashnik Ester, their children

Potashnik Nehemia, his wife Hana, their children Chaim, Isroe

Pozniak Yakov, his wife Dobrushka

Providla Michael, his wife Rivka, their children Hanara

Radushevski Peysah, his wife Sonia, their children Genia, Moshe, Reuven

Rahmilevich Yosef, his wife Avrom, their children Dov, Moyshe

Rapoport, his children Avrom, Yosef, Yehiel

Rapoport Eliezer, his wife Lea, their children Gitl, Zelda, Freydke

Rapoport Moshe

Rapoport Yehezkl, his wife

Rapoport Yhoshua, his wife Sarka, their son Isar

Rapoport Zeev, his wife Ester, & their children Gitl, Yosef

Rayher Zeev, his wife Fruma, & their children Shula, Itshok

Rogovin Aron, his wife Sora

Rogovin Avrom-Itshok, his wife Sheyna, & their children

Rogovin Avrom-Leyb, his wife Henia, & their children Hana, Ida, Yehuda

Rogovin Dovid, his wife Eshka, & their children Gala, Motl

Rogovin Ele-Yakov, his wife

Rogovin Eliezer

Rogovin Etl

Rogovin Hanan, his wife Beyla-Rivka

Rogovin Chaim, & their daughter Tsipora, Rivka

Rogovin Hirsh-Leyb, his wife

Rogovin Hirsh, his wife , & their son Nehemia

Rogovin Isroel, his wife Sora, & their daughter Freydl, Yakov

Rogovin Itshok, his wife Hana, & their daughter Feygl

Rogovin Itshok, his wife Batia, & their daughter Hana

Rogovin Kopl, his wife

Rogovin Mordhay, his wife

Rogovin Moyshe, his wife Reyzl

Rogovin Nehemia

Rogovin Shevah, his wife Golda

Rogovin Shmuel, his wifdaughter Chaim, Rivka

Rogovin Tsvi, his wife Gitl, their son Yosef

Rogovin Yehuda, his wife Haya, & their daughter Elka, Zeev

Rogovin Yohanan, his wife Rivka-Dvora, & their daughter Batia

Rogovin Yosef, his wife Rivka

Rogovin Zalman, his wife Tema

Rozen Chaim, his wife Freydl

Rozenberg Reuven, his wife Gitl, & their son Yoel

Rozenberg Shlomo

Rozensheyn Moyshe, his wife Elka, their daughter Beba

Rozensheyn Tsvi, his wife Yoheved, their daughter Ester

Rubin Elka, & their son

Rubinshteyn Faytl, his wife

Rubinshteyn Haya

Rubinshteyn Solem-Leyb, his wife Lifsha, their children Broha, Golda

Rubinshteyn Tamara, their children Yakov-Yosef

Rudenski Dovid, his wife

Rudenski Meir, his wife

Rudenski Yakov, his wife Ruda

Rudenski Yehezkl, his wife Fruma

Rudenski Yohanan, his wife Dvosha-Elka

Rudnia Rohl

Rudnitski Gitl, his wife Haya, & their children Meratsl

Ruhamkin Yakov-Shmuel, his wife Tsviya

Sapir Naomi

Savitski Alta

Savitski Osher, his wife Bashe, their children Rivka, Yeheskl

Segalovich Alter, his wife Dvoshe, & their son Avrom

Segalovich Chaim, his wife Matke

Segalovich Moyshe, his wife Sora, their daughter Sonia

Sepetnitski Moyshe, his wife Bunia

Sepetnitski Yehusa, his wife

Shabtay-Note, & their son Shmuel

Shaker Avrom, his wife

Shalman, & their children, Leyba, Shlomo

Shalman Elka

Shalman Chaim, his wife Ester & their children

Shalman Tsvi, his wife Gitl & their children Miryam, Rosa, Ayzik

Shalman Yehoshua, his wife

Shaybl Mendl, his wife Slava & their children Libe, Mule

Sheyniuk Tsvi, his wife Rivka

Shif Avrom-Moyshe, his wife Reyzl & their children Golda, Shimon

Shimkin Yehuda, his wife wife

Shimshelevich Alter, his wife Haya-Lea

Shimshelevich Moyshe, his wife Batia

Shishko Mordehay, his wife Dvoshe

Shklar , & their children , Pesah, Kopl

Shklar Eliyahu, his wife Rohl, & their children Golda, Ben-Sion, Chaim

Shklar Sara

Shlosberg Arye-Leyb, his wife Yoha, & their children Rohl, Grunem, Yosef, Itshok

Shmerkovich Yehoshua, his wife Rivka, & their son Isroel

Shmid Mordhay, his wife Maryasha, & their children Yosef, Shlomo, son

Shmukler Eliezer, his wife wife

Shnayder Arye-Leyb, his wife Ester & their children Hana-Merke, Zelig

Shnayder Dovid & their children

Shnayder Chaim, his wife Nehama

Shnayder Moyshe, his wife Merl & their daughter Sore-Rohl

Shnayder Tsvi, his wife Tsirl & their daughter Miryam

Shptsiner Isroel, his wife Bela

Shriro Heshl, his wife Rivka, their children Dreyzl, Shmuel

Shriro Itshok, his wife Anetl & their daughter Avigayil

Shulevich Shmuel, his wife Rohl & their children Eliyahu, Mordehay

Shuster Tsvi, his wife Yona

Shvarts Yakov-Dovid, his wife Rivka

Shvartsberg Alter, their daughter Rayne

Shvartsberg Ele-Iche, his wife Dveyre-Elke, their son Leybl

Simernitski David, his wife Doba

Simernitski Chaim, his wife

Simernitski Michael, his wife Malka

Simernitski Yaakov, his wife Sora-Ester

Sklut Alter, his wife Feyga

Sklut Avrom-Itshok, his wife Shifra

Sklut Berl, his wife

Sklut Dvora-Ester

Sklut Eliyahu, his wife Feyga

Sklut Gita-Rohl

Sklut Chaim-David, his wife Rohl

Sklut Chaim-Shaul, his wife Rashe-Dvosh Sklut Hilel, & his family

Sklut Itshok-Getsl, his wife

Sklut Itshok, his wife Bashe-Elka, their children Rohl, Reyzl, Chaim, Yaakov & Shimon

Sklut Leya-Bashe

Sklut Leyb, his wife Riva-Yenta

Sklut Leyvik, his wife

Sklut Michael, his wife, their daughter Musia

Sklut Shimon, his wife

Sklut Shlomo, his wife Shimka, their children Pesia, Shmuel

Sklut Shmuel-Itshok, his wife

Sklut Yakov, his wife wife

Sklut Yehoshua, his wife Dobrushka

Sklut Yehoshua, his wife Hana

Sklut Zlata

Sosenski Itshok, his wife Pesia

Spector Dov-Ber, his wife their daughter Tsila

Stekolshchik Yehuda, his wife Meytl

Stolar Eliezer, his wife Liba, & their children Berl, Moyshe, son

Stolar Kopl

Stolar Yehiel

Tabahovits Yakov, his wife Haya

Tabahovits Yosef, his wife Bela

Taf Arye, his wife Musia, & their children Tova, Isroel

Tiuf Zalman, his wife Leya, & their children Avrom, Isroel

Tsart Avrom, his wife Tsviya, & their children Nehama, Aron, Hirsh

Tsart Gdalya, his wife Ester, & their children Aron, Shmuel

Tsart Tamara, & her family

Tsart Yosef, his wife Rohl, & their children Berl, Pesia,

Tsimerman Lipa, his wife Reyzl-Feygl

Tsimerman Note, & his family

Tsipin Benyomin, his wife Rohl-Lea, & their son Pinhas, ,

Tsirulnik Chaim, his wife Hayka

Vayner Moyshe, his wife Rachel, their children Lea, Mordehay

Vaysbord Eliyahu, his wife Hasia

Vaysbord Haim-Izhak

Vaysbord Michael, his wife

Vaysbord Moyshe, his wife Haya

Vaysbord Shimon, his wife wife

Vaysbord Yakov, his wife Matke

Vaysbord Yakov, his wife Sheine-Riva, their children Mihla, Heynah

Velvel Leybl

Vidrovich Yosef-Haim, his wife Haya-Sara, their children Hinda, Efraim

Volkin Rabbi Haim, his wife Beyla, their children Dreyzl, Haya-Lea

Volkomich Malka, her daughter Shulamit

Volkomich Shmuel, his wife Elka-Haya, their children Moyshe, Sara

Yankelevich Alta

Yazgur Dovid, his wife Elka

Yazgur Mordhay, his wife Sonia, their children Haim Ishayahu

Yofe Avrom, his wife Sore-Beyle, their children son and daughter

Yurshner Haim, his wife Sonia, their children Mindl, Reyzl

Yuzefovich Zvi-Meir, his wife Sima, their daughter Elka

Zalb Isroel, his wife Yente, their family

Zalb Yosef, his wife Merke, their children Binyomin, Isroel

Zarin Yosef, his wife

Zeltser Tsvi, his wife Sonia

Zhale Shlomo, his wife Feygl, their son Michael

Zlotnik

[Page 617]

From One Generation to Another and to Eternity

[Page 618] Blank [Page 619]

Bar-Ilan University & it's President Professor Pinchas Churgin

by Eliezer Leoni

Translated by Meir Razy

The Bar-Ilan University grew forth from a tree, a tree from an orchard in Volozhin. It is named after a son of Volozhin, Rabbi Meir Bar-Ilan, a son of the NATZIV. Its founder and first Rector was Professor Pinchas Churgin,[1] a student of the Yeshiva Etz-Chaim in Volozhin. However, there is a difference between the university[2] on the hills of Volozhin and the one built on the plain surrounding Ramat-Gan.

The Yeshiva Etz-Chaim was forced to close because of its resistance to the Russian Government's demand to add non-religious classes to the curriculum, an idea that was also promoted by "the Movement of Enlightenment". Its founder, Rabbi Chaim, believed that "there is nothing which is not alluded to in the Torah". He referred to the Midrash Tehilim Chapter 19,5[3] "Shmuel Bar Abba said: I know the stars in the Heavens as well as I know the streets of Nehardea [his city in Babylon]. We know that he did not ascend to the Heavens, but he studied the Torah and thus developed his knowledge about the stars." This teaches us that a person who knows the Torah also acquires knowledge of all the Sciences. For example, Rabbi Shmuel became an astronomer through studying the Torah.

Bar-Ilan University, on the other hand, was destined to merge Torah with Enlightenment, Judaism and non-Jewish knowledge. Professor Churgin identified the basis of this link in the writings of the GAON of Vilna (the HAGR"A - Hagaon Rabenu Eliyahu) who was the teacher of Rabbi Chaim. The HAGR"A wrote that "all the Sciences use the knowledge of the Torah, and the Torah includes all the Sciences". Therefore, a person who wants to have a deep understanding of the Talmud must also have knowledge of the "external" Sciences such as Astronomy, Geography, Mathematics, or Medicine.

The HAGR"A said: "A person must be erudite a hundred times more in the Torah than in the Sciences because the Torah and the Sciences are linked." He asked Baruch Shick to translate the Geometry book of Euclid from Greek to Hebrew. He himself wrote the book "A Triple Ram" where he explained mathematical problems which appear in the Talmud.[4]

Pinchas Churgin was born in Pahost (in the Minsk area) on November 25, 1894, son of Rabbi Reuven Yona and Devosha.

[Page 620]

His father was the Head of a famous Yeshiva in which he was educated. When he was eleven years old, the family moved to Eretz-Israel and settled in Jerusalem. He attended a Yeshiva in Jerusalem but wished to go back to Etz-Chaim. He believed that this was the best Yeshiva in the world. Consequently, he returned to Volozhin and spent four years under the tutelage of Rabbi Raphael Shapiro.

He then moved to the U.S.A and after studying there he became a professor of Jewish History at Yeshiva University in New York.

Rabbi Meir Bar-Ilan, the founder of the American branch of the Mizrachi Movement, took note of him and nominated him as the head of the School of Jewish Teachers, a part of the Rabbi Yitzhak-Elchanan Yeshiva in New York. Churgin led the School for over thirty years. The thousands of graduates of the School are the leaders of today's Jewish education in the country.

Churgin steered the schools towards a blend of Biblical and modern Jewish culture that served as a cornerstone of national Jewish strength. He did not see any conflict between the Torah and Science. Moreover, he reminded us that there were Jewish scholars who were scientists, engineers, mathematicians and physicians among the writers of the Talmud in Babylon, during the Middle Ages in Spain and down through the ages in Europe.

Churgin was a Torah Scholar but he himself was humble and modest. He adored small trees. When his brother asked him why he preferred smaller trees he said that small trees reminded him of everyday honest people who do not look down on others. Tall trees are scary and reminded him of people who pursue power. Those trees keep the sunlight for themselves and cast big shadows around them, depriving the small ones of sunlight.[5]

Churgin adapted the learning method of the NATZIV, a method that emphasized researching the sources of Jewish Law and taught the students how to identify these sources. The students were educated both to understand the history of Jewish ideas and concepts and to be able to trace their development.

He followed Rabbi Chaim's pedagogical method which believed that the mind of the student is flexible and inventive and that a good teacher must not suppress the student's creativity. On the contrary, he should promote free thinking.

[Page 621]

Churgin was aware of the limited availability and capacity of higher education during the early years of the State of Israel and started devoting his time and connections into forming a new University. He defined the vision for it as "We hope to educate a generation of people who would be committed to our ancient Torah. Losing the Torah, G-D forbid, as a cornerstone of the Nation may bring about the demise of the Nation. On the other hand – science and research do not contradict the belief in G-D."[6]

In 1949, Churgin was elected President of the American Branch of the Mizrachi. In 1950, he visited Israel and met Government officials to discuss the creation of the university. On July 26, 1953, the cornerstone of the University was laid. The "Foundation Scroll" (Megilat HaYesod) was placed in a cavity in the cornerstone. The text of the Scroll reads:

"With the grace of the One who gave mind to man and granted wisdom to humans, on this Sunday the fourteenth day of the month of Menachem-Av in the year of five thousand seven hundred and thirteen since the Creation, that is the sixth year of the independent State of Israel, in the presence of Torah Sages and Ministers of the State, people of wisdom and Science, leaders of Institutions and generous donors in the city of Ramat-Gan, let it blossom like a lily in the Valley of Sharon. Today we lay down the cornerstone to an Institution of Torah and Wisdom named after our leader, the President of the worldwide Mizrachi movement, our Rabbi Meir Bar-Ilan z"l, the son of Rabbi Naftali Zvi Yehuda Berlin z"l. Let this Bar-Ilan University be a Tree of Life (Etz Chaim) for the heritage of the Eternal Nation, for the everlasting values of the Torah, wisdom and morals, justice and world peace. Let it be an oasis for intelligent people where science and research, skills and arts, creation and resurrection of the people and of the State can flourish. The University will be a source for the Jewish spirit, a place of creation and preservation for the spirit of young people. Belief will be the foundation and Science will be the crown of its students. It will be a Lighthouse to the nation of Israel and a place of wisdom to all Nations of the world."

The Inauguration Ceremony took place on August 7, 1955. In attendance were one hundred students who represented the "Ingathering of the Exiles": people from South America, Morocco, Egypt, Iraq, and other countries. Professor Churgin's opening remarks laid down the goals he set for the creation of the University:

[Page 622]

"There is a dichotomy among the people of Israel. One view believes in the study of the Torah and nothing else, ignoring scientific progress and the improvements made to human life and its condition. The other view opposes consecrated Jewish values and follows a spiritual nihilism when it comes to Jewish traditions. Our role is to develop the synthesis between our traditional life and the world's general culture. This blend existed during the times of the Talmud and the "Golden Era" in Spain and delivered manifolded benefits to Judaism.

He told the students "we pray that you will follow that great man who gave his name to this home, Rabbi Meir Bar-Ilan z"l, who dedicated his life to the resurrection of the Nation and its people and to their spiritual foundations: the love of G-D, the love of every Jew and the love of all humanity. We hope Rabbi Meir Bar-Ilan will be a model to you and to future generations. His way of life is a worthwhile symbol for this Institution and for your life."

It is appropriate to quote the Chief Rabbi of Israel, the GAON Rabbi Herzog, who said:

"Two great forces are struggling for control of the human spirit since time immemorial, the presence of G-D and Science. However, it is not surprising that in our era, when Science discovers so many secrets of nature, some of the greatest scientists voice their opinion that Science does not conflict with 'In the beginning G-D created'. They realize that the power of Nature is not random, but that there is a Supreme Creator who shaped the world in an intelligent and wise way."

The first year offered courses in Judaism: Talmud, Biblical Studies, Jewish History, the Hebrew Language and Literature, Linguistics, English, French, Spanish and Arabic. Science courses included Mathematics, Chemistry, Physics and Biology.

Professor Churgin was elected President of the University. He dedicated much of his time to admitting candidates. He interviewed each registered candidate trying to understand their personalities and knowledge and admitted only those that satisfied his criteria: their commitment to Judaism, their morals and their level of knowledge. In so doing, Churgin followed the custom of Rabbi Chaim who personally screened each candidate to his Yeshiva. He admitted only those who were committed to his own views of the kind of education the Yeshiva should instill in its students.

[Page 623]

Professor Churgin had an important principle: the student's financial ability must not hinder his admission. He remembered the Talmudic story of Rabbi Hillel who was not able to enter the Beit Midrash where Shemaiah and Avtalion were teaching. Hillel climbed on the roof and listened to their voices through the chimney. Churgin did not want to see this happening under his watch and admitted all worthy students, whatever their financial means.

Sadly, Professor Churgin did not have long to oversee the University. He died in the U.S.A. on November 29, 1957. The day before his death he asked his brothers and daughters to cover him with his Tallit, to put his Tefillin on him and to sing HaTikva ("The Hope", Israel's national anthem). These were the two great foundations of his life – Jewish hope and the belief in national redemption by studying the Torah.

Pinchas Churgin's determination and insistence that the Torah is the foundation of the Jewish Nation was a direct continuation of Rabbi Chaim of Volozhin, who wrote "a person who did not involve himself with the Torah could not perceive the utmost holiness and purify his soul." (Nefesh Hachaim, Vol 4 Ch 22).

This note is not just about the story of Bar-Ilan University. It explains the motivation for establishing it and what its inner essence and goals are. It also tells a little about Professor Pinchas Churgin who was a modern Rabbi Chaim of Volozhin and about his motivation for creating the University. His drive to create Bar-Ilan University was based on his fear that the Nation might forget the Torah; the same fear that drove Rabbi Chaim to create the Yeshiva Etz-Chaim in Volozhin.

We do not know if the University has a faculty of "Volozhin Studies", nor do we know if the book "Nefesh Hachaim" is mandatory reading for its students. In any case, we consider the University to be a part of Volozhin, a modern incarnation of the Yeshiva Etz-Chaim.

[Page 624]

"The whole commandment that I command you today you shall be careful to do, that you may live and multiply, and go in and possess the land that the LORD swore to give to your fathers." (Deuteronomy, Ch 8, 1)

"that you may live" the soul is not complete until they arrive at Eretz-Israel

("Look Deep", the NATZIV)

Translator's footnotes:

1. His picture is shown on page 167
2. Eliezer Bran described it as "the only and the special university that educates rabbis in Lithuania". HAMELIZ, Issue 45, February 22, 1891
3. Nefesh Hachaim, Vol.4 Ch. 20
4. See "The History of Jewish Literature" Vol. 3 Ch. 5 P. 293 by Dr. Israel Zinberg
5. Gershon A. Churgin Memoires, included in the Bar-Ilan University Yearbook 1963, page 11
6. Bar-Ilan News, No.17, October 1957

[Page 624]

Kibbutz "Ein HaNatziv"

by Eli Avisar

Translated by Meir Razy

Our Kibbutz, Ein HaNatziv, is in the valley of Beit-She'an near the crossroads of Jericho – Beit-She'an – Tirat-Zvi. It was the third Kibbutz in the "religious block". It was founded after Tirat-Zvi and Sde-Eliyahu. Later, a fourth Kibbutz, Shluchot, was founded during the War of Independence.

The Kibbutz founders came from three groups of young people who had assembled in different locations: one was in Kvutzat "Rogers" (Kvutza is a collective group in Israel, working a farmstead cooperatively on national land) that later became "Kvutzat Yavneh", a second was in Moshav "Sde-Yaakov" in the Valley of Izrael, and the third was in the "Ein-Ganim" neighborhood in the Bay of Haifa. The members of the three groups met in an agricultural training camp on the dunes of Nachalat Yehuda near Rishon-LeZion. When they realized they would not be able to find jobs in that vicinity, they started dispatching "work details" to any place where they could secure employment. This was during the time of the "Arab Revolt" of 1938. One work detail worked near Gaza, another one - in the Bay of Haifa and the third one worked near Jericho. The lack of permanent work, however, was instrumental in forging the group together in order to face future challenges.

The Second World War brought the Holocaust and the loss of our families in Europe. It was a period of rapid economic growth which created many work opportunities. After years of working in separated, dispersed groups, we gathered all our members in one location and hoped to finally start building our new settlement. However, the leaders of the Jewish Community in Eretz-Israel supported enlistment in the newly created Jewish units ("The Brigade") in the British Army. Many of our members wanted to join the military and to fight the Nazis (most of our members were of Austrian and central European origin) but we eventually agreed on a limit of 10% in order to keep the group unified and to fulfill our main objective of starting a Kibbutz. The leaders of the Jewish Community directed some of the volunteers to join the local "army" (the PALMACH) and the rest of them joined the British Army.

[Page 625]

While living in the work camp it was not easy to find additional members for our group. We did, however succeed in recruiting several graduates of "Aliyat HaNoar" from the Mizrachi House for Women, from the "Mikve-Israel" Agricultural School and from the Religious Youth Village.

Although by now we were high on the priority list for land allocation by the Jewish Agency, the rules of the "White Book" of the British Government did not allow the creation of new settlements. By the end of the War, most of the arriving survivors from Europe did not want to join a group that promoted a life of sharing, a cornerstone of the kibbutz movement. Moreover, the method of building a new kibbutz at the time "Homa u-Migdal" (Tower and Stockade) brought back nightmarish memories for them. They did not want to live inside a fenced settlement. We assisted these people by linking them up with others who had come from their hometowns and with the social services that were available.

Towards the end of 1945, we finally received an allocation of 500 dunams (123.5 Acres) of land that was held by several Kibbutzim around the city of Beit-She'an. This land area was surrounded by thousands of dunams of the British Mandate Government land that was cultivated by Arabs. On January 17, 1946, "Tu Bishvat Day", a convoy of trucks loaded with small huts, tents and tools left Kibbutz Sde-Eliyahu and drove to the north. It stopped in the middle of a barley field and our settlement was ready a few hours later. "Hagana" soldiers and Jewish policemen stood on guard until we built the surrounding fence. Tents and huts were ready to house the people and a "security room" held our weapons. Tu Bishvat was commemorated by planting 12 trees – one for each settlement in the Valley of Beit-She'an. Dignitaries, including Moshe Shertok – the Head of the Diplomatic Branch of the Jewish Agency (later Sharett, the second Prime Minister of Israel), as well as Moshe Shapiro - the Head of the Immigration Branch of the Jewish Agency and many other representatives from the nearby settlements came to congratulate us and help us celebrate.

The Jewish population in Eretz-Israel was struggling with the British authorities for the right to bring survivors of the Holocaust from Europe into our independent State. No one knew how long this might take but it was clear that our situation, where our group was divided into two locations, was not sustainable. Moreover – we wanted to bring the women and children who had remained in Nachalat-Yehuda to live together with us.

The only land that the JNF owned in the area lay between Kfar-Ruppin and Sde-Eliyahu. However, we did not want to be "squeezed" between two already existing Kibbutzim. We had to wait for another year to pass until an appropriate area of land was transferred to us from Kibbutz Messilot. We immediately started building houses for the children and the Kibbutz members. We then built a cowshed and workshops and sowed the fields for animal fodder and vegetables.

[Page 626]

We had not yet named the Kibbutz before we moved to the location, but on the following day a news item in the DAVAR Daily newspaper announced that "The NATZIV has settled in the Valley of Beit-She'an". Only a few people in the country knew who the NATZIV was and many people mistook him for the British Governor of Eretz-Israel. He was a hated person in the country at that time (the Hebrew word for governor is 'natziv'). The newspaper clarified that the NATZIV was Head of the Yeshiva of Volozhin, a teacher of the National Poet, Chaim Nachman Bialik, and the person that Bialik described in his famous poem 'HaMatmid'.

The settlement received the name "Ein-HaNatziv" (the Fountain of the NATZIV) on Lag BaOmer of that year, in May 1946. The name was proposed by Rabbi Meir Berlin (later: Bar-Ilan) who was the son of the NATZIV, the President of the Worldwide Mizrachi Movement and a Director of the JNF.

There are many water springs in the Valley of Beit-She'an. Three springs flow near the Kibbutz and their names are related to the NATZIV: The Naftali Spring, The Zvi Spring and The Yehuda Spring.

Our members, including the women and children, were waiting in other parts of the country. They joined us just two weeks before the historic vote of the United Nations in Lake Success on November 29, 1947. We hoped to dedicate all our efforts to building and developing the Kibbutz, but soon we found ourselves becoming soldiers with "part-time jobs" as farmers.

It was around that time we lost two of our members: Yoseph Kopler was killed with the 35 men who died on the road to Gush-Etzion and Yoseph Immerglick died on Mount Gilboa near the town of Jenin.

We committed ourselves to integrating and educating the refugee children found in churches and the homes of Christian citizens in Belgium and France by Alyat-HaNoar and the soldiers of the Brigada.

The time then came to focus on developing our own home. We prepared a plan for agricultural production; we bought equipment and formed different agriculture branches. Being a religious Kibbutz, we had to find ways to deal with such religious requirements as working on Shabbat, avoiding mixed crops or mandated donations. The most important question was educating the children. We allocated our best people to be teachers and along with the other three nearby religious Kibbutzim, we built a shared school. Each child receives 12 years of education in either one of two streams: Humanities or Science. The boys in grade 10 also spend some time at a Yeshiva.

In addition, we helped the State by sharing our facilities with "Youth Seed Societies" – people with no prior experience in farming who were preparing themselves to build new Kibbutzim. These Societies would spend two to three years with us (and provided manpower to our small-sized Kibbutz).

After 23 years of existence in the Valley of Beit-She'an, we can feel satisfied with our many achievements. These achievements did not arrive "on a silver platter". We are a Kibbutz with 150 members, 12 of them belong to one "Youth Seed Society", and 160 children. We cultivate 8,000 dunams of land (3,100 sq. miles), about one-quarter of which is irrigated. We also care for 1,060 dunams of fishponds.

[Page 627]

The Synagogue in Kibbutz Ein-HaNatziv

There are two special buildings in the Kibbutz. One is the Beit-HaMidrash, which was built in our fifth year through the initiative of Rabbi Meir Bar-Ilan and which was named after his mother, the wife of the NATZIV. The second is the synagogue that was inaugurated on February 5, 1966, the day that marked 20 years from the founding of our Kibbutz.

The people of our Kibbutz, who maintain our Jewish religious beliefs, symbolize the eternal future of the Jewish nation, the eternal existence of the Torah, and the eternal presence of the spirit of Volozhin.

[Page 628]

Israel Rogozin

by Yitzhak Yaakobi

Translated by Meir Razy

Israel Rogozin was born in Volozhin. His father, Rabbi Shalom Eliezer Rogozin, was sent to America by the NATZIV to raise donations for the Yeshiva.

Before he left for the U.S.A., Rabbi Shalom bought his wife a knitting machine. This machine knitted socks and was able to make the family financially independent while he was away.

Six years later, his wife and children joined Rabbi Shalom Eliezer Rogozin in New York. His wife brought the machine with her and this gave the family a head-start in their new country. In 1895 Rabbi Shalom opened a small knitting factory. In this factory Israel learned all about production, marketing and sales. He was only 12 years old when he became a "traveling salesman" for the family business. His first business trips were to Brooklyn and were followed later on by more trips to many other cities. By the age of 14 he had mastered all the different jobs in the company. In fact, when necessary, he was even able to repair the machines.

By 1903, his father, who was not interested in manufacturing and sales, became a teacher in the Yeshiva of Rabbi Yaakov-Yoseph. Israel, who was 16 years old by then, became the General Manager of his family's company.

Israel Rogozin dedicated a lot of time and effort expanding the factory. During this process, he became a major industrialist in the U.S.A. He was interviewed by the "Jewish Press Weekly" and was asked about "the secret of his success". He said "I worked hard and I am still working hard. I had always believed that hard work and doing business fairly would bring success. I built up and grew the "Bonit" Company through many years of effort and dedication."

Rogozin started expanding his business in 1912 at a time when he employed about 200 workers. By 1920 the Company owned 5 plants and employed one thousand workers. In that year he purchased his sixth plant – a factory that manufactured synthetic silk. The demand for this product grew very quickly and Rogozin's companies became an empire of synthetic silk and nylon products which employed ten thousand workers. Israel Rogozin sold "Bonit" in 1963 when annual sales had reached 150 million dollars and its products enjoyed an excellent reputation.

[Page 629]

However, Mr. Rogozin's goal in life was not increasing his personal wealth. He always shared his prosperity with the public and donated many millions for scientific and educational causes both in the U.S.A. and in Israel.

His relationship with Eretz-Israel started over fifty years ago. He helped with the financing of a factory that manufactured roof tiles in Motza and, over the years, invested about 30 million dollars. Recently, he donated four million dollars for educational projects in Israel through the charity organization managed by Rebbetzin Sara Herzog, the wife of Israel's Chief Rabbi. As well, he donated to Bar-Ilan University and built a Cultural Center for his workers in the city of Ashdod. He then donated all of his shares from this Ashdod company to several charities. In 1966, he donated a million dollars to the Yeshiva University in New York in order to create a Faculty for Ethics. Presently, thirty young Rabbis - Orthodox, Conservative and Reform study in this Faculty.

His investments in Israel are very successful. Half of the production from his tire factory is exported while the production and export levels grow greater every year.

Mr. Israel Rogozin is 83 years old now. He is very energetic and still developing new business plans.

Once, someone asked the GAON of Vilna how he had become a GAON (genius). He answered, "If you want it, you too can become a GAON." Mr. Rogozin is proof of the goals one can achieve if one is strong-willed and hard-working.

[Page 630]

The Association of the Descendants of Volozhin in Israel
(Acts, events and words of Torah)

by Eliezer Leoni

Translated by Meir Razy

The early news about the Holocaust in Volozhin

The Association and this book are direct outcomes of the destruction of Volozhin. However, the difference between the book and the Association is that the book immortalizes the lives that were lost while the Association's goal is to maintain the living spirit of Volozhin.

The terrible news about the Holocaust took several years to reach the world. It was in 1947, five years after the destruction of the town of Valozhin, that we finally learned of the scope of the calamity that overtook the Jews of our town. This was when the first few survivors arrived in Eretz-Israel. They were Fruma Lipsitz, Pessia Potashnick, Yehuda-Yoseph Potashnick and Yaakov Kagan.

They were "the Bearers of Bad News" who told us about the destruction of our town and its Jewish population. The Nazis and local Christians had devastated the city and its Jewish residents, and we, its survivors, were left alone and desolate.

These terrible revelations scared our souls. Before the Holocaust we used to say these words in the prayer for the dead: "Let G-D remember the souls of my mother and father" but now we say "Let G-D remember the souls of my mother and father, aunts and uncles of both my father's and mother's side, the Rabbis and Torah Scholars, who were murdered, burned, killed and drowned". It was terrible to realize that we had lost all our families. There is no one to send or receive a letter from, a photograph or even just a "hi, how are you" message.

The realization that nothing was left of Volozhin planted a burning yearning in our hearts for its past glory. We remembered lines from the Poem "Farewell" by Bialik, lines that expressed sorrow and loss. Bialik wrote:

> " You are all very dear to my heart
> The way you are, the twisted, falling fences
> Piles of garbage everywhere and your presence so miserable

[Page 631]

> And yet you are very dear to my heart, sevenfold more,
> I see you purified from all your slag and I adore you
> Beautiful, perfect and glorious. "

The first literary appearance of the Holocaust was in 1948. Mr. Yoseph Schwartzberg published a Lamentation in the June issue of the publication "Fun Letzten Churban" (The Latest Disaster). The poem "Der Umkum Fun Volozhin" (The Destruction of Volozhin) impressed many people. Mr. Schwartzberg published his memoir in which he mourned the annihilation of the many thousands of men, women and children.

Welcoming our Sisters and Brothers

As more and more survivors began to arrive in Eretz-Israel, a meeting was held at the home of Ms. Bella Slisternick (Kramnick) and the decision was taken to create "The Association of the Descendants of Volozhin in Israel". The organizers were Rabbi Shimon Langbard, Binyamin Shishko (Shafir), Pesach Berman, Chaim Golobenchich, Dov Levitt, Bella Slisternick, Yitzhak Perski, Yaakov Kagan and Zipora Shepshenwol. Rabbi Shimon Langbard was elected Chairman and Dov Levitt – Secretary.

Bella Slisternick's home became a center for all the survivors who arrived in Eretz-Israel. Bella and other volunteers listened to the new immigrants and assisted them in their first steps in their new country. Bella's husband, Mr. Yaakov Sliternick, although not a native of Volozhin, also helped in this endeavor.

One of the first actions the Association took was to help find survivors who were in the camps of Displaced People (DP camps) in Germany. The survivors were asked to help document the destruction of their hometown. They were also asked to relate their personal experiences from the Holocaust. One reply to this request was a letter from Yoseph Schwartzberg dated April 5, 1948:

"I met Simcha Perski and we discussed your request for a description, dates and our personal experiences during the destruction of Volozhin. Our sorrow and pain are beyond description. We lost our beloved families and community; we are all orphans. Moreover, our situation now is desperate.

[Page 632]
The supporters of Hitler are still killing Jews and we are not sure about the future. We want to come to Eretz-Israel. This is the only place in the world for us.

Rabbi Shimon Langbard asked a group of survivors from Volozhin, who had gathered in Salzburg, to provide details about themselves and other survivors they knew of. To this outreach came a reply from Chaya Skaliot asking for the address of her relatives in Israel. This was the first established link between the survivors in Germany and Israel.

The survivors in both Europe and Israel were penniless. Our Association realized that we must provide financial aid but we ourselves did not have the financial means. The Association of the Descendants of Volozhin in Israel sent an appeal to the Volozhin Association of Etz-Chaim in New York asking for their help. It reads:

"The murderous hand of the Nazis eliminated our parents, brothers and sisters in Volozhin. Only a few were able to survive by escaping to the forest and returning to the town once the War had ended. Only 15 or 20 remained of the two thousand Jews who had once populated Volozhin. They could not stay in the town where each street and building reminded them of their slaughtered families. Exhausted and crushed, they migrated to Germany, to Italy, to Austria. Their desire was to come to Israel and once more rebuild their lives.

Many of the survivors who arrived in Eretz-Israel and those still in the European DP camps are not capable of working. Therefore we, members of The Association of the Descendants of Volozhin in Israel, are committed to helping both those who are planning and those who have finally arrived in Israel and have no family to help them.

However, we cannot do this on our own. We are asking you to join our efforts and "help us help them".

[Page 633]

The goals of The Association of the Descendants of Volozhin in Israel are:

- To contact the survivors of Volozhin who are concentrated in DP camps in Germany
- To assist Volozhin natives in the DP camps and in Israel
- To build a memorial for Volozhin
- To document and archive Volozhin's history
- To rebuild the Yeshiva of Volozhin in Israel

In the meantime, the Association did all it could to help those who had already arrived in Israel. It assisted a family that was evacuated from the city of Jaffa. As soon as the road to Jerusalem was opened, the Association sent boxes of food to our comrades in that city, many of whom were in dire straits during the Arab siege.

While in besieged Jerusalem, the Rebbetzin Fridle Drachinsky (Ben-Sasson), a descendant of a family with a long history in Valozhin, wrote a very moving letter to the American Volozhin community:

"Two months ago, The Association of the Descendants of Volozhin in Israel mailed you a detailed letter about our duty to help the survivors from Volozhin.

We are now in the middle of a cruel battle to secure our destiny in the Holy Land. We trust that with G-D's help, we shall succeed. Our condition, however, requires your help. We are sending food packages to our Volozhin brothers and sisters wherever they are, especially in the besieged and hungry city of Jerusalem, but our means are limited.

Dear brothers! A friend in need is a friend indeed! We are asking for your participation to help the survivors NOW! Any delay may cause this help to arrive too late. You must remember the Talmudic quotation: "Whoever saves one soul, Scripture accounts it as if he had saved the world".

The following sections were translated by Jerrold Landau

The Founding of the Gemilut Chesed Fund

As we have seen, the concern to bring the survivors of Volozhin into the circle of life directed the organization from the time of its founding. In the year 5709 (1949), the first organization was created – the charitable fund.

On 23 Iyar 5709 (May 22, 1949), the organization received a letter from Mr. Y. Grazovski, a relative of Mr. Yitzchak Bunim of New York, announcing that Mr. Bunim has donated five hundred dollars to found the charitable fund in memory of his parents Moshe and Mina Bunimovich.

Mr. Grazovski describes Mr. Yitzchak Bunim in the following words: "Mr. Bunim is one of the princes and champions of Volozhin – a prince from his origins and a champion in his deeds. He wove the chapter of great deeds of

[Page 634]

Volozhin, and has sanctified its name in public, in America and Israel. His heart was always alert toward every important activity that involved a continuation of the faithful Jewish chain, especially of the chain of the great *Gaonim* of Volozhin."

Moshe and Mina Bunimovich

In Mr. Grazovski's letter, dated 1 Kislev 5710 (November 22, 1949) in honor of Rabbi Shimon Langbard, we learn that the organization decided to name the charitable fund in the names of Moshe and Mina Bunimovich. In that letter, Mr. Grabovski urges the workers of the organization to hasten the practical realization of that decision in a legal fashion – that is to prepare the charter of the charitable fund and have it certified by the government.

Mr. Grazovski promises that after the certification of the charter, the activists of Volozhin in the United States would be prepared to offer assistance in order to aid the Volozhin natives in settling in the Land. Indeed, they were aroused to action. Mr. Moshe Bunimovich of New York informs the organization, "I have succeeded in organization a committee of important householders. We will attempt to collect the necessary money to help the survivors of Volozhin in the State of Israel. We hope that we will succeed in collecting a significant sum."

In order to certify the fund from a legal perspective, the following directors were chosen: a) Binyamin Shishko

[Page 635]

(director), b) Dov Lavit (treasurer), c) Chaim Botwinik, d) Bella Slitarnik, e) Chaim Potashnik, f) Yitzchak Perski, g) Yosef Schwartzberg.

The organization concerned itself with affiliating the fund to the charitable fund headquarters in the Land of Israel under the auspices of the Jewish Agency and the citizens loan agency of the Land of Israel. The charitable headquarters affiliated with the Jewish Agency would grant loans of significant amounts of all the charitable funds that it certified.

In its letter to the organization dates 2 Adar 5710 (February 19, 1950), the charitable headquarters in the Land of Israel that, "We hereby inform you that the charitable headquarters has decided in its most recent meeting to include your fund in its network." In its letter of 25 Av 5710 (August 8, 1950), the charitable headquarters attaches the official certification of the fund, as was announced in the newspapers. It was written as follows:

The office of the District Director
Tel Aviv, PO Box 1763
Number 421/99
13 Tammuz 5710 (June 28, 1950)

To Serlin, lawyer, 68 Ahad-Ha'am Street, Tel Aviv.

Greetings:

"In response to your letter of 16 Sivan 5710 (June 1, 1950), I am honored to confirm the receipt of the following documents:

a) The declaration of the founding of the organization named "The Moshe and Mina Bunimovich o.b.m. Charitable Fund" by the organization of Volozhin natives in Israel.

b) The charter of the organization.

With great respect

(–) Y. Kuperman
Responsible for the Tel Aviv District

With its modest sums, the fund will not only support the immigrants from Volozhin who are in need of most urgent assistance, but also the needs of security, to strengthen the State of Israel.

The donation of the organization of the sum of fifty Lira to the benefit of *Keren Magen* touches the heart. The organization received a letter of thanks from the director of the security office, as follows:

[Page 636]

Hakirya, 6 Kislev 5617
November 21, 1955

To
The Organization of Volozhin Natives
11 Moledet Street
Tel Aviv

Dear Sirs,

I hereby acknowledge with gratitude your donation that was transferred to use through the means of *Yediot Achronot*.

Blessed are you to our country, dear citizens. Congratulations, and may your efforts be blessed. The donation was transmitted to *Keren HaMagen* to purchase arms.

With great honor,

(–) Sh. Zelinger
Delegate of the General Director

In an invitation sent to the natives of Volozhin to a memorial in the year 5718 (May 12, 1958 – 23 Iyar 57180, we read that in that year, the charitable fund distributed five loans of the total sum of 1,000 Lira. The treasury of the fund reached 1190.18 Lira (1190 Lira and 18 Agorot). On 17 Tishrei 5719 (October 1, 1958), the fund balance showed a surplus of 826.44 Israeli Lira. That balance proves that the fund grew with the passage of time. It should be noted that the loans were given without the signing of documents and without interest. Many Volozhin natives who were living in economic straits were helped by the charitable fund.

The Bringing of the Books of the Etz Chaim Yeshiva Library to the Land

One of the splendid and wonderful activities that the honorable, active member of the organization, Rabbi Shimon Langbard performed was the bringing of about two hundred books from the library of the Etz Chaim Yeshiva of Volozhin from the United States to the Volozhin Yeshiva of Bnei Brak.

As is known, the Etz Chaim Yeshiva in Volozhin was closed during the First World War, and Rabbi Rafael Shapira and his household were exiled to Minsk. Rabbi Rafael concerned himself with the Yeshiva library. In accordance with his directive, the books were packed in twenty-four large crates and shipped to Minsk.

The city authorities asked about the content of those books, and they were told that they were books of wisdom and study. Since they thought that the books dealt with logic, metaphysics, and philosophy, they gave

[Page 637]

them over to the leadership of Byelorussian University in Minsk. There was a sensitive Jew whose heart was very pained that the gentiles were dishonoring the Torah. He redeemed with his own money, at full price, approximately two hundred books and sent them to the United States. The late Dr. Yitzchak Rivkind, who worked in the Shechter Library in New York, ensured that the books become part of the library, and remain under his supervision.

Dr. Rivkind informed Rabbi Langbard that approximately two hundred books of the Etz Chaim Yeshiva library of Volozhin had been redeemed, and he recommended that they be brought to the Volozhin Yeshiva of Bnei Brak. The books were transported to Israel. All were stamped with the seal of the library of the Etz Chaim Yeshiva, and were placed in a special room in the Volozhin Yeshiva of Bnei Brak.

The seals of the Etz Chaim Yeshiva library

Most of the books are volumes of Mishnah and Talmud. Several of the volumes of Mishnah were published in the year 5611 (1851). Among them, there is also a book of novellae of the Meiri, which is a commentary on Tractate *Shabbat*, published in Vienna in the year 5622 (1862). That book had been first published in Livorno in the year 5530 (1770).

Among the old, rare books is *Minchat Shai* – a *chumash* published by a rabbi A. Sh. Feivish, published in Nadworna in the year *Uvamishor* (*vav* – 6; *beit* – 2; *mem* – 40; *yud* – 10; *shin* – 300; *vav* – 6; *reish* – 200; total 565 – that is the year 5564 – 1804), one year after the founding of the Etz Chaim Yeshiva of Volozhin. The book includes several commentaries on the Torah, including the *Aderet Eliyahu* commentary by the Gr'a, the *Baal Haturim*, and Rashi.

That book has special significance because it was published with the approbation of Rabbi Chaim of Volozhin. Among the rest, the Gra'ch writes:

"My heart speaks with awe: Where is the weigher and where is the scribe who can count all the letters of the Torah, so that the Torah of G-d shall be complete, without missing one letter or having one letter extra, so that the entire world will not be destroyed.

"Due to the length of the exile and the wanderings that we have suffered on account of our multitude of sins, exile after

[Page 638]

exile, and wandering after wandering, with frequent tribulations and disturbances, without any place to even look into the essence of the Torah to the extent necessary, and even though (and especially) to the fence around the Torah, which is the tradition, having been placed into a corner without anyone seeking after them, being covered over with the thorns of confusions, until it has become a sealed book."

Rabbi Chaim of Volozhin praises A. Sh. Feivish, the son of our rabbi and teacher Shlomo Zalman, who removed the "thorns" (that is the confusions) from the Torah and published a large volume with several of the finest and choicest commentaries, which will assist us in the understanding of the Torah.

There is an additional level of holiness to that book in that it was used by the Yeshiva heads of the Etz Chaim Yeshiva of Volozhin. The students of the Yeshiva were taught the weekly Torah portion from that book, with the additional of their own commentaries and novel ideas.

We have included only a few examples from that important collection of books that is found in the Yeshiva Volozhin of Bnei Brak, under the supervision of the Yeshiva head Rabbi Shimon Langbard. The books are replete with secrets. They tell of the strength of Volozhin with their mute mouths. From them, the wonderful voices of the Yeshiva lads burst forth, lamenting the destruction of their holy sanctuary. Everyone entering the room with the books gathers in the atmosphere of Volozhin. There, one hears different hymns, hymns of a wonderful world that set. There, one hears the far-off singing of stars.

Rabbi David Rodinski
The final *shamash* of the Etz Chaim Yeshiva of Volozhin

There is a wonderful Jewish legend that in the future days of redemption, all the synagogues and houses of study in the Diaspora will be uprooted and will come to the Land of Israel. There, one feels as if the Etz Chaim Yeshiva has been uprooted from its place in Aroptzu and transported to the Land of Israel. You can see with your senses the "giant," the Yeshiva building, which was taller than all the houses in Volozhin for many generations.

We are verry sorry that we are unable to literally bring the Yeshiva building to Israel. This beacon of light now stands on the top of the hill. It stands there barren. Whom does it illuminate there? To whom? It is bad for us that the permission has been removed from us to bring the holy stones of the Yeshiva building and to establish the building in accordance with its structure and form as it was in Volozhin, so that we can agree completely the splendor of Volozhin and the splendor

[Page 639]

of Judaism; so that we can see the holy sanctuary that served as a magnificent structure for scholars, geniuses, sharp minds, and Torah giants for more than a century.

In that corner, hidden in the building of the Volozhin Yeshiva in Bnei Brak, the lights of the Etz Chaim Yeshiva are secluded and hidden away. It contains the wellsprings of the "Mother of Yeshivot" in Lithuania, which was a sort of *Chatan Bereishit*[1] of the new era of Torah study, and cast its supreme authority upon a sizable portion of Eastern European Jewry.

Everyone who stands in front of that modest bookcase, found in holy secrecy, will utter the following words of Bialik:

> Of all the pleasant things of the wide world
> Only you yourselves knew my youth
> In kindergarten, you were to me like the heat of a summer day
> And for my head, a pillow on winter nights
> And I will study bound in your parchments the charge of my spirit
> And weave into your lines holy dreams.
>
> ("In Front of the Bookcase")

Another poem of Bialik ("If Your Soul Wishes to Know") "Then your heart will tell you, that your feet shall tread upon the threshold of our house of life, and your eyes will see the treasure of our soul" – stands before our eyes.

The Annual Memorial Ceremonies in Memory of the Community of Volozhin

The annual memorial ceremonies in memory of the community of Volozhin were unusual events, for famous people appeared at those memorial ceremonies, delivering their speeches, and granting us from their talents and their knowledge of the city and the Yeshiva. We are very sad that their words have sunk into the abyss of neglect, for nobody tried to record those wonderful words. However, even the little that remains are an important national cultural possession. It is worthwhile that they be recorded – for our generation and for coming generations.

From the mouths of the survivors, we know that on 23 Iyar 5702 (May 10, 1942), the second slaughter took place in Volozhin, during which most of the Jews of the city perished. Therefore, that date was established as the memorial day for the martyrs of the community of Volozhin, and as a day of mourning in which the survivors of the city in every place shall unite with the memories of their dear ones. The organization placed the organizing of the first memorial ceremony for the martyrs of Volozhin at the top of its concerns. A great deal of energetic work preceded it. It was necessary to collect the addresses of all the Volozhiners in Israel. Bella Slitarnik and Dov Lavit, who served as the secretary of the organization from its inception, were involved in that tedious task. They were very successful at that task, and the success of the first memorial ceremony is due in no small part to their efforts.

The first memorial ceremony took place in the year 5707 (1947) in the Strauss Building in Tel Aviv. Almost

[Page 640]

all the survivors of Volozhin came to that memorial ceremony, to shed tears and unite with their dear ones. Pnina (Pesia) Potashnik and Yaakov Kagan spoke of the atrocities that were perpetrated against the Jews of Volozhin. Their words aroused weeping and groaning.

It is told (*Devarim Rabba*, *Parsha* 11, section 7) that Moses our Teacher was unable to leave Egypt without the coffin of Joseph. Segula (a nickname for Serach the daughter of Asher) showed him the place, and the coffin of Joseph immediately began to flutter and rise from the depths. Moses took the coffin and placed it upon his shoulders. Pnina Potashnik, Yaakov Kagan, as well as other survivors from Volozhin placed the "coffin" of the martyrs of Volozhin upon their shoulders before the left Volozhin. Their memories of what was done to those martyrs are this holy "coffin" that has been buried in our hearts until the end of time.

A portion of the crowd at the memorial ceremony

The center point of the first memorial ceremony was a powerful mourning speech delivered by the honorable Rabbi Shimon Langbard:

"An evil man with an evil government entered the world. Wickedness came and brought wrath. The attribute of judgement became strong[2]. The Divine face was hidden, and powerful wrath was spattered upon our brethren the House of Israel in the lands of Europe. The terrible "reproof"[3] has been fulfilled in our days and before our eyes – the cruel destruction of the Nation of G-d, the likes of which has never taken place since man was created in the Divine image. We have lost that which is dear and holy,

[Page 641]

the finest of the human race, the majority in number and in structure of our brethren the House of Israel in Europe. The entire rich, beautiful history of thousands of years has been wiped out from beneath the skies of G-d in a deluge of blood and tears of millions of our holy brothers and sisters, including myriads of school children, whose blood was spilled like water at the hands of the evil enemy that mauled and annihilated our nation. We have no prophet or prophecy that can give expression to the scope of the destruction, the depth of the travesty, and the Holocaust that has been perpetrated in our days.

"The praiseworthy city of Volozhin, which had been a host of Torah for more than a hundred years, has been turned into a cemetery. Buried within it is the period of greatness, glorious strength, and treasuries of preciousness and blessing of the great "fortress of Torah" in Israel[4]. We stand silent, bereaved, and forlorn, next to the holy graves, as our hearts roar.

"The holy community of Volozhin, and its dear people, upright of heart and upright in their ways, people of benevolence, great in Torah and in fear of Heaven, have perished in sanctification of the Divine Name. Their blood has been spilled with terrible cruelty by the impure murderers, along with the other holy communities.

"Its miniature sanctuaries[5] have been destroyed, and its institutions have been laid waste. In the center of the city, the splendid house, adored with holiness, the Yeshiva building that fluttered in glory over the heights of the city – the cruel enemy has destroyed everything."

A portion of the crowd at the memorial ceremony

[Page 642]

The memorial ceremony of the year 5709 (1949) was very impressive, for two eulogies of great inspiration were received, one from Rabbi Meir Bar-Ilan of blessed memory, and one from the honorable Rabbi Yisrael Isser Shapira – may he live long. In his words of eulogy, Rabbi Shapira (the son of the Gaon Rabbi Rafael Shapira, may the memory of the holy be blessed), writes as follows:

"The city of Volozhin was one of the special cities that merited to be anointed with the oil of the light of Torah, with a large measure of holiness, purity, nobility, wisdom, and knowledge for the entire world. It has all fallen to the sword, a downfall of torture, torture of their bodies and torture of their souls.

"Would it be that our heads were water, and our eyes sources of tears, we would weep day and night[6] for those who were beloved and pleasant to us in their lives, and from whom we cannot separate in their deaths[7], for the victims of Volozhin, its elders, its youth, who were murdered and slaughtered.

"Even though we are unable to bring their remains to our Holy Land – we are not exempt from reviving them and bringing them here through our deeds – good deeds in accordance with the Holy Torah, to continue the oil lamp of the atmosphere of Volozhin, an atmosphere of the homes of our forbears, in our own homes – to kindle memorial lights during or lifetime, with lives of Torah and fear of Heaven. Would it be that we merit this – and that they rest in peace in their repose, and let us say Amen. They should be good intercessors for us and for all of Israel, upon us and upon our children, until G-d above calls out, 'Arise and rejoice.' etc."

A portion of the crowd at the memorial ceremony

[Page 643]

Rabbi Meir Bar-Ilan of blessed memory, who was unable to attend the memorial ceremony due to his weak state of health, sent a letter to the memorial, which included words of memory and appreciation for his native city of Volozhin.

Rabbi Meir Bar-Ilan of blessed memory writes in his letter:

"I did not know of the existence of your organization to this point. I was also unaware that a specific day was designated for the natives of Volozhin to mourn for the hundreds of martyrs of our dear city, which is affixed to our souls and hearts.

"To my sorrow, I cannot promise to participate in the memorial day, for my state of health does not permit me to determine up front whether I can leave my house and travel to Tel Aviv. However, even if I will not be present, let it be as if we sit together, and my tears will be dripping over the destruction of Israel in general during the terrible days that befell us, and over the Jews of Volozhin, the place of my birth, in particular. Let them join the tears of all those who are mourning, and let our prayers be as one together, so that G-d will hear our prayers and comfort us and the entire Nation of Israel with the rise of our State in its greatness and breadth, headed by Jerusalem our Holy City."

Rabbi Meir Bar-Ilan of blessed memory added to his letter wonderful words of appreciation of Volozhin, that typify its spirit and essence. It is worthwhile that these words be etched and embedded in the hearts of every Volozhin native, and in the hearts of those who research Volozhin, for these things will stand forever. Rabbi Meir Bar-Ilan of blessed memory writes:

A portion of the crowd at the memorial ceremony

[Page 644]

A portion of the crowd at the memorial ceremony

"It was not necessary to directly express the name 'Volozhin Yeshiva.' If one said 'Volozhin' alone, it would be understood that the Yeshiva was intended. It was as if there was no city of that name with its residents, travails, and life. Just as when one mentions the names of Pumbedita and Sura[8], one sees in a vision only the Yeshivas and *Reish Galutas*[9], and forgets that, aside from those famous institutions and personalities, there were certainly also ordinary folk and regular affairs. It was like that with the name 'Volozhin' among the Jewish people, where the concept was tied only to the Yeshiva, its heads, and students, and no more. Even within the city itself – the residents of the city with their wealthy people and leaders, were considered subordinate to the Yeshiva students. The permanent ones, the citizens of the city, were below, and those who had came to live there for a certain time only to study Torah were on top.

"Teaching went forth to Israel from Volozhin, not just in the restricted areas of what is ritually permitted or forbidden, guilty or exempt – but rather in all questions of the nation, in all areas of the life of the people. The Torah with the three fathers of the Yeshiva burst forth and rose to the pinnacle of communal and national life of the entire nation. Their four ells spread to all the borders of Jewry, and all areas of the Nation of Israel. Therefore, the Yeshiva heads of Volozhin were like the *Reish Galutas* in their times. The crown of Torah was also on their heads, the splendor of holiness on their countenances, and the manners of royalty in all aspects of their lives. It is not an exaggeration that the expression relating to *Beis Harav* [The rabbinical household or dynasty]

[Page 645]

in Volozhin – "the royal family" was a sort of kingdom of "The honor of Torah" during the three generations of the Yeshiva of Volozhin, of the form that used to exist in the Yeshivot of Babylonia. The Yeshiva of Volozhin was a center of Judaism. All the focal points turned their eyes toward it, and through this they would rise up and be elevated. It too cast its rays of glory afar, and gave of its honor and splendor to far off places. When this center was destroyed, the focal points lost their life force and came down from their greatness."

A portion of the crowd at the memorial ceremony

The honorable Chief Rabbi of Israel, Rabbi Isser Yehuda Unterman, participated in the memorial ceremony of the year 5720 (1960). Rabbi Unterman presented interesting memories of important householders of Volozhin and of the place of the city within Jewry.

The honorable Rabbi Moshe Tvi Neria, participated in the memorial ceremony of the year 5722 (1962). The Volozhin natives do not recall what the rabbi spoke about, but from the thank you note that the secretary of the organization, Mr. Yosef Schwartzberg, sent to Rabbi Neria, we can learn that the words were very important. In his letter of 9 Tammuz 5722 (July 11, 1962), Mr. Schwartzberg writes to Rabbi Neria: "We hereby thank your honor from the depths of our heart in the name of the Organization of Volozhin Natives for your appearance at the memorial ceremony for the martyrs of our town.

"Your honor certainly felt during your speech that your words raised the spirits of the audience and contributed to the atmosphere of unity with the people of our community who perished at the hands of the enemy."

[Page 646]

A portion of the crowd at the memorial ceremony

At the memorial ceremony of the year 5728 (1968), Rabbi Isser Yehuda Shapira sent a letter of lament about Volozhin. We include sections of it:

"We are still shaken up, shaken to the core of our hearts, as we bring forth memories of honor and reverence for our native city, the lofty city of Volozhin, which turned into a cemetery and has become a disgrace and shame. For the wicked enemy spread forth and brought with his own hands wrath on all that was precious to it, on its children-builders[10] on its householders, residents, students, honorable ones, pure ones, upright ones, great in Torah and commandments, people of benevolence and of an upright path, good in deeds. These are our parents, fathers mothers, brothers, sisters, relatives, friends, all so honored, who were hauled to slaughter, who were murdered and killed in unusual manners, with terrible cruelty, among the rest of the holy communities who gave their souls in the sanctification of the Divine Name during the days of tribulation and downfall, at the time of wrath, during the destruction of the Jewish communities in many countries at the hands of the accursed evildoer, the wild beasts, who had no mercy or compassion for men, women, and children, as they shed their blood as water. May He Who Dwells in Zion avenge their blood.

"The eyes further shed choked tears as we recall that the enemy succeeded. They came to its sanctuaries, which are the *Beis Midrashes* of the city from which the sounds of prayers and supplications to our Father in Heaven burst forth into the atmosphere from the mouths of the elderly and children, older lads and young children more precious than gold.

[Page 647]

"How great is the pain still and the agony as we remember that the enemy has destroyed these holy places, high in the holiness of Torah and the commandments, with their great luminaries, the splendor and glory that emanated from them into the recesses of the heart, encouraging pure faith in He Who Dwells In Heaven, the King Of The Worlds, illuminating the recesses of the soul and the spirit.

"This will be our comfort – to believe and hope that the day will come, the great day, when the Blessed G-d will remember the disgrace of His servants, and will rebuild our Holy Temple, with our redemption and the liberation of our souls. We will then be able to once again see the faces of our martyrs when the Supernal Glory will call out, great in deeds, He Who Dwells In the Heavens may His Name be blessed, the support of all creation.

A portion of the crowd at the memorial ceremony

Mr. Shimon Zak (a student of the Etz Chaim Yeshiva during the period of Rabbi Rafael Shapira) participated in the memorial gathering of 5628 [1968]. He spoke about the Yeshiva and the city of Volozhin. Among everything, Mr. Zak said:

"The Yeshiva of Volozhin, as the mother of Lithuanian Yeshivot, took an honorable place among its fellows. Its heads were recognized as the great ones of the generation, with the eyes of the heads of the other Yeshivot looking toward them. Every Yeshiva student saw it as a merit for himself if he succeeded in studying for a certain period in the Yeshiva of Volozhin, to be perfumed with the aroma of its Torah. In the latter years, a spirit of simplicity and naturalness pervaded that Yeshiva. This was the spirit of its original founders,

[Page 648]

the spiritual students and heirs of the Gaon of Vilna, who, for the most part, inherited the doctrine of simplicity and straightforward understanding of the study of the Talmud and its commentaries. The thread of spiritual grace and splendor that was spread over the Yeshiva of Volozhin, and its ancient charm – the charm of a tradition from the past and the spirit of generations – that hovered over it, also influenced the souls of the youths who came there in a calming manner.

"The person educated in Volozhin has a straightforward understanding and clear intellect in his spirit. He is calm and deliberate in his knowledge, pleasant with his fellow, honored and dear to them. The student of the Volozhin of Yeshiva was a desired, dear guest in the circles of householders, who related to him as their own kith and kin. They recognized his superiority in his general spiritual development. Therefore, they revered him, and honored and loved him with the love of parents. His opinions were accepted and heeded also in communal affairs and needs.

The editor, Mr. Eliezer Leoni, speaking about the Book of Volozhin at the memorial gathering in the year 5729 (1969), that took place in Beit Hachalutzot in Tel Aviv

"The world of the Volozhiner was not only expressed in the life of the Yeshiva and its internal affairs. His heart was alert to everything that took place in his surroundings He knew how to celebrate 'a lovely tree and a lovely field'[11], views of nature and the beautiful landscape that surrounded the city of Volozhin. Whoever has not seen the youth and young men of the Yeshiva of Volozhin going out on a summer evening to stroll in the outskirts of the city, enjoying the glory of nature, benefiting from the splendor of the world of the Holy One Blessed Be He in the wild fields,

[Page 649]

discussing important topics of the world and of Judaism during their stroll – has never seen a heartwarming scene in his life[12].

"The lives of the Yeshiva students were very much rooted in the lives of the residents of the city, until it seemed at times that they directed the course of their lives in accordance with the needs of the Yeshiva students. Many residents added special rooms to their homes, and at times even a second story, so as to host the students in those rooms. A hallway divided their space with that of the householders so that the students would not be bothered by the members of the hosting family.

"A deep soulful connection to the Yeshiva of Volozhin remains in the hearts of its students throughout all the days of their lives. All those who merited to bask in its shadow will remember and always recall their youthful grace. They would speak of it with great warmth and abundant love. Even those who left it and 'set up their altars far from its bounds' (in the words of Bialik), whether in the world of action or the world of general knowledge and culture – even they maintained faith in it, and would talk about their memories from their period of study in Volozhin These memories were guarded in a hidden corner of their hearts, and would always warm their souls and feed their spirits.

"The Yeshiva of Volozhin stood for approximately 140 years. Throughout all those years its existence, it served as wellspring that watered the manifold roots of Judaism, spread throughout the entire world, with its clear, pure water. The worth of the Yeshiva of Volozhin is not confined to the hundreds of Torah giants that came from its midst, and not even to the excellent, talented students, whose names became famous later as creators and innovators in the fields of literature, science, and society. Its influence was especially deep through its anonymous students, natives of various countries and states who brought with them upon their return to their native countries, some of the human purity, moral wholesomeness, and spiritual beauty that pervaded the Yeshiva. They brought streams of the warm life of love of Torah, love of their fellow Jew, and knowledge of Judaism into their difficult, gray, day-to-day lives. They illuminated the Jewish street with sparks of the light, song and beauty hidden in the treasures of fundamental Hebrew culture."

Rabbi Yedidya Frankel[13] participated in one of the memorial ceremonies. He spoke about what he had seen in Poland after the war. Professor Chaim Hillel Ben-Sasson also participated. He discussed Volozhin as a host of Torah. The words spoken at these memorial ceremonies blend together into a sublime chapter of elegies and words of appreciation for Volozhin.

The Participation of the Organization in Memorials Conducted by the Holocaust Cellar [Martef Hashoah]

The organization participated in memorial ceremonies organized by Martef Hashoah on Mount Zion. The committee for moral perpetuation of the martyrs of the Holocaust on Mount Zion, directed by Rabbi Dr. Sh. Z. Kahana, invited the natives of Volozhin to participate in the *Tikkun Leil Hashimurim*[14] organized by Martef Hashoah, where the ashes

[Page 650]

Those on the dais of the memorial of the year 5729 (1969)

Right to left: a) Bella Slitarnik, b) Shoshana Neshri, c) Yisrael Ben-Nachum, d) Binyamin Shapir, e) Pesach Berman (speaker), f) Meir Shiff, g) the editor Eliezer Leoni, h) Mr. Namiot, i) Dov Lavit

[Page 651]

of the martyrs of the Holocaust are buried. The Leil Shimurim takes place on the night of the 27th of Nissan (*Yom Hashoah Vehagevurah*) [Holocaust Remembrance Day], and includes the study of Mishnah, the recital of Psalms and penitential prayers, and noting the memory of the bravery of the martyrs.

In order to include the Volozhin natives in the general memorial day for Holocaust victims, the committee sent a letter to Mount Zion, dated 6 Nissan 5719 (April 14, 1959), stating: "We hereby inform you that with respect to the designation of the day of the liquidation of the martyrs of your community on 23 Iyar 5702 [1942], we will light on Sunday, 23 Iyar of this year (May 31, 1959), a memorial candle in memory of the martyrs of your community in Martef Hashoah in Jerusalem, where the ashes of the martyrs of the death camps are interred. Prayers and traditional study for the elevation of the souls of the martyrs, parents, children, brothers, and sisters, will be conducted.

"It would be appropriate, in accordance with the custom accepted in Israel, to send a delegation of members of your community on that day to ascend Mount Zion, kindle the memorial candle, and participate in the memorial and prayers, so that you can unite yourselves with the ashes of the martyrs."

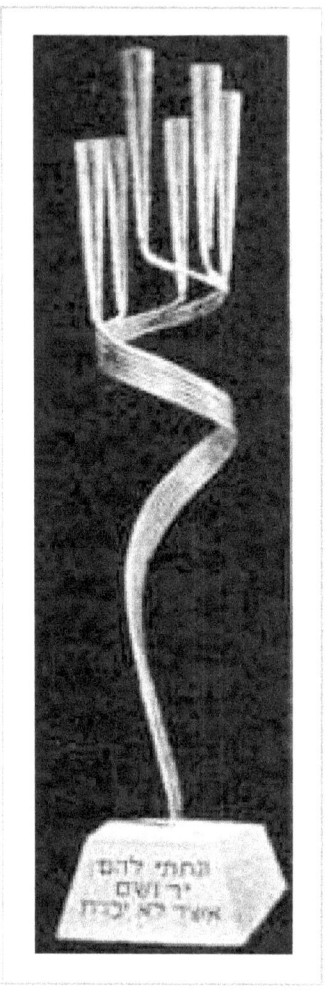

Memorial Lamp of Yad Vashem

The organization participated in the Yad Vashem memorial candle event. With the aspiration of "ensuring that the day that the Knesset designated as the memorial day for the Holocaust and the heroism become rooted within the Land and the entire nation, and to nurture a sense of united memory for the heroism and the victims." (As is written in the Holocaust and heroism memorial law), the custom of lighting memorial candles at Yad Vashem began. Each one is a small light, designated for a household and a family, and is lit on the evening of the 27th of Nissan. It remains burning until the conclusion of the central closing ceremony on the Mount of Remembrance in Jerusalem. The second has six branches, and is designated for institutions and organizations. Lighting it serves as the leading role during the memorial gatherings. The candle symbolizes the human soul, as is written, "The candle of G-d is the soul of man" (Proverbs 20:27). For generation after generation, it has been the Jewish custom to kindle a light on the memorial day [*yahrzeit*] of parents and family members. The organization obtained a large and small memorial candle.

The organization maintained contact with the organization of *Olim* from Poland and the directorship of Yad Vashem. The "union" invited the representatives of the organization on 22 Adar I, 5722 (February 26, 1962) to the convention of organization of natives of cities and towns in the vicinity of Volozhin, in connection with the publication of the Yizkor Book that was to include all the cities and towns of the region.

The editorial board of the Yizkor Book, published by Yad Vashem, also sent a letter to the organization, in which was written: "As is known to you, Yad Vashem is preparing Yizkor Books for the underground fighters in the ghettos and the partisans in the forests who fell in the war against the Nazis.

[Page 652]

We have in our hands the names of the fighters of your city who fell in battle. To perpetuate their memories, we require full biographies. We are interested in meeting with you to figure out means and possibilities of obtaining comprehensive details on the fighters from your city."

Several of the Volozhin survivors responded to this invitation. Their words of testimony are stored in the archives of Yad Vashem in Jerusalem.

Memorial Tablet for Volozhin in Martef Hashoah

Martef Hashoah on Mount Zion is an awe inspiring museum on the great destruction of the Nation of Israel in Europe. Rising from it is the outcry of millions of Jews who perished in Treblinka, Belzec, Auschwitz,

The memorial tablet in memory of the community of Volozhin in Martef Hashoah on Mount Zion in Jerusalem

Text on the tablet is as follows:

May G-d remember
the souls
of our fathers and mothers
brothers and sisters
of the community of

Volozhin
(Vilna region)
With the Yeshivot of our generation
who were murdered on the day of Iyar 23
5702 [1942]
Survivors of Volozhin

[Page 653]

Sobibor, Majdanek, Ponar, and other places. It symbolizes the slaughtered Nation of Israel.

The cellar serves as a central focal point for all the longing, wishes, nostalgia, sorrow, and grief over a wonderful Jewish world that has passed from the world and is found in the "world of truth." It also serves as a holy spot of pilgrimage for the masses of Jews in Israel and the Diaspora in order to hear the voices of the millions that rise up and burst forth from the marble tablets. For such a tablet is not a cold marble tablet. It is incarnated with the souls of our dear ones. Judaism describes as memorial tablet as a *nefesh* [soul], for we learn (Jerusalem Talmud, *Shekalim* 47a), "Excess [money] of the dead – one builds a *nefesh* over his grave." This refers to a memorial monument.

It is self evident that the organization concerned itself with perpetuating the city of Volozhin and the Etz Chaim Yeshiva of Volozhin by erecting a memorial tablet in Martef Hashoah. On 25 Nissan 5718 (April 14, 1958), the organization wrote to the "Committee of Mount Zion" requesting details on the payment for the tablet.

The lighting of candles in memory of the six million at the unveiling ceremony of the memorial monument of the community of Volozhin (Mr. Namiot is lighting the candle)

In a letter dated 30 Nissan 5718 (April 20, 1958), the committee responded that "the place of the tablet does not cost anything, but you must prepare a tablet of the size forty by fifty centimeters. The text must be

[Page 654]

general, without mention of individual names, in the style of the other tablets affixed to Martef Hashoah on Mount Zion in Jerusalem."

The organization tasked Mr. Yonah Ben-Sasson, a scion of the "Volozhin Dynasty" with dealing with all matters related to this. Mr. Ben-Sasson took this holy task upon himself with awe and love. He discussed this with Dr. Kahana (director of the Ministry of Religion) and ensured that the choicest location would be designated for the memorial tablet of Volozhin. He also composed the text that was to be engraved on the tablet. The text was accepted unanimously, for it expressed the essence and preciousness of Volozhin as the mother of Yeshivot of our generation. An honorable location was assigned to the tablet, not far from Vilna the crown, the city of the Gra, the rabbi of the Gra'ch (the Gaon Rabbi Chaim of Volozhin). The tablets that adorn the tablet of Volozhin are woven into a holy tapestry, demonstrating openly and covertly that these towns and communities were all nurtured from the holy, pure wellspring of Volozhin.

On the memorial day of the year 5726 (1966), 24 years after the destruction of Volozhin, the unveiling ceremony of the marble tablet took place. Almost all the survivors of Volozhin came to this awe inspiring, impressive ceremony.

Prior to the ceremony, the local rabbi taught two chapters of Mishnah. One is the seventh chapter of Tractate *Mikvaot*, and the second was the 24th chapter of Tractate *Keilim*. The seventh chapter of Tractate *Mikvaot* concludes with the word *tehora* [purity], and the 24th chapter of Tractate *Keilim* concludes with the word *tahor* [pure]. This is a form of honor to the memory of the deceased. Through this study, we wished to state that every soul of the community of Volozhin is pure, and every martyr of Volozhin is pure.

Mr. Binyamin Shapir (Shishko) directed the ceremony. He related to the Volozhin natives the wonderful legend of Rabbi Chaim of Volozhin, as is written in the articles on the Etz Chaim Yeshiva (see page 96). That legend symbolizes the essence of Volozhin, and the responsibility that Volozhin took upon itself for the redemption of the Nation of Israel and of all humanity. That legend states that the Gra'ch did not want to enter the Garden of Eden on his own. He remains standing and waiting at the border that separates between heaven and earth – until the Messiah will come. The natives of Volozhin heard this legend and were silent, with the awe of Rabbi Chaim on their faces.

In the year 5726 from the creation of the world, twenty-four years after the destruction of Volozhin, from the summit of the City of David, the natives of Volozhin released the vow of Rabbi Chaim of Volozhin. Through the agreement of the martyrs of Volozhin, through the agreement of the Yeshiva lads, through the agreement of the Jews of the towns surrounding Volozhin, and through the agreement of the slaughtered Nation of Israel – we permit you "my father, my father, the chariot and horseman of Israel"[15], Rabbi Chaim of Volozhin, to leave the border that separates between heaven and earth, and to enter the Garden of Eden. You already no longer have

[Page 655]

Volozhin natives at the unveiling ceremony of the memorial tablet in memory of the community of Volozhin at Martef Hashoah [the Holocaust cellar]

[Page 656]

anyone to wait for, for the Jews of Volozhin, and all the Jews from near and far that were so dear to you have already been cut off from the land of the living. They are all already "the crowds above" and not "the congregations below." They are already seated the heights of the world, basking in the shadow of the wings of the Divine Presence. You were a faithful shepherd to your Nation of Israel, and all creation knows that you made efforts before Our Father In Heaven to ensure that the rule of evil passes from the world, for His mercies are great.

During the time of the release of the vow of Rabbi Chaim of Volozhin, I recalled the statement in Tractate *Sanhedrin* (chapter 11, folio 98) regarding the coming of the Messiah. Rabbi Yehoshua the son of Levi asked Elijah, "When will the Messiah come?" He responded, "Go and ask him." "And where is he sitting?" "At the entrance to the city of Rome." "And what are his signs?" "He is sitting among the indigents who are suffering from illnesses, and all are untying the bandages from their wounds and retying them all at once. However, he (the Messiah) unties one bandage and replaces it immediately, because he says: Perhaps I will be summoned to go and redeem Israel, and then I must not tarry. If I am occupied with tying two bandages, I will have to tarry.

There is a fundamental connection between this Talmudic legend and the release of the vow of Rabbi Chaim of Volozhin. It is not only that the Gra'ch can already leave the border separating between heaven and earth, but the Messiah can already leave the entrance to the "city of Rome," for the indigents suffering from illnesses are already no more, for the Nebuzaradan of our day has already annihilated and destroyed them all. The Messiah has nobody for whom he must unbandage and rebandage their wounds. He can already arise and set out on is way, whereas "an indigent riding on a donkey, upon a colt the foal of an ass" (Zecharia 9:9) or through some other means, for his time has arrived. The time has arrived for the Gate of Mercy to be opened to greet the coming of the Messiah.

At that unveiling ceremony, the ceremony of uniting with the martyrs of Volozhin and with Rabbi Chaim of Volozhin, the spiritual father of the community of Volozhin – the natives of Volozhin expressed their longing for the true redemption of the Nation of Israel, as we envisioned by Rabbi Chaim of Volozhin.

The Literary Perpetuation of Volozhin

When the days were still as they were, many years prior to the Holocaust, Volozhin was perpetuated by naming a street after it, on the border of Jaffa and Tel Aviv. To our sorrow, we have not succeeded in finding out when the street was named for Volozhin, just as we have no information about the initiator of that idea.

From its outset, the organization has set the idea of perpetuating Volozhin at the head of its concerns, and there is no perpetuation other than through a book. For from ancient times, the Jewish people have realized that the life of the individual and the pubic are only perpetuated through a book. Did Job not say, "O that my words would be written, o that they would be inscribed in a book" (Job 19:23). In the latter generations, the author Shmuel Yosef [Sha'i] Agnon wrote: "Paper is superior even to a monument, for if it is tall and beautiful, the gentiles steal it and place it

[Page 657]

in their buildings. And if it is small, it sinks into the ground. That is not the case with paper, for if one publishes a book, it is distributed throughout all Jewish communities, and it has existence for generations." ("A Guest for the Night" page 332).

When Mr. Schwartzberg was chosen as the secretary of the organization, he began to concern himself and make significant effort toward the publication of the book. He sent a letter, dated 15 Sivan 5722 (June 17, 1962) to the committee of the Kehilat Etz Chaim Anshei Volozhin in New York, in which he stressed the painful fact that twenty years have already passed since the destruction of Volozhin, and no memorial has been created. He also requested material help, for the Volozhin natives in the State of Israel are unable to publish the book through their own means.

However, it became clear that the main issue is the problem of literary material, for the material found in the hands of those working in that holy endeavor was few and meager, not even sufficient to publish a regular book, let alone a book such as the Book of Volozhin, which is not designated solely for the natives of the city but also for the broad community of erudite people, scholars, intellectuals, and anyone to whom issues of Judaism is close to their hearts.

The organization decided to connect with a professional editor and to give him the task of collecting the material, arranging it, editing it, and bringing it to publication. In 5725 (1965) the writer of these lines (a native of the city of Kowel – Volhyn) was invited to edit the book.

Street named for the Yeshiva of Volozhin, on the border of Jaffa and Tel Aviv

[Page 658]

The writing of the book was fraught with many difficulties. I will not burden the readers with the details. These matters are from the crucible of creativity, and we do not discuss them. In order to deal with the special problems, an expanded editorial council was formed, as follows: a) Chaim Eshlagi, b) Chava Baksht, c) Yisrael Ben-Nachum, d) Professor Chaim Hillel Ben-Sasson, e) Yona Ben-Sasson, f) Mina Dwik, g) Mendel Wolkovich, h) Yisrael Levinson, i) Fania Levitzky, j) Dov Lavit, k) Shoshana Neshri, l) Bella Slitarnik, m) Chaim Potashnik, n) Yitzchak Perski, o) Fruma Zwobner, p) Fruma Cytryn, q) Efraim Rogovin, r) Tzvi Rogovin, s) Rachel Rubinstein, t) Binyamin Shapir (Shishko).

Two committees were formed from the members of the council: the book committee and the financial committee. The first committee was composed of the following members; Binyamin Shapir, Shoshana Neshri, an Yisrael Ben-Nachum. That committee examined the material and accuracy of the various details together with the editor. The second committee consisted of Pesach Berman, Dov Lavit, Chaim Potashnik, and Fruma Zwobner. That committee was busy with the collection of money for the book. We must note the great dedication of all those active on both committees.

A meeting with Mr. Benyamin Wolper in the Dan Hotel in Tel Aviv

Standing (right to left): a) Yisrael Ben-Nachum, b) Dov Lavit, c) Chaim Potashnik
Sitting (right to left): a) Fruma Zwobner, b) Mrs. Wolper, c) Mr. Binyamin Wolper, d) editor Eliezer Leonie, e) Shoshana Neshri, f) Sara Ben-Nachum

[Page 659]

They performed their work with dedication, faithfulness, and no ulterior motives. We will not give marks to those who did more and those who did less. All of them deserve thanks and blessings. May the merit of Volozhin stand for them and their descendants.

Since the Book of Volozhin is one of a kind, we were faced with the issue of what to call it. The book is composed of two books, so it had to express the essence of both of them. We turned to Dr. Yitzchak Rivkind, who always expressed great interest in the Book of Volozhin, and carefully followed the process of its writing. Dr. Rivkind responded as follows: "Since we are talking about Volozhin, I would express that in the name of the book. My advice is that the book should be called 'Supernal Volozhin,' and its subtitle should be 'A book of testimony and memorial to the great Torah center, to the city and the mother of Lithuanian Yeshivot.' If that recommendation is not acceptable, I would word it: 'A book about the city and the Etz Chaim Yeshiva,' or 'The story of the city and the supernal Yeshiva.' As is known, Dr. Rivkind's recommendation was not accepted. Rather, the recommendation of Mr. Yona Ben-Sasson (with slight emendations by Mr. Meir Madan, the secretary of the Academy of the Hebrew Language) was accepted: 'Volozhin, the Story of the City and the Etz Chaim Yeshiva'."

During the period of the writing of the book, several Volozhin natives who live in the United States visited Israel. I recall the visit of Mr. Yehuda Chaim Kotler, who contributed an interesting chapter to the book. Mr. Kotler perpetuated his name and memories with a classic statement on the essence and purpose of the Book of Volozhin. He stated that the Book of Volozhin must be written in such a way that professors and scholars at universities could read it and find content in it. Mr. Kotler had no doubt that the Book of Volozhin would be read in universities, so the editor must know before whom he is standing and before whom he will have to ultimately render an accounting[16].

The ancients used to say *Habent sua fata libelli* (Books have their own fate, each book to its fate); or as it says in the Zohar (Part 3, Torah portion of *Naso* 134) "Everything depends on its luck, even a Torah scroll in the ark"[17]. Books, like humans, are subject to the vicissitudes of luck. The fate of the Book of Volozhin cannot be determined from the outset. However, with an unbiased view of the "spiritual treasury" embedded in the book, we dare to think that this book will not be embarrassed or shamed even in the world of professors and scholars.

Chaim Nachman Bialik differentiated between a book [*sefer*] and a *bichel*[18]. According to Bialik, a book [*sefer*] is a large structure, a creation for generations, worthy of the recognition or feelings of the nation. A *bichel* is crumbs that do not merge into creativity. We hope that our composition is a *sefer* and not a *bichel*. Volozhin shall merit the honor of which it is worthy.

From among the Volozhin natives living in the United States who visited the State of Israel during the time of the writing of the book, we should note in particular the visit of Mr. Wolper and his wife. The editorial council hosted a meeting with the visitors in the Dan Hotel, in which the financial difficulties involved with the writing of the book were disclosed. We told Mr. Wolper that all the organizations that have published Yizkor Books did so with the assistance from the natives of the city in the United States,

[Page 660]

The Book Committee of Bnei Volozhin in the United States

Mr. Benjamin Wolper

Dr. Abraham Jablons

Mr. Ezra Shapiro

Mr. Yitzchak Meir (Irving M.) Bunim

[Page 661]

Pesach Berman

Mr. Samuel Rudin

Mr. Yehuda Chaim (Julius) Kotler

Rabbi Menachem Mendel Potashnik

[Page 662]

and that we hope that the Volozhin natives who live in the United States would conduct themselves similarly. Indeed, our request was fulfilled. Our Volozhiner brethren in the United States took it upon their shoulders and extended a brotherly hand. They fulfilled the task of Zevulun[19] and provided the majority of the "material sustenance" for the book.

From among the Zevulun natives in the United States, a book committee was chosen, composed of the following members: a) Dr. Avraham Jablons, b) Mr. Benjamin Wolper, c) Mr. Yitzchak Meir Bunim, d) Mr. Ezra Shapiro, e) Mr. Samuel Rudin, f) Mr. Pesach Berman, g) Rabbi Mendel Potashnik, h) Mr. Yehuda Chaim Kotler.

That committee acted with dedication of heart and soul for the success of the Book of Volozhin. For this, we extend a heartfelt thank you to them all.

And You Shall Love Volozhin

We will conclude the history of the organization with words of Torah. In *Saarat Eliyahu* (the book is a eulogy by Rabbi Avraham, the son of the Gr'a, for his father the Gr'a), a fine parable is included (page 14): A certain king had a son of his old age. He sent him to a large city filled with scholars and scribes to study all sorts of wisdom and sciences. The king said that if his son were to tarry for several years in the large city, in which many stumble in theft and all types of disgraceful things, his son might also stumble. Therefore, he decided that his son should remain in the city only for the duration of his studies, and should be hosted for the rest of the time in a village near the city. The host will supervise his steps. From this, benefit will accrue to the villagers who will learn from his traits and hear on a daily basis the wisdom that he learned in the city. That is what the king did. After two years, the king sent a letter for his son to return home. All the villagers burst out in weeping. One village asked his friend, "Why are you weeping?" He responded, "My heart is anguished because the son of the king has left the beautiful village filled with vegetable gardens. Where will he find such a spacious residence such as the one in the village?" He responded, "It is not for this that we must weep and be anguished. Even though I have never seen the royal palace, I nevertheless imagine that is certainly as beautiful as our fine village houses, and perhaps even more so. However, it is for this that we must weep, that will no longer hear his words of Torah or his words of wisdom.

"The son of the king" – that is Volozhin with its Jews, its *Gaonim*, its scholars – "left" us, and we can no longer enjoy ourselves with them in words of Torah. However, their words exist. They are written in books. What we have included in the Book of Volozhin is only a check, whose actual value is invested in the bank. The millions and billions of Volozhin are stored in the mighty "financial securities" of the writings of Rabbi Chaim of Volozhin, the writings of the Netzi'v, the writings of Rabbi Yosef Dov Soloveitchik, the writings of Rabbi Yitzchak Yaakov Reines, the writings of Rabbi Rafael Shapira, the writings of Rabbi Kook, the poetry and prose of Chaim Nachman Bialik and all the virtually endless, rich literature regarding the Yeshiva of Volozhin. These are books high in spirit. They reach the pinnacles of the highest spirits. These

[Page 663]

are the "financial securities" of Volozhin. Its "finances" are stored within them. There, its spiritual real estate treasures are stored. Love of those writings is the love of Volozhin.

The more we age and get older, we become cognizant of the vanity of our money, we distance ourselves from light and unimportant matters, and connect ourselves with human creativity that has eternal value. We find our happiness in creative activities, that which the Yeshiva lads referred to as the "meat and fish" of the Gemara and the human spirit in general.

A person from Volozhin must act from the starry heavens above him, and the Torah of Volozhin within him. Through reading and studying these writings, we can connect ourselves increasingly to Volozhin, and its light will never extinguish.

Let us permit ourselves to end our words by paraphrasing the words of the poet: "Volozhin, our spiritual birthplace! You are compared to health! Only a person who loses it, his soul aspires and knows how to value you."

Translator's footnotes:

1. The term used for the first aliya of the new annual Torah reading cycle on Simchat Torah. Here it means the very first.
2. According to tradition, the world is run via two attributes: the attribute of mercy and the attribute of justice. When the attribute of justice is in control, bad things may happen. The next sentence refers to the hiding of the Divine Face (*Hester Panim*), which is a term for G-d withdrawing direct control in the world and allowing nature to take its course. Needless to say, these concepts, mentioned in this speech, are very difficult theological concepts, which would take pages to explain properly. These concepts are not meant to imply that G-d caused the Holocaust, or that the human perpetrators are in any way not responsible. They represent a theological grappling with the age-old question of why bad things happen to good people.
3. *Tochacha*, referring to the sections of reproof in the Torah in Leviticus 26:14-4 (in *Bechukotai*), and Deuteronomy 28:15-68 (in Ki Tavo). Both are read in an undertone in the synagogue.
4. The term 'Israel' here and in the subsequent rabbinical letters refers to the Jewish people, and not the country.
5. A term for synagogues, as opposed to the major sanctuary of the Holy Temple.

6. Based on Jeremiah 9:1.
7. Based on II Samuel 1:23 – the eulogy of King David for King Saul and his son Jonathan.
8. The names of the cities that contained the two major Talmud academies of Babylonia.
9. The titles of the leaders of the Diaspora community during Babylonian times. The *Reish Galuta* took on almost a regal position, and had a great deal of power.
10. This is a Talmudic play on words, as the Hebrew word for its children *baneha* and its builders *boneha*, are the same other than the vowels. See Tractate Berachot 64a.
11. Based on *Pirkei Avot* 3:9.
12. This structure is based on Mishnah *Sukka* 5:1.
13. Served as chief rabbi of Tel Aviv. He was the father-in-law of Rabbi Yisrael Meir Lau.
14. The term for this event is based on *Tikkun* – a ceremony of 'rectification' involving Torah study on the night of Shavuot, and to a lesser extent on the nights of the Seventh Day of Passover and Hoshana Rabba. *Leil Shimurim* [Night of Watching] is a term for Passover night (Exodus 12:42). Some of the ashes of Holocaust victims were indeed brought to Israel and buried in a symbolic grave in Martef Hashoah. Martef Hashoah has largely been eclipsed by Yad Vashem, but it preceded it, and remains a very worthwhile place of pilgrimage on Mount Zion in Jerusalem.
15. A term of honor, used twice in the book of Kings: 2 Kings 2: 12 (Elisha lamenting for Elijah), and 2 Kings 13:14 (King Jehoash lamenting for Elisha).
16. Paraphrased from a phrase in Tractate *Berachot* 28b, and *Pirkei Avot* 3:1 – in both cases referring to G-d, but here referring to academic scholars.
17. The meaning here is that some Torah scrolls are read weekly or even several times a week, some on special occasions, and some may only be taken out once a year on Simchat Torah for *Hakafot*.
18. A Yiddish diminutive of book – indicating a book of lesser importance.
19. Referring to the tradition that the tribe of Yissachar occupied themselves with Torah study, while being supported materially by the tribe of Zevulun. To this day, an arrangement where one side provides the financial assistance for the other side to engage in spiritual pursuits is known as a Yissachar-Zevulun arrangement.

[Page 664]

Fallen Sons of Volozhin in Israel's War of Independence

by the Editorial team

Translated by Meir Razy

Benyamin was born in Karkur, son of Malka and Moshe-Yaakov, on August 22, 1927. He studied in the local elementary school, continued in the Agriculture High-School in Pardes-Channa and found employment as a clerk at the Yitzhar Oil factory in Nachalat-Yitzhak.

He was known as a friendly man, always smiling and happy to help everyone.

He was a member of the HAGANAH and received some military training. When the War of Independence broke out, he enlisted in a religious unit, was sent to a Squad Commanding Course and fought with the Alexandrony Brigade in all its battles in the Sharon, Shomron and Lod's regions. His battalion was then sent to the Negev Front. During leaves, in order not to alarm his parents, he did not tell them any 'heroic' stories. Another soldier in the same Company was Chaim Reches. He too was born in Karkur and he and Benyamin were childhood friends who grew up together, fought together and were killed together in the battle for the Irak el-Manshiya Fort in the "Faluja Pocket" on December 28, 1948. The people of Karkur said: "Two candles were extinguished together the night of the second candle of Chanukah".

Benyamin Perach

He was buried in the Faluja Temporary Cemetery and was moved to the Nachalat-Yitzchak Cemetery on December 8, 1949.

He was a fighter like his father. Moshe-Yaakov (let him live for many more years) was a fighter for the Torah since his youth in Volozhin. The son sacrificed his life for the Holy War that gave us our Independence. We shall carry his memory in our hearts forever.

[Page 665]

Chaim Persky was born in 1911 in Volozhin, son of Shmuel and Galia. He was educated in the Tarbut School and was a member of the Chalutz movement. He practiced sport and came to Eretz-Israel in 1932 as an athlete in a team for the Maccabia Games. He settled in Kiryat-Chaim and joined the "Hapoel Haifa" work teams as well as its music band. He was a member of the Haganah and worked as a "Noter" (an armed guard protecting busses and trucks on the roads) during the Arab Revolt of 1936-8.

He was drafted by the Army for the War of Independence and fought in the region of Acre. He was killed in the battle for the village of Miar. During that battle, the situation was dire and some of the soldiers retreated from their positions. Chaim stayed behind, refusing to leave his post without a direct order from his commanders. He was killed on September 4, 1948 and was laid to rest at the Kfar-Ata Cemetery on September 9, 1948.

Chaim Persky

[Page 666]

Eliezer was born on May 6, 1922, son of Zvi and Toibe Rogovin. The family was poor, but his parents gave him a Zionist education and he excelled at school. During the Holocaust, the family was trapped in the Ghetto. When the Ghetto was liquidated, he managed to escape to the forest and, with his friend Bernstein, joined the partisans of Tzkalov near Nalobok-Stopltz. He was a brave fighter and earned several medals, including "a Hero of the Soviet Union" and the rank of lieutenant. In 1943 he became the commander of a team of explosives experts whose task was to lay mines and to sabotage railroads and bridges.

At one point his unit faced a large group of German soldiers. He ordered his soldiers to fight the Germans "'til their last bullet". The battle lasted for a whole hour and Eliezer's leg was hit. Nonetheless, he continued fighting and when the Germans approached him, he threw a grenade and killed them.

He spent two months in a hospital and then returned to the front.

After Volozhin was liberated by the Soviets, he was appointed as Commander of the Secret Police. He was responsible for shooting and killing a peasant while trying to repair a machine gun and was punished by being sent to the front. In Vilna, he found and killed the collaborator, the person responsible for helping the Germans kill his family.

After the war, he returned to Lodz where he joined the "Gordonia" Group and tried to reach Eretz-Israel. He was an activist in the DP camps of Salzburg, Vienna and in Italy. He was a Hebrew teacher and active in the "Aliya Bet" – the effort to smuggle Jewish survivors into British-ruled Eretz-Israel. In Italy, he joined the "Etzel" underground movement and sailed to Eretz-Israel. The British Navy stopped the ship and the survivors were detained in refugee camps in Cyprus. Twice he tried to escape but was arrested. After a year in Cyprus, he arrived in Israel in 1948 and served in ZAHAL as an Explosives Officer.

Towards the end of the War of Independence he was sent to defuse mines in the Negev. On December 26, 1948, he was killed while defusing a mine. He was buried the following day in Rehovot.

Eliezer Rogovin

[Page 667]

To Leyzer Rogovin's Memory

Written by Yafa Abramovitsh (Sheyna Lidski from Horodok)

Translated by M. Porat z"l

I recall
Leyzer Rogovin
The rebellious hero
The Partisan from Volozhin

Gun in hand
I've seen you in the woods
Your blond forelock flashing
in the wind,
Young and alert,
To the brutal battle.

Your words: "Revenge!
Vengeance!
For our holy martyrs,
For Volozhin,
For my burnt Jewish home"

"Deep in my body and soul
Is an open ugly wound
But my injuries will heal
When on the battlefield
I will fight, win, and fall."

Camp Krasno you fled,
With enemy weapons
abounding,
At the darkness of night
Deep into the forest you ran.

Many times I have seen you
On guard,
You told me
With a smile on the face:
"Today, rails will blow up"

[Page 668]

To the bandits it will be shown
They must die and see
Their own mortality
Through their blind eyes!

Yes, you have gone
On your fighting battle way
With the Horodok hero
Partisans
Nazi trains to blow away.

Returned back into the woods
Happy and joyful
The command was fulfilled
Efficiently, clean, and fast.
I'll remember forever
Your winner's mood,
Your young and smiling face.

After the war we met again,
In the Austrian Alps
You had a sermon
Revealing a victory saga.

You joined the Betar rank
To lead to your land
To preserve there
The remnants left after Hitler's hell
Breathing, suffering souls,
You transformed your battle
Versus the closing gates

You, Leyser the Partisan
You could not
Let go of your gun

Our triumph you did not see
That victory you so sought to experience
You fell in battle
Hero among heroes
Your death in the combat
Was for the liberty,
Of our own land.

[Pages 669-678]

Volozhiners in America

This section is equivalent with the English section pages 15-25

[Page 679]

Expressions of Gratitude

by Binyamin Shapir (Shishku)
(chairman of the Organization of Volozhin Natives in Israel)

Translated by Jerrrold Landau

I regard it as a pleasant duty to express my feelings of gratitude, and the feelings of gratitude of the Volozhin natives in the State of Israel and in every other place, to the editor of the Book of Volozhin, Mr. Eliezer Leoni, who did a great deal for the success of the book.

Mr. Leoni collected detail after detail from the few Holocaust survivors. He delved deeply into the entire rich literature of Volozhin. His compositions published in the book excel in their great expertise and broad, deep knowledge about Volozhin.

Those who should be blessed: Mrs. Shoshana Neshri (Berkowitz), the secretary of the book committee, who invested great toil into the organizational effort.

Mrs. Fruma Gurwitz (Kiwilowitz), treasurer of the committee.

Mr. Dov Lavit, who took the financial responsibility upon himself, even though he did not have the means.

Mr. Chaim Potashnik, who was active, and enlisted others in organizational matters.

Special thanks to Mr. Pesach Berman, who organized the financial means among the Volozhin natives living in the United States.

Also remembered for a blessing are all the friends from among the Volozhin natives, as well as those who are not Volozhin natives, who assisted and participated in the effort toward the book.

May the Book of Volozhin be a source of encouragement and comfort for all who research the city.

[Pages 3-8 - English]

Sefer Volozhin, the Book of Volozhin

Introduction

Eliezer Leoni

This section is equivalent with the Hebrew section pages 11-16

[Page 9 - English]

Our synagogue - 209 Madison street
(Between Rutgers and Jefferson Sts.)
New York, N. Y.

[Page 10 - English]

Our "Little synagogue" - where services are held 75th Anniversary celebration 1886 - 1961

[Page 11 - English]

Some of the old standbys – 1886 - 1961

Top row, left to right: Samuel Bonder, Doctor Abraham Jablons, Rabbi Nathan Rothstein, Morris Heicklin, Harry Silverman
Bottom row, left to right: Abe Rogovin, Sam Miller, Jack Stark, Benjamin Wolper, Ruby Rogovin, Harry A. Brookman

[Page 12 - English]

Second and third generations – celebrating the "75th Anniversary Celebration"
1886-1961

Top row from left to right: Seymour Bloom, Al Kirshner, David Wolper, Benjamin Wolper, Irve Rubin, Jack Kronenberg, Bernard Wolper, Sidney D. Wolper
Middle row from left to right: Abe Rogovin, Harry Silverman, Jack Stark, Samuel Bonder, Rabbi Nathan b, Morris Heicklen, Dr. Abraham Jablons, Ruby Rogovin, Samuel Miller, Harry A. Brookman
Bottom row from left to right: Mrs. Dinah Stark, Ruth Silverman, Mrs. Sarah Rogovin

[Page 13 - English]

First, second and third generations – celebrating the "70th Anniversary Celebration"
1886-1956

[Page 14 - English]

Our first banquet committee - celebrating the Fortieth Anniversary of the founding of Congegation Etz Chaim Anshei Volozhin 1886 - 1926

[Page 15 - English]

Volozhiners in America

By Abraham Jablons M.D.

Executive Director, American Committee

Edited by Judy Montel

Prologue

It cannot be said that the publication of this Volozhin Commemoration Book is like any others because its contents embody in three languages – Hebrew, Yiddish and English – important factual data, which, like a golden chain, give the glowing and fascinating history of orthodox Jewry in the nineteenth and twentieth century in the city of Volozhin, which it is meant to memorialize.

The very name of "Volozhin" conjures up an academy of Talmudic learning which became famous throughout Europe and other parts of the world. This Academy – The Yeshiva of Volozhin – founded in the year 1803 by Rabbi Khayim, of blessed memory, flourished for close 160 years, then, due to the devastation of the Nazi Holocaust of the Second World War, the Yeshiva, bearing the name of Volozhin, was reconstituted in Israel.

The transplant of Volozhiners who voluntarily immigrated to the United States, pioneered the establishment of a Khevra; and those who by grace of G-d, escaped the Nazi onslaught, finally to reach Israel, subsequently formed the Irgun (Society) of Volozhiners. These subjects are dramatically covered in the text.

The sole purpose of the Yeshiva was to foster Torah-true Judaism. From the Yeshiva ordained Rabbis and scholars went forth who adhered strictly to the prescribed tenets in observing and disseminating the Judaic faith.

The importance of this volume is that posterity may learn of the trials and triumphs of Volozhiners and their contribution throughout the Diaspora in perpetuating the religious heritage of what was the city of Volozhin.

Acknowledgements

It is with a profound sense of gratitude to those who were actively engaged in having the English section included in this publication that they are thankfully mentioned.

Space does not permit listing the many names of those who contributed

[Page 16 - English]

toward the book; therefore sincere credit is extended, in their behalf, to the congregation Etz Khayim Anshei Volozhin and the American Committee for the memorial (Yizkor) Volume of Volozhin.

A great debt of thanks is due to the individuals named below, not only for their tireless endeavors in connection with the book, but also for activating the interest and assistance of Volozhiners in America:

To both the assistant directors: Rabbi Mendel Potashnik for initiating the project in the United States, and Julius Kotler, who on his return from a visit in Israel persistently worked to the very end of the undertaking,

To Irvin Bunim, honorary chairman; for his veneration for Volozhin and for his assistance in every possible way,

To Ezra Shapiro of Cleveland, Ohio, for his interest and ready response,

To the Honorary Presidents of the Congregation E.C.A.W; Albert Kirshner, Irve Rubin, Harry Silverman and Benjamin Wolper for their participation and devoted support,

To Pesah Berman, who acted as a liaison between the United States and Israel on his frequent visits to Israel, and was of tremendous help in the furtherance of this book.

Finally for me as editor of "Volozhiners in America" indulgence is asked of all who read this historical narrative, should any omission or error unwittingly be committed. It is with pardonable pride that I submit this "labor of love".

Volozhiners in America

"And let them grow into a multitude in the midst of the Earth"

Genesis, Ch. 48, v. 16

Introductions

From the shtetl of Volozhin, historically famous throughout World Jewry because of its Yeshiva, to the cosmopolitan city of New York, is a distance of approximately 5000 miles over land rails and the Atlantic Ocean.

This narrative, which covers a span of close to 90 years (written in 1970), cannot state with precision the date of the first arrival of the "landsleit" of Volozhin but the year 1881 can be accepted as the year of departure from the Yeshiva City of the earliest immigrants to our shores.

[Page 17 - English]

Before departing from their birthplace these pioneer travelers bade farewell to the venerable Gaon Rabbi Naftoli Zvi Berlin (then Rosh Yeshiva) for his rabbinical blessing. The scholarly and sagacious Rabbi, with a smiling countenance on his holy face - to lessen the sad and serious of their visit - gave them his holy blessing for a safe and healthy trip and his only fatherly request of them was that they should always keep in mind that they are Jews.

In retrospect, we see our travelers departing from their wives, children, friends and acquaintances, with the prayer shawl and phylacteries (talith and tefilim) in one hand and a small sack of hard tack in the other for sustenance of the journey.

With a final glance at the homeland of their youth and adult life, and with heaviness of heart, they knew little of the hardships and difficulties of crossing the land borders, confronting the steamship agencies and discomfort of travel in steerage of three weeks over the stormy Atlantic Ocean to the land of freedom in which they staked their future.

Commemoration

"Give me… your huddled masses yearning to breathe free…
I lift my lamp beside the golden door."

Inscription of pedestal of Statue of Liberty
Emma Lazarus

Despite of the uncertainty of their lot in this land, the vanguard of Volozhiners, with fortitude and steadfastness in trust of the Ever-Living G-d, and instilled with love and adherence to Torah-true Judaism, endured the hardship and inconveniences of the journey and landed safely ashore at Castle Garden (Battery) New York.

It can readily be understood that the first arrivals to the new country missed the comfort and conveniences of family life, and as newcomers had to become boarders with strangers; whereas in the old country they had their own homes and family entourages. In order to overcome their saddened loneliness, which at first was somewhat embittered, they sought the companionship of comrades and friends of

Volozhin. This led to the gathering of Volozhiners on Saturdays and Holidays where a Minyan or more assembled for religious services.

[Page 18 - English]

These get-togethers offered exchanges of news and developments in their homeland based upon letters that were received by individuals amongst the group.

This arrangement continued for about five years until the death of a Volozhiner "landsman", by the name of Yochanan Halevy, which occurred on the final day of Passover in 1885. The decedent was the brother of Abraham Samuel Levy and the father of Trustee Joseph Rudensky. Fifteen of the Landsleit came together in order to arrange for the burial and not having burial grounds of their own, obtained a grave from the Radushkevitsher Congregation.

Realizing the need for burial grounds, the group took steps to form an Organization (Khevra), and not long thereafter, purchased grounds in Washington cemetery, Brooklyn, N.Y. The Organization became a "fait accompli" on October 13, 1886, on which date the Charter was granted by the Sovereign State of New York. Included in the designation of the Congregation, in honor of the founder of the Yeshiva, was that of (Reb) "Khayim", who made Volozhin the great citadel of Talmudic learning. The initial officers of the "Congregation Etz KHAYIM Anshei Volozhin," as it was officially named, were: Moses Pierson, President; Jacob Hurvitz, Vice-President; Treasurer Herman Rogovin; Secretary Jacob J. Jablons; Trustees Samuel Bunimovitz, Moses Chafetz and Isac Meltzer.

The meager earnings of the membership permitted them only a rented space for the holding of Religious Services and meetings. The first of several rented places was 36 Eldridge Street. The group subsequently moved to 101 Hester Street and thence to 20 Orchard Street. At the later location, a diversity of opinion occurred regarding how to conduct the Congregation's affairs and as a result, a small number of members resigned to form their own group. They held services at 21 Bowery and were known as the 21'ers. This splintering did not last long and at a later date a reconciliation took place.
The treatment accorded the Congregation by the Landlord of the Hall at 20 Orchard Street was so offensive that it was imperative to move again – the third move- this time to a 2nd floor at 16 Ludlow Street. From then on, progress and growth of the Congregation was evident. Services were held every day of the year. They were held previously only on Saturdays and Holidays. The new sign literally translated read - "A Place to Worship Mornings and Evenings and Every Day of the Year".

[Page 19 - English]

An epochal event took place on June 8, 1891, which to this very day attests to the zeal and fervor of the young Congregation. The group, while only in existence for five years, undertook to purchase the structure at 209 Madison Street. This property was previously owned by missionaries who, because of the changing neighborhood, with no candidates to proselyte, were compelled to place the property on sale.

The emblematic Six-pointed star – the Mogen David – adorns the top most part or pinnacle of the structure to this very day – replacing the crucifix that had been there prior to the acquisition of the building. In connection with this event a sad occurrence took place at that time in the untimely and accidental tragic passing of one of the members, Mordekhai Yonah, an iron worker who, in his zeal to remove the crucifix, fell to his death.

In less than a decade, to be exact, eight years from the time the building was purchased, the organization has advanced to a stage where it became necessary to have a set of rules governing its affairs in accordance with parliamentary procedure. A booklet was printed bearing the caption ... CONSTITUTION... dated 1899. Also fascinating reading, space does not permit of more than the PREAMBLE – its unique wording translated as follows:

"As we are immigrants in this country, and as is our custom, we, being G-d fearing, therefore have subscribed to establish a Khevra with its holy name: Etz KHAYIM ANSHEI VOLOZHIN

In brotherly bond to serve G-d with prayer and Torah, a bond in friendship, a bond to assist one another when unfortunately there is a need, when there unfortunately is an illness, or when unfortunately, G-d forbid, a death occurs, to extend consolation, to help with advice and deed, and also to provide for widows and orphans.

Being signers (to the Constitution) it is our duty to abide by the laws in a strong bond for all times; and in this meritorious undertaking, the Almighty will help us in our ways to protect us from all evil, and Peace to be with us and to all Israelites. Amen."

With the acquisition of the building, the members were enthusiastically aroused to active efforts in altering the building to conform to a house of worship (Synagogue) wherein the religious services were held as was the custom (minhag) in the Yeshiva-city of Volozhin."

[Page 20 - English]

By the time the 21'ers returned, and the Volozhiner Verein was formed, the membership increased to more than several hundred.

The coalition of the three separate factions into a unified organization so strengthened the Khevra which was afford the engagement of an eminent Rabbi as spiritual leader, and from time to time, distinguished cantors were contracted to lead in the services.

Worthy to mention in this narrative is the assiduous assistance given by the womenfolk who gave unstintingly of their time and effort along with the male members in furnishing the many holy ritual objects that make for a Hebrew sanctuary. One of the first donations, as evidence of their devotion, was that of a holy scroll (Sefer Torah).

As time does not stand still but marches on, so the number of deceased members increased during the period 1886-1926. Among the spiritual leaders who held the Rabbinate seat were: Rabbis Abraham Youdelovitz, Mordekhai Klatzko, Burak, Dameshek, Ralbag, Charlip who through our Congregation became renowned throughout American Jewry.

Deserving of mention is Abraham Isaac Meltzer for his record of 28 years of devoted service as Sexton (Shamesh), Reader of the Torah (Baal koyre) and blower of the Shofar (Baal Tkia).

In their lifetime the pioneering members established a House of Worship with all that pertains to Torah-true regimen. In addition they instituted a free loan found -Gmilos Khessed – a sick benefit fund known as Bikur Kholim and purchased additional burial grounds.

By 1926, the Organization having made substantial progress, with a membership of 268, it was deemed of sufficient importance by the officers and members to mark the four decades since the charter was granted (1886-1926) with a celebration called an Anniversary Banquet.

On Sunday March 21, 1926 at Beethoven Hall, 210 East 5th Street, New York, the 40th Anniversary Banquet was held, Many of the "Old Timers" had lived to participate in this millstone occasion. It was a heart-warming scene to behold the gathering of those who came and greet life long "landsleit". The toastmaster of the evenings' affair was Isidore Jablons – a son of Jacob Jablons and grandson of Samuel Banovitsh , both of whom were founders of the Congregation.

Rabbi Meyer Berlin (Bar-Ilan) graced the dais as the Guest of Honor. He was a native born Volozhiner, and while distinguished in his own right, was the descendant of a line of renowned Rabbis who were

[Page 21 - English]

"Rosh" (head of) the Volozhiner Yeshiva. Within the memory of those who attended the banquet, the highlight of the evening was his stirring address of the glory of Volozhins' contribution through the Diaspora (Centers of Judaism) and an interesting account of the renowned Rabbinical leaders and scholars who emanated from the Yeshiva. At the conclusion of his address, he was given a standing ovation.

The officers of the Congregation at this time were: Jacob Joshua Jablons, President; Moses Banovitsh, Treasurer; Barnett Harisson, Vice president; Harris Rudnick, Secretary; Trusties Louis Henkind, Abraham Garellick, Eli Solof, Joseph Rudin; Gabais Isaac Bunimovitsh and Eliezer Khayim Rabinovitsh.

The Jubilee journal, printed on this occasion, is of special interest in that most of its contents are printed in Yiddish with Hebrew characters in the traditional order from right to left.

Two items of special interest appear in the journal , the first item: a photograph of twenty six "Old Timers" pioneers of the Khevra.

The second item was a fascinating history of the Congregation covering the span of 40 years from the inception of the Volozhin Congregation in the United States.

The 50th Anniversary of the Congregation was celebrated with a banquet in a festive spirit befitting the golden millstone of its existence. It took place on Sunday, March 1, 1936 at the Broadway Center Hotel. The chairman of the celebration was Benjamin Wolper and together with his committee, made it an outstanding success. In the fall he was elected President in recognition for his devoted services to the Congregation. The synagogue was completely renovated and Dedication Ceremonies were held at which the prominent Rabbis A.D. Burack, B.L. Rosenbloom and B.D. Ruditski addressed the capacity gathering that filled all the seats of the Synagogue.

Samuel Rudin and his family rendered valuable "know-how" to renovate the entire interior of the synagogue to a most attractive and inviting structure for worship and praying.

In 1941, Moses Banovitsh was elected President, by acclamation,

[Page 22 - English]

succeeding Benjamin Wolper. He was born in Volozhin, son of one of the founders Samuel Banovitsh. After three years of presidency he served as Gabai than as Treasurer of the Loan fund. The marble pillars on the Volozhiner burial ground, Beyt David Cemetery in Elmont Long Island, were his donation.

The 55th Anniversary Celebration was held on March 1941 at the River Side Plaza Hotel (3rd gala).

During the World War II years (1942-1945), the sons of many members served in the US Army. By the grace of Almighty G-d, none were lost.

Due to the 2nd and 3rd generations the Congregation members increased to 215.

The 60th Anniversary Celebration was held on November 24, 1946 at the River Side Plaza Hotel. At this 4th gala the attendance was overflowing.

In the several years that followed, the Congregation lost the last of the founders in the passing of Victor Klein one of the early Presidents. Shortly thereafter Moses Banovitsh, a recent President, passed on, as well as Isaac Bunimovitsh, affectionately called "Reb Itsele". The membership was greatly saddened by their passing.

The Congregation memorialized the name of Moses Banovitsh by establishing "The Moses Banovitsh Memorial Welfare Fund", which is under the Directorship of his nephew Dr. Abraham Jablons. The fund continues to perform the many charitable services that his uncle had administered.

It was in the evening of Armistice Day (of WWI) November 11, 1951 that the Congregation celebrated its 65th Anniversary – the fifth in the series of these events.

In its 45 page souvenir journal a number of young officers, offsprings of the older members, is listed: Albert Kirshner, born in Volozhin was elevated to the presidency in 1952. Assisting Vice Presidents were Harry Silverman,

[Page 23 - English]

Morris Heiklin and Charles Skloot; Tresurer – A. Brookman; Trustees- Jack Kornberg, Abe Rogovin and Ruby Rogovin.

On Benjamin Wolper the distinction of Honorary President, was conferred after Jacob J. Jablons having been the first honored.

On the 18th November 1956 the 70th Anniversary (6th one) took place. Of historical significance highlighting this Banquet was the symbolical burning of the mortgage which lifted the encumbrance of 63 years from the property.

Harry Silverman, son of Samuel Silverman a founder and early President served as presiding officer for the 195-1959 years. He was assisted by Jack Kronenberg, Morris Helckin, Abe Rogovin, and Jack Stark. His gracious manner and soft spoken words made harmony and comradeship amongst the members. Rabbi Natan Rothstein's services as spiritual leader were and are still held in great esteem.

In 1959 Irve Rubin assumed the duties of the Presidency.

The Diamond, 75th Anniversary (7th in the series) was held on November 13, 1966. The ceremonies master was Isidore Jablons. Irve Rubin, the President delivered a very interesting history of Volozhin (which is published in the Volozhin Yizkor Book – page 26). The honorary President, Benjamin Wolper rendered an account of the splendid achievements of the Congregation for the many years during he was its member and officer.

President Irve Rubin in greeting the assembled stated: "Our congregation has withstood the changes of time and customs in its steadfast adherence and observation of Torah-true Judaism for which special thanks is due to Rabbi Nathan Rotshtein for his spiritual guidance and supervision of the ritual and Talmud Study in our Synagogue".

Epilogue:

It is hoped this narrative will be an incentive for others to devote time and effort for a more extensive dissertation on Volozhiners in America.

It can truly be said that be of the lineage of a Volozhiner, bears the hallmark of distinction.

The American committee of the congregation "Eytz Chaim Anshey Volozhin"
When publishing the Volozhin Yizkor Book
"The book of the city and of the Eytz Chaim Yeshiva"

HONORARY CHAIRMEN:
Irving Bunim
Israel Rogosin
Samuel Rudin

CHAIRMAN:
Irve Rubin

VICE CHAIRMAN:
Albert Kirshner

EXECUTIVE DIRECTOR:
Dr. Abraham Jablons

ASSISTANT DIRECTORS:
Julius Cutler
Rabbi Mendel Potashnik

ASSOCIATES:

Dr Ahil L. Aison, Chicago
Rev. Jacob Bakst
Ben Bennet
Charles Benovitz
Pesah Berman
Seymour Bloom
Samuel Bonder
Joseph R. Cohen
William Ginsberg
Dr. J. L. Gordon
Benjamin R. Gutterman
Dr. Louis Harrison, Lakewood N.J.
Sidney Heicklin, New Bedford Mass.
Morris Heicklin
Seymour Herbst
Dr. Benjamin Jablons
Isidor Jablons
Al Kelly
B.S. Kirshner
Rev Eli Meltzer
Artur L. Morris
Prof. A.P. Nazatir, San Diego, Calif.
David Pecker
Herman Pecker
Irving Pecker
Dr. Nathan Portnoy
Louis Rabinovitz, Greenwood S.C.
Rabbi N.H.J. Riff, Camden N.J.
Prof. Isaac Rivkind
Barney Rogovin, Los Angeles Calif
Rabbi Natan Rothstein
Michael Ruden, Miami Beach Fla.
Sidney Rudy
Aaron Shneider, Los Angeles Calif
George Seligman, Sherman Oaks Calif.
Ezra Shapiro, Cleveland Ohio
Harry Silverman
Michael Sipkin
Charles Skloot
Jack Stark
Lewis Steinman
Dr. Edward Weisman
Benjamin Wolper
Bernard Wolper
David Wolper

[Page 26 - English]

I Remember Volozhin By Irving Bunim
(son of Reb Moshe and Minnie Bunimowitz / Grandson of Shmerl der Melamed)

I left Volozhin in 1910 at the age of 9. Born and brought up in the central life of this small, peaceful, lovable and very human ghetto town, I look back with nostalgic memories of my Shtetel.

It was a small locality and topographically divided into two parts: one which was on a hill and called "Arufzu". There was the aristocratic Wilner Gass, the Mark, the Kleisel of the Wilner Gass and the world-renowned Yeshiva and the Beis Medrash to the left of the Mark. The other part of the shtetel was down the hill and was called "Aropzu". There was a small lake in Wilner Gass and a small river after "Aropzu" setting the boundary of Volozhin. It was a township in the state of Wilno, county of Oszmiana. The government officials were the Pristoff, the Uradnik and the Baron. The Graff had had estates to the right of the Mark. He very rarely was seen or heard of except that he permitted the residents of Volozhin to take pleasure walks through his estate.

The centre of life and portance was the Yeshiva, worldly renowned and officially titled Yeshiva Etz Chaim of Volozhin. This was the first Yeshiva of Higher Learning established in Lithuania and it was the mother Yeshiva of the many great citadels of Torah that enriched Lithuania, and in fact, the entire Torah world. It was established in 1802 by the great scholar, Saint and Sage, Reb Chaim Volozhiner, the disciple of the great Gaon of Wilno. This Yeshiva was later headed by Rabbi Yoshe der Soloveichik, Reb Naphtaly Zvi Yehuda (Hirsh LEIB) Berlin and by Rabbi Raphael Shapiro. Thousands of great scholars owed their Torah learning to Volozyn, among them, Rabbi Abraham Isaac Kook and Yibodel L'Chaim Rabbi Isser Yehuda Untermann, former and present Chief Rabbi of Israel.

The community was poor. A few families, the richer ones found their income from clerical work and management of the lumbering that was done in the vicinity of Volozhin. The rest of the township lived from commercial enterprises, buying and selling their wares from and to the peasants that lived in the "Bondras", the boundaries of Volozhin. Yes, there was a watchmaker, a barber, a shochet, a butcher, an innkeeper,

[Page 27 - English]

a baker, a Scribe who wrote Sifrei Torah and Tfillin, a dyer of woollens, several tailors and several shoemakers, and of course Melamdim.

With that economy, the community supported the students of the Yeshiva, named Yeshiva leit (not Yeshiva Bochurim). The Yeshiva paid for the lodging of the students but the meals were supplied by the residents of the town. These young men used to eat "Tag" – a day here and a day there. Let it be said to the credit of the "Baalebostas" of Volozhin that the meals so offered and given were on a much higher standard than the housewife gave her own husband and children. It was a holiday meal and several Kopeks stealthily put into the pocket of the Yeshiva man. Of course, there were some affluent Yeshiva leit who were supported from home and a goodly number received scholarship maintenance from the great philanthropist, Brodsky, a sugar manufacturer from Petersburg. They were the "Gvirim", the rich ones. The Yeshiva leit were very friendly with the local people and there was a mutual convivial spirit among them. Several of the Yeshiva leit married local girls and the residents of Volozhin picked up the phraseology, the Torah expressions, the Torah spirit that permeated the very air of Volozhin.

Like every other Jewish Community, it had its public bathhouse, the Mikvah, the Linath Hatzedek, Bikur Cholim, a miniature perambulating nursing service, a charity chest, etc. There are a few very interesting moments in the life of Volozhin that give it local colour. I should like to dwell upon them briefly.

Almost all the houses were of wooden structures except the Yeshiva and a few brick buildings, single or two-floored – on the Mark. Every so often, the Goyim from the neighbouring villages used to put fire to one or two houses and almost the whole town would burn down. So, Volozhin established a volunteer fire department, the "Paziarna Komanda" and each night, several young men used to walk the streets and side paths of the town as vigilantes against the arsonists. When a fire broke out, all residents came with pails of water, water hoses pumping water from the river, the Yeshiva leit with their long jackets and yarmulkes trying to chop down the wood that was burning to keep the fire from spreading.

For Passover, the affluent citizens used to join four or five families, kosher a house and the stove for Passover and bake the Matzos necessary for the Holiday. Of course, they consumed much more Matzos than we do here today, because the other parts of the menu were much more

[Page 28 - English]

expensive and Volozhin did not count calories. Then, one large house was Koshered and the community chest contributed the necessary money for flour. The sons and daughters of the richer families were the labourers to knead, to reddle, to bake and to wrap the Matzos for the poor. This was called the "Padrat", (the contract).

Friday was a busy day for the housewife. After the chicken was slaughtered by the schochet, she had to pick the feathers, singe the small feathers, examine the chicken if it had no Shaylo (a physical defect that might render it treif), soak, salt it and of course, cook it. She baked her own Chalah and Kuchen and cake. She made her Tzimes, her Tscholent, set the Samovar, fed the geese and the chickens then cleaned the house and set her candlesticks, the white tablecloth and linens for Shabbos. One could tell the menu by the fragrance that came forth from each house.

Some houses had no wooden floors so the housewife would sprinkle a generous quantity of yellow sand on the ground in honour of Shabbos.

If a resident went to the schochet to slaughter a chicken in the middle of the week, it was a case of either the chicken was sick or the master was sick.

There was a doctor in Volozhin, intermittently. Well, one day, an epidemic of diphtheria broke out and no doctor was in town. The Pristoff was cold to the danger of Jewish life and did nothing to relieve the situation. Papa notified the Gubernator in Wilno and he sent down a commission to study the situation. The Pristoff, afraid of being held for negligence, sent a policeman around town, ordering the parents to take their sick children out of bed and set them at a table around the house. The Commission found no cases of diphtheria and if it were not for Reb Raphael's intercession, sad results might have followed for papa.

The pogrom reports came in almost daily from Odessa and other big cities. The Russo-Japanese War of 1905 was a catastrophic failure for Czar Nicholas and he had to divert the minds and attention of the Russian people. He blamed the Jews and set off a series of murderous pogroms. Schools and colleges were closed to the Jewish boys and girls. Manufacturing and commerce on a broad scale was forbidden. A Jew could not reside in a large city across Russia without a special permit. The horizon was indeed very small and low. The more alert and progressive citizens of Volozhin saw the handwriting on the wall and emigration of one or more families was a daily event. It was, of course, coupled with great hardship; to leave parents and relatives; to travel

[Page 29 - English]

into space, where? – to seek a trade for the bread-winner and a healthy religious atmosphere for the children; to get the necessary funds for travelling expenses, etc. etc.

Of course, we had family names and given names. There were a number of popular family names such as Bunimowitz, Persky, Rogovin, Potashnik, Berman, Kotler, Jablon, etc. But nobody was known by his family name except for the draft (sluzba) or the post office. People were known either by their calling, their parents or by the nickname. I can remember the following: Simcha der Kneiper; Chaim Meier, Hirshel Neches, Avram Chaim die grosse kop; Shlomo der Chassid; Moshe der steiptzer; Schmerl der Melamed; Monya der Zeigermacher; Mendel der Pochter; Icha Tana der wasser treger.

The Yeshiva leit were also known by the town which they came from – Der Raduner, Der Pruziner, etc.

There was ample humour, boyish pranks, a cast of amateur players that performed "Mechiras Joseph". Everybody attended everybody else's Simcha, invitations were announced by the Shames in schul. The Shames had other duties. Friday approaching sunset, he would go up and down the mark calling "In shul arein", and all the stores closed. During the High Holy Day season, he went from house-to-house before dawn, knocked on the windows and with his melodious voice, he would cry out: "Shteht Uf Yisroel Am Kidoshim, Shteht Uf l'Avodas Haboireh".

Half the emigrants went to Eretz Israel and the others to America. Volozhin had indeed reason to be proud of its children that she had sent to Eretz Israel. Some of the leading men in political, economic and military life in Israel are Volozhiner, and America certainly owes a debt of gratitude to Volozhin for the fine productive citizens, doctors, lawyers, Rabbis, philanthropists and industrialists that Volozhin sent forth to enrich the American community.

Volozhiner of America and Israel never forgot the poor of the shtetel that they left behind. Regularly and steadily the widow, the orphan, the handicapped, were remembered. For half a century, money was sent to the needy, privately and through organized effort by the Congregation Anshei Volozhin, 209 Madison St., New York. The Yeshiva was remembered regularly. As of today, the Congregation Anshei Volozhin continues to subsidize the Yeshiva in Bnei Brak, bearing the name of Etz Chaim Yeshiva of Volozhin.

This was Volozhin, and the murderous Huns cruelly wiped out such a beautiful segment of Noble humanity.

[Page 30 - English] [Page 542 - Hebrew]

The Destruction of Wolozhin

Mendel Wolkowitch, Natania

The Germans entered Wolozhin on 1st Tammuz 5701 (25th July, 1941). Before their entry, they bombarded the city with artillery and bombed it from the air. When they entered, they engaged in a small-scale massacre of Jews. Those murdered included Alter Berman, Pesach Mazeh, Eliahu Perski and Alter Shimshelewitz.

A fortnight later, a Judenrat or Jewish Council was appointed by order of the Gestapo. It had twelve members and was headed by Jacob (Yani) Garber. The purpose of the Judenrat was to carry out the orders of the Gestapo, i.e., to conscript people for work and to supply money, jewellery, furs and cloth to the authorities.

The non-Jews welcome the Germans joyously and at once said that they would collaborate with them. Advocate Stanislaw Torski, a notorious "Endek" (the Endeks or National Democrats were the most anti-Semitic political group in Poland), returned to Wolozhin from the Concentration Camp at Kartoz-Braza. His time had come at last. He contacted the local Jew-haters, the barber Baranski and others and they began to conduct atrocity propaganda against the Jews. Advocate Torski was appointed mayor. On his second day in office, he sent to prison the popular physician, Abraham Zart with his daughter Nehama, Chaim Zirolnik, Aaron Galperin, Simeon Lavit, Lippa Zimmerman and Hasia Leah Perski. The next day, they were all executed. The local police were made up of worthless wretches who were brought from the neighbouring villages and placed under the orders of the S.S. men. These policemen used to attack the Jews and beat them murderously. One of them, Minkowitch, first broke the hands of Freidel Rosen and afterwards, shot and killed her. Rosa Berman and Shachna Partzki were savagely beaten and killed.

In the month of Av that year (August 1941), the Ghetto was established in "Aroptzu" within the "Krummer Gass" (crooked street), Dubinski Street and Minsk Street. Some 3500 people were crowded together in a few dozen houses. They included the Jews of Zolozhin and the Jewish refugees from the small neighbouring towns of Wizhniewa, Olshan and Oshmina.

[Page 31 - English]

We went out to forced labour together. We had to clean the streets, dig pits and sweep away the snow in winter. I worked in the Yatzkeve Forest near Bielokortz, in a group of about eighty Jews. We lived in a miserable little cabin where we were all crushed and crowded together, broken and depressed. Everything saddened us and lowered our spirits. No food was given to us. We had a few belongings in return for which the gentiles gave us bread.

While we were working on the road that leads to Minsk, we saw some dreadful sights. We saw the Germans maltreating Soviet prisoners of war in a horrible way. While their blood was flowing, the torturers made them sing the song "Katiusha". They were starving and naked. The Germans were seated on a cart carrying grass and spring onions. From time-to-time they flung the prisoners some of the grass as though they were animals. The unfortunate men fell on it and crazily swallowed it.

On the Sabbath, they permitted us to return to Wolozhin. Before entering the Ghetto, we were very carefully searched and woe to the man who had with him a piece of bread or a bottle of milk. He was beaten murderously and the food was taken from him. Sometimes, a Christian who felt sorry for the imprisoned Jews would approach the Ghetto fence with a loaf of bread or a bottle of milk. He was savagely beaten by the police and a few of these kind hearted people paid with their lives. Koppel Rogowin received a little food in return for kerosine from a non-Jew who went and denounced him. When Rogowin learnt of this, he ran away to the Yatzkeve Forest. We were all lined up there and Koppel was taken out of the line. The murderers beat him so cruelly that he begged them to kill him, but they did not do him that favour at once. They put him on a waggon and brought him, almost dead, to the "Priest's Hill" where they executed him.

On 7th Heshvan 5702 (28th October, 1941) Moka, of the Gestapo, entered the Ghetto and demanded a large supply of boot soles at once. They gave him the soles assuming that they had done their duty with that gift. But he turned up again at the Judenrat accompanied by several S.S. men. He ordered all the Jews in the Ghetto to be summoned to a meeting in order to listen to "an interesting lecture" by him. The members of the Judenrat hurried out and passed on the word of the ruler. Not everybody responded. My little daughter, Shulamit, begged

[Page 32 - English]

me: "Daddy, don't go to the meeting!" The child's heart forewarned her. I listened to her and did not go to the meeting.

When a large number had assembled, Moka sent most of them back to the Ghetto. He imprisoned the rest in the cinema hall. From there, he took out groups of ten people at a time, conducted them to the neighbouring sports ground and killed them. In this "action", more than 200 Jews were killed including Jacob (Yani) Garber, head of the Judenrat.

Jacob Finger, Tzapin and Zacharia Beikilin succeeded in escaping from this action. They returned to the Ghetto and told what they had seen. When it was immediately, the White Russian police came with the peasants of the neighbourhood, stripped the clothes off the corpses, took away any rings and jewellery and pulled their gold teeth out of their mouths. Then a group of Jews were brought and ordered to bury the dead.

Life in the Ghetto grew harder and harder. One day, several S.S. men entered the house which served as a House of Prayer. They took a Torah scroll, spread it out on the ground, made several dozen Jews lie down on the sheets and killed them.

The 23rd Iyyar 5702 (10th May 1942) arrived and marked the destruction of the Wolozhin community. A few days earlier, three Germans had been found dead between Wolozhin and Zadzhezha. Gestapo men arrived from Wileika and visited several places in town. It later became known that they had come to select a suitable place for general slaughter.

I was told by a very reliable source what was being planned. My daughter was ill and had a very high temperature. I hastened to summon Dr. Faminski, a friend of the Jews. While treating the child and giving medical instructions, he informed me that the time to exterminate the Jews was approaching. He used to come and go among the heads of the Gestapo and knew their plans for the Jews. So, the information he gave me was absolutely reliable.

After I had heard what the doctor had to say, I fell fast asleep but a nightmare woke me up. In my dream I saw that they had surrounded the Ghetto. The murderers entered our house and killed everybody. I was very much worried by the dream and told it to Rachel Leveiner,

[Page 33 - English]

my brother's sister-in-law. She listened to me but did not believe my words and quietly went out into the courtyard to bring something into the house. But she came back at once with her face as red as fire, trembling as she said to me: "There is something terrible all around – they are banging and yelling and shooting".

I looked out of the window and saw that the murderers were driving the Jews out of their houses. When they approached our house, I said to Malka (my first wife): "The murderers are coming. Let's take the child and run away". She did not listen to me but stayed where she was because she saw nowhere to escape to. When I saw the police and the S.S. men approaching our house and mounting the stairs, I called my father-in-law, Sana (Nathaniel) Lavit and my brother-in-law Leiba, and we slipped out through the back door into the barn. We then climbed up into the attic.

On 23rd Iyyar 5702 (10th May, 1942) at 5 a.m. the Ghetto was cordoned off by S.S. men and Polish and White Russian police. First, they killed Yohanan Klein and Isaac Naroshevitz, the two Jewish policemen standing at the entrance to the Ghetto. They then began shooting at Jews and many fell. They led the prisoners towards the smithy which the Russians had built in Moszczitzki Street, not far from the synagogue, and there they imprisoned many Jews in the building. Opposite the building they placed chairs and a table which was set out with all kinds of liquor. Around it sat policemen and S.S. men, bright and cheerful with machine guns next to them. Between one drink and the next, they shot into the building in order to silence the weeping of the children and the outcry of the adults.

Among the prisoners was Rabbi Reuben Hadash, the Rabbi of Olshan. He appealed to the people not to go like sheep to the slaughter, and called on the prisoners to destroy the stoves and ovens. Let each one take a brick, a stone or an iron bar in his hands, break down the doors and attack the murderers. But Rabbi Israel Lonim opposed this quoting: "Even when a sharp sword is pressed against a man's throat, let him not cease to hope for mercy".

The chief of the gendarmerie summoned Aaron Kamenietzki, a member of the Judenrat, and ordered him to polish his knee boots. As soon as Kamenietzki bent down, the chief shot him. When the prisoners saw this murder, a deadly commotion began and they started to break

[Page 34 - English]

out through the roof. The murderers shot them but still a few succeeded in escaping, Mordechai Malot among them.

On that dreadful and hot day, they kept the people crowded together from five in the morning until five in the afternoon. They then took them out in groups – children separately and men and women separately. A few Jews went to their deaths in their prayer shawls and phylacteries. They conducted the Jews of set purpose through the streets of the Christians in order that the later might rejoice at the fall of their Jewish enemies. A gang of young men and women came out of the houses with their mouth organs and played and sang cheerful songs and began dancing. They gathered around us and mocked us.

Those who were being led to death were taken to the House of Bulowa next to the Jewish graveyard where they were killed with automatic weapons. After the murders, they set the house on fire and the Jews of Wolozhin went up to heaven in flames. On that day, many other Jews were killed having been shot in attics and other hiding places. When these corpses were taken for burial, the gentiles flung dead cats, dogs and all kinds of rubbish on to them.

After the slaughter, the gentiles entered the Ghetto with their carts and looted whatever they saw. One woman raised her hands high and shouted joyously: "Father in Heaven, I thank thee for having purified us of this Jewish filth". It should be added that her husband was a decent and upright man who treated us kindly. He very much grieved at the bitter fate of the Jews which broke his heart.

When the sun set, we left the barn and crept towards our house. We came near the stable. The doors were open. "Is there anybody here?" we asked in a whisper and heard a whisper back: "I am here!" It was the voice of my brother-in-law Hershel Perski. We then heard the voices of Hershel and Zivia Lonim. Under cover of darkness, we set out for the forest near Volozhin. I went with Nathaniel (Sana) Lavit, my brother-in-law Leiba Lavit and Hersh Rogowin. We reached the forest where we found a couple of dozen Jews. It was a marshy spot. Weary and hungry, we asked on another where our help could come from?

Hunger and thirst distressed us very much. We decided to go and look for food and water and were firmly resolved to defend ourselves

[Page 35- English]

if we were attacked. We set out wearing peasant clothes. We crossed the river Berezina and reached a village where we went to the home of a peasant whom we knew. He gave us bread, salt and cheese. His wife warned us to be careful because there were police wandering around who had killed several Jews the day before.

We stayed fourteen days at the village. When the food gave out, Sana Lavit said to us that there was no choice but to go back to Wolozhin. It was not easy for the roads and paths were patrolled day and night by police and S.S. men. Still, we reached Wolozhin where we found Mottel Chaiklin in a house. I asked him whether any of my family were alive? He answered that peasants had told him that my brother Munia (Samuel) was Zabzhezha. I went there and found him in a peasant's home. One leg was swollen. Although it was hard for him to walk, he accompanied me and we reached Volozhin together.

Translations by Jerrold Landau

Translator's note:

The Volozhin Yizkor Book contain a supplement. The page numbering begins once again from 1. On the NYPL site (https://digitalcollections.nypl.org/items/ade5e2b0-2ff3-0133-6e56-58d385a7b928) this addendum can be found on scans 720-760. On the Yiddish Book Center site (https://www.yiddishbookcenter.org/collections/yizkor-books/yzk-nybc314103/leoni-eliezer-voloz-in-sifrah-shel-ha-ir-ve-shel-yeshivat-Etz-hayim) this addendum begins on page 721.

Supplement to the Book of Volozhin

[Page 3]

Volozhin Natives Who Perished in the Holocaust

Merciful Father!
Pour out your wrath upon the nations that do not know You;
And on the nations who do not call in Your name.
For thy have consumed the house of Volozhin
And destroyed the beauty of the natives of Volozhin.[1]

The Family of Aryeh Leib Berman

Right to left: a) Mina Berman, b) Aryeh Leib Berman, c) Esther Berman (on his lap), d) Elka Berman, e) Tzipora Berman, f) Shmuel Berman, g) Chaya Sara Berman, h) Chana Berman

"And they killed all those pleasant to the eye" (Lamentations 2:7)

Perpetuator: **Yitzchak Berman** (United States)

[Page 4]

The Family of Yitzchak Meir Berman

Standing (right to left): a) Chaim Meir Berman, b) Mina Berman (his wife), c) their daughter, d) Shoshana (Roza) Berman
Sitting: a) Eli Moshe Brudna, b) Henia Mereh Berman, c) guest, d) Rivka Berman, e) Yitzchak Meir Berman

[Page 5]

Sonia Yurshaner (Berman)

Chaim Yurshaner

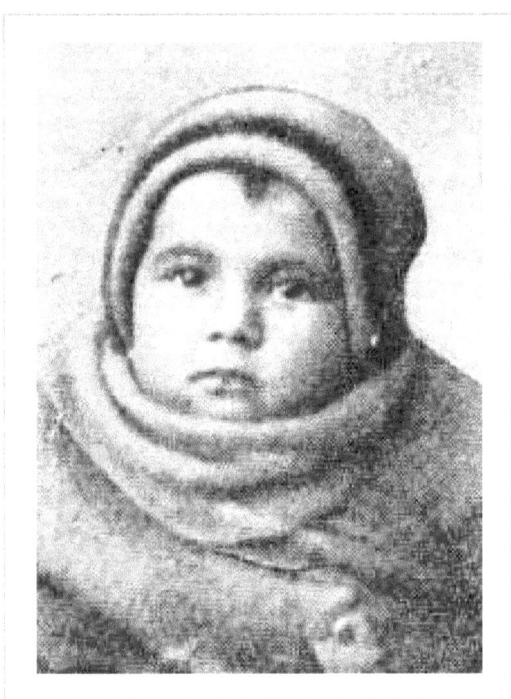
Mina Yurshaner

Natan Berman

"The spilled their blood like water… and there was none to bury them."
(Psalms 79:3)

Perpetuators: **The brothers Pesach and Shlomo Berman, and cousin Mina Mandel**

[Page 6]

Berkowitz Family

Keila Berkowitz

Avraham Berkowitz

Yisrael Berkowitz

Yaakov Berkowitz and his wife Sonia (nee Dubinsky)

This was a vibrant and bubbly family. The father and two sons were active in communal life in the city. The mother bore the yoke of livelihood with endless dedication. Thanks to her efforts, the children studied in Vilna and obtained a general and professional education.

Leibele – the son of their old age – was a wise and talented student. A precious family was cut off before its time. May their memory be blessed forever.

Perpetuator: **Daughter Rosza (Shoshana) Neshri (Berkowitz)**

[Page 7]

Gelman (Kotler) Family

"Woe to me over my hurt. My wound is grievous." (Jeremiah 10:19)

My sister Reizel (Shoshana), her husband Yitzchak Gelman, and their children

[Page 8]

Wand-Polak Family

Dr. Hirsch Rozenstein, daughter Esther,
and his wife Yocheved (Yatza) (nee Wand-Polak)

Riva Sheiniuk (Nee Wand-Polak)　　　　Nechama Wand-Polak

Dr. Rozenstein, a native of Riga (Latvia), graduated medicine from the University of Prague (Czechoslovakia). He came to Volozhin in 1932 and married Yocheved (Yatza), the daughter of Mr. Michael Wand-Polak. When he was in the Volozhin Ghetto, he extended medical help to all in need of such. He was murdered during the third slaughter.

Perpetuators: **The Wand-Polak, Schwartzberg, and Kaminer families**

Translator's footnote:

1. A paraphrase of the *Shefoch Chamatcha* prayer of the Passover Seder.

Volozhin Natives Who Perished in the Holocaust {cont.}

[Page 9]

Cheiklin Family

Masha Cheiklin

Netanel Cheiklin

Reizel Cheiklin

Zecharia Cheiklin

"My spirit is destroyed, my days are cut off, graves await me." (Job 17:1)

Perpetuator: **Son, Zisel Cheiklin**

[Page 10]

Tabachowitz Family

Standing (right to left): a) Yosef Tabachowitz, b) Shimon Tabachowitz, c) Chenia Tabachowitz (Kahanowitz), d) Yaakov Tabachowitz, e) Chaya Tabachowitz, f) Velvel Tabachowitz
Sitting: a) someone not from Volozhin, b) not from Volozhin, c) not from Volozhin, d) Sonia Perski (Tabachowitz) and her daughter

Yaakov Tabachowitz had a splendid countenance. He served as a Torah reader and prayer leader, and he would enchant the worshipers with his fine voice in his prayers. Yosef, his eldest son, was also graced with a with a sweet voice and acting talent. He played the primary role in many plays by the amateur troupe. He married Bella Shoker.

Sonia, the eldest daughter, married Velvel Perski, a grain merchant and owner of a grocery store. Sonia did not live long. She died during pregnancy.

The daughter Henia married Yeshayahu Kahanowitz, an enthusiastic Zionist and one of the founders of the Tarbut School in Volozhin. The son Shimon joined the pioneering [chalutz] movement while still a student at the Hebrew Gymnasja of Vilna. He was one of the first chalutzim of Volozhin to make aliya to the Land of Israel. He lived in Petach Tikva, and earned his livelihood with the toil of his hands throughout his entire life. He lived a modest life until his sudden death at the age of 61. With his death, the candle of this family was extinguished. Nobody of this family survived.

Perpetuators: **the group of friends**

[Page 11]

Josefowitz Family

Tzvi Meir and Sima Josefowitz

About Grandfather's Household

My grandfather, Yaaov Weisbord, settled in Volozhin during the latter half of the 19th century. He bult a large house on Narutowicz Street that was called "The Troktir." His daughter Sima married my father.

My mother excelled with her good heart and generosity. She was a mother to many orphans. She would feed them and clothe them with new clothes.

During the First World War, many Jews from nearby villages escaped to Volozhin. My mother took in a family of refugees to our house, and they lived with us for a certain period. Three lads from the Etz Chaim Yeshiva of Volozhin were also hosted in our house. They ate with the family on the Sabbath.

My father was graced with a musical soul. During times of sadness, he would play the violin. My sister Sara gained her great love of music from him.

A great fire broke out in Volozhin in the year 5678 (1918), and our house burnt down. My father was weakened from this great tragedy, but my mother's spirit did not fall. She planted all sorts of vegetables in our yard, and we lived from this. She also distributed vegetables to poor people for free. The family remained in that impoverished state until the deluge of blood came and wiped out everything.

Perpetuator: **daughter Fruma Guzman (Josefowitz)**

[Page 12]

The Family of Reuven Lavit

Ita and Reuven Lavit

Mordechai Yehuda Lavit and his family

[Page 13]

Lea Weiner

Eliezer and Rodel Lavit

Elka Chaya Wolkowitz (nee Lavit)

Shmuel Wolkowitz

[Page 14]

Rachel Weiner (nee Lavit)

Moshe Weiner

In eternal memory of my wide-branched family who perished in the Holocaust of Volozhin. Pour out your wrath upon the nations that do not know You, and on the nations who do not call in Your name. For they have consumed my family members and have destroyed their beauty.[1]

Perpetuator: **son Dov Lavit**

* * *

Yaakov Levinson

My brother, Yaakov the son of Moshe and Yocheved Levinson, was born in Volozhin in the year 5666 (1906). He received a Torah education (our father was ordained as a rabbi by the Netzi'v and Rabbi Chaim Soloveitchik).

With the influence of the times, he stopped his studies at the Ramailes Yeshiva of Vilna and turned to secular studies. He studied for one year at the Dr. Epstein Hebrew Gymnasja of Vilna. Then he studied in the Polish Gymnasja and earned his certificate of matriculation. He was accepted to the faculty of law at the University of Vilna at the age of 19. In his time, he was the only Jewish student in Volozhin. He served as a Polish teacher in the Tarbut schools in the towns of the area of Volozhin.

His name will be etched in my heart forever.

Perpetuator: **His brother Yisrael Levinson**

Translator's footnote:

1. A paraphrase of the *Shefoch Chamatcha* prayer of the Passover Seder.

Volozhin Natives Who Perished in the Holocaust {cont.}

[Page 15]

Children of Yisrael Lunin

Children of Yisrael Lunin
Right to left: a) Tzvi Lunin, b) Tzvia Lunin, c) Nechama Lunin

Perpetuators: **Shulamit (nee Brener) and Chaim Golobnechitz**

* * *

Moshe Yehuda Bunimovich

Rachel and Shlomo Avraham Liberman

Both were born in Volozhin in the year 5673 (1913). They received a traditional education, starting in the cheder, and continuing in the Tarbut School. Both believed with perfect faith in the rise of the Jewish state.

Shlomo Avraham Liberman was involved in communal life in the chapters of Hashomer Hatzair and Hechalutz. He went on *hachshara* in the Hashomer Hatzair kibbutz, and was certified for *aliya*.

Moshe Yehuda Bunimovich – after completing his studies at the Tarbut School, he turned to religious studies and learned in Yeshiva. When the stream of *aliya* to the Land of Israel increased, he left the Yeshiva and joined the Hapoel Hamizrachi religious kibbutz movement. He traveled to a kibbutz in Vilna and was certified for *aliya*. However, the gates of the Land were locked, and his *aliya* was postponed.

When the Second World War broke out, Shlomo Avraham Liberman was drafted to the Polish Army. As far as I know, he fell into German captivity, and he was lost track of. The fate of Moshe Yehuda Bunimovich was the same as that of all the Jews of Volozhin. He perished in the ghetto. May their memories be a blessing.

Perpetuator: **Chaim Tzvi Potashnik**

[Page 16]

Lipshitz Family

Yaakov Lipshitz

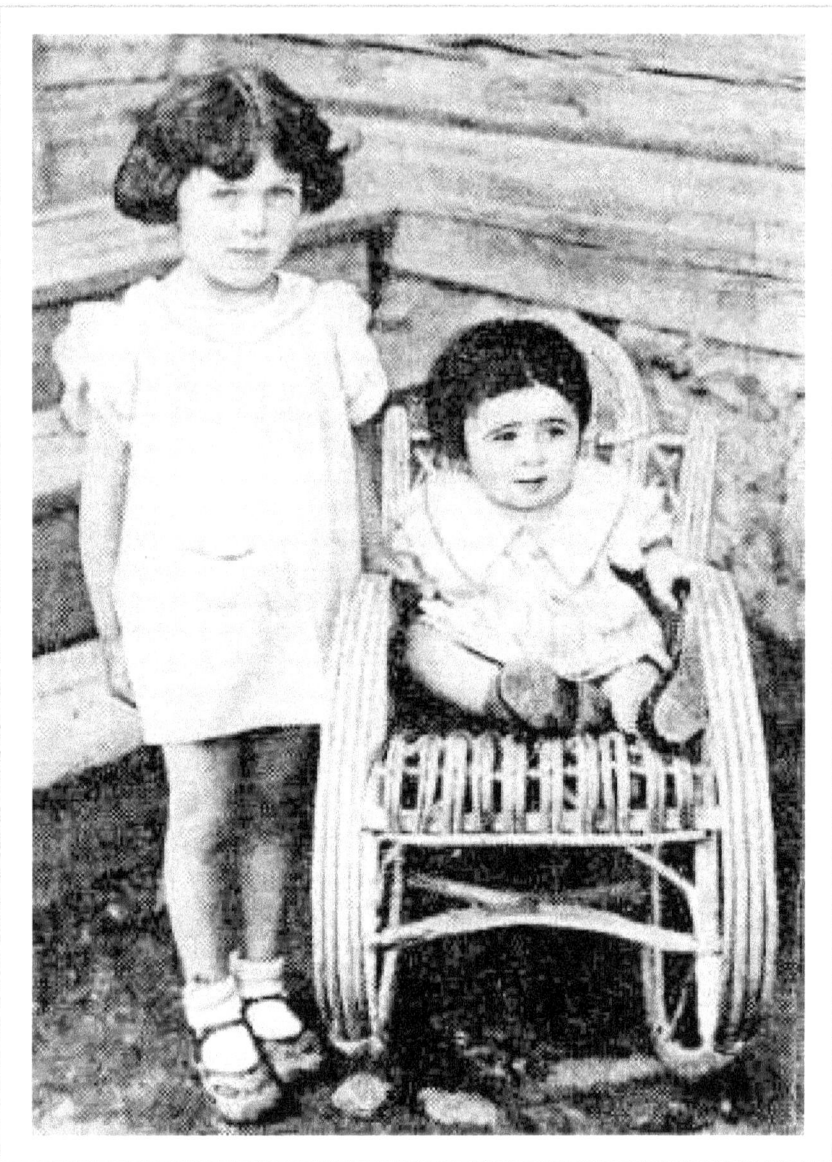

Chayale and Shoshanale Lipshitz

In eternal memory of my daughters.

Shoshanale was born in Volozhin on Friday, 13 Tammuz, 5693 (July 7, 1933). She was shot and burnt on Thursday, 24 Tammuz, 5702 (July 9, 1942).

How refined, intelligent and Talented were you! You excelled in your studies. Your desire to know Hebrew was so strong that you taught yourself.

When the Soviets arrived, you received a prize for the dance and song olympiada, in which the choicest powers of the school appeared.

Swarthy Chayale was born in Volozhin on Friday, 2 Iyar 5696 (April 24, 1936). She was shot and burnt on Thursday, 24 Tammuz 5702 (July 9, 1942).

When you were quite small, you already demonstrated your musical talent. You would take the guitar – twice your size – while sitting on a low sofa, and play and sing, accompanied by Shoshanale's dancing.

And suddenly you, my dear daughters, were murdered by the German, Lithuanian and Byelorussian murderers who knew no mercy. Your blood was spilled while you were still very young, without fault and without sin.

My G-d, my G-d, why have You abandoned me! Chayale and Shoshanale, would it be that I had died instead of you. How can I enjoy eating and drinking, or how can the light of day be sweet in my eyes, while I still see that you were stolen from me at the spring of your days.

Your mother Fruma Lipshitz-Gapanovich (United States) who weeps for you until the end of my days.

[Page 17]

Yitzchak Sosinski, his wife Pesia, their daughter Rivka

Shimon and Rivka Elishkovich

Yisrael and Lipsha Elishkovitz "the Rosalishkeer"

"For – He who demands blood will remember you; the outcry of the modest ones will not be forgotten." (Psalms 9:13)

Perpetuators: Shalom Elishkovich and Chaya Eidelman (Elishkovich)

* * *

Perski and Schwartzberg Families

Standing (right to left): a) Sonia Perski, b) Aryeh Schwartzberg
Sitting (right to left): a) Zeev Perski, b) Genesia Perski, c) Yitzchak Perski, d) Rasia Perski, e) Nisan Perski, f) Dvora Elka Schwartzberg, g) Eliahu Yitzchak Schwartzberg
Sitting on the ground (right to left): a) Chaim Perski, b) Golda Perski, c) Feivel Perski

"The righteous have perished from the earth, and the upright of people is no more." (Micha 7:2)

Perpetuators: **Simcha Perski and his family (United States), and the Schwartzberg family (Israel)**

[Page 18]

Family of Dov Ber Potashnik

Nechemia Potashnik   Dov Ber Potashnik   Chana Lea Potashnik nee Girzon)

Our lofty family that was destroyed in the Holocaust and has become pillaged and plundered.

A memory in the book is dedicated to a pure, refined man, who performed merciful deeds regularly, that is our dear father, our honor and splendor, a pillar of benevolence in our city, Rabbi Dov Ber HaKohen Potashnik.

He was a precious man, above others, pure and straightforward. He performed his good deeds without fanfare. He did not give out his money with interest. He performed benevolent deeds to wealthy people, merchants, poor, indigents, shopkeepers, and those who attended fairs. He enjoyed the fruits of his labors. He sustained others, as he did his own children.

He attended the *Beis Midrash*, and the doctrine of benevolence was upon his lips. He did good deeds for thousands. He was a support for the poor and a refuge for the persecuted. He knew no rest, worked diligently, and sanctified the name of Israel before the people of the land.

Our mother, the crown of our heads, modest and with internal honor, generous, wise, upright, clear, and straightforward – Mrs. Chana Lea, who guarded her mouth and tongue, and conducted the household with wisdom and raised her children in Torah and faith.

Our honored brother, very sublime, a unique person, who grasped the deeds of his ancestors and followed their paths, Mr. Nechemia and his prominent wife Chana (from the nearby city of Rakow), who built together a splendid house, a pleasant dwelling, and gave birth to sons – Chaim and Yisrael.

[Page 19]

Chana (wife of Nechemia Potashnik) and their son Chaim

Perpetuators: **son Rabbi Menachem Mendel Potashnik (United States)**
daughter Chaya Ziskind (nee Potashnik (United States)
son Chaim Tzvi Potashnik
daughter Pnina Chait (Potashnik)

* * *

Yaakov Rogovin

"As for you, go to your end, and rest, and arise for your destiny at the end of days" (Daniel 12:13)

Perpetuator: **brother Reuven Rogovin**

[Page 20]

An Eternal Memorial for my Family Members
(Perski, Tzart, Golubnochich, Sklot, and Lungen families)

Eliezer Golubnochich, his wife Beila, their son Nachum, and daughters Miriam and Fruma

My wife Yehudit Perski and my daughter Beilinka; My brother-in-law Eliezer Golubnochich, my sister Beila (his wife), and their children Nachum, Miriam, and Fruma; my brother-in-law Gedalyahu Tzart, my sister Esther (his wife), and their children Ahrele and Shmuel; my brother-in-law Shlomo Sklot, my sister Shimka (his wife), and their children Pesia and Shmuel; my brother-in-law Moshe Lungen, my sister Sara (his wife), and their children Pesia, Rachela, and Shmuel; my brother Yisrael Perski, his wife Batya, and their children Avraham and Shmuel.

"For my sighing comes before my bread, and my outcries pour out like water" (Job 3:24)

Perpetuator: **Genedi Perski**

[Page 21]

Feigenbaum Family

Bluma Feigenbaum (Mechanik)

Nachum Feigenbaum

Hinda Feigenbaum   Yosef Feigenbaum

Our father, the crown of our heads, was an intelligent man. On Sabbaths, when he rested from his toil, he studied a page of Gemara. He would serve as the prayer leader on festivals. He was a Zionist activist. He lived a life of toil all his days in order to sustain his six children. He suffered a great deal in his life.

Our mother (stepmother) had a refined soul. She loved us as if we were her own children, and dedicated herself to us with the entire warmth of her heart. He Who Dwells On High shall reward her for all the good that she bestowed upon us.

Our brother Yosef was a talented lad. He obtained broad knowledge through his own powers, and a bright future was predicted for him were he to have survived. He ascended high on the ladder of human values. Woe to us for we have been pillaged. The precious personalities of our dear ones flutter before our eyes always. We will mourn for them until the end of times

Perpetuators: **daughters Dina Lechi (Feigenbaum) and Lea Baksht (Feigenbaum)**

[Page 22]

Kagan Family

Nachum Kagan

Batya Kagan

Malka

"The crown of our head has fallen" (Lamentations 5:16)

Perpetuators: sons and daughters: **Yaakov Kagan (Israel), Kopel Kagan (Mexico), Feigel Trutner (Kagan) (Mexico), Charna Robinson (Kagan) (Mexico)**

* * *

Hinda Bomrash (Rudnia)   Rachel Rudnia

We will never forget the nobility of your appearance and refinement of your souls with which you were graced, our dear sisters Hinda and Marishka. Our dear mother, there is a great deal to write about your dedication to us, your daughters. You were widowed at a young age and bore the yoke of the family. You were a refined soul a pure spirit. We are proud of you mother.

Perpetuators: **daughters Esther Greenberg and Pnina Hochman**

[Page 23]

Lipshitz Family

Sonia Berman (Kivilevitch)

Rachel Kivilevitch (nee Meltzer)

Shneur Kivilevitch

Moshele Berman

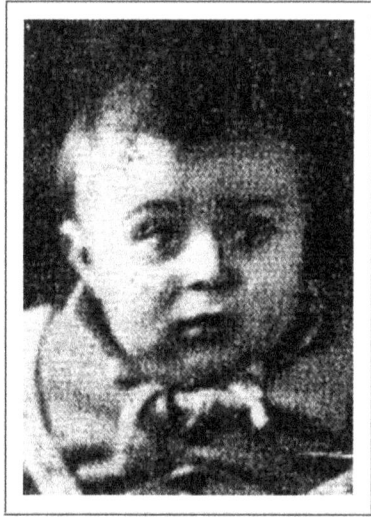
MunialeBerman

Yigal Kivilevitch

"The joy of our hearts has ceased, our dance has turned to mourning." (Lamentations 5:15)

Perpetuators: **Sisters: Ethel Shiff (Kivilevitch), Leah Hutman (Kivilevitch), Fania Levichki (Kivilevitch), Fruma Gurvich (Kivilevitch)**

[Page 24]

A Permanent Memorial to my Parents and Family Members

My father Tzvi Kleinbord

My mother Rivka Kleinbord

My sister Hinda and her husband Noach Kagan, and children

My sister Tzirel and her husband Zev Gurvich

My sister Esther and her husband Mordechai Maretski

My sister Lea and her husband Zalman Teif

My uncle Yosef Pozniak, his wife Chasia, and their children Eizik, Nachum, and Hinda

My aunt Chaya Rubinstein

My uncle Yitzchak Berman, his wife Malka, and their children

My wife's parents Yisrael Zigel, Shifra Zigel, and their entire family

Perpetuator: **son Binyamin Kleinbord**

* * *

A Meeting of Friends in the Home of Freidel Kramnik

Standing (right to left): a) Chana Weisbord (Luzin), b) Chaim Yitzchak Aharon Weisbord.
Sitting (right to left): a) Yisrael Berkowitz, b) Mina Berman, c) Shlomo Meltzer, d) Miriam Luzin, e) Eliezer Mezia, f) Freidel Kramnik, g) Mordechai Meirson

Perpetuator: **the daughter Bela Slitarnik (Kramnik)**

[Page 25]

Family of Shevach Rogovin

Our father Shevach was born in the year 5640 (1880) in Minsk. He later settled in Volozhin and married our mother, Golda. They had seven children.

Our father was liked by people, and occupied himself with communal affairs – not for any remuneration. He served as the *gabbai* [trustee] in the synagogue and was among the founders of the Tarbut School of Volozhin.

Our brother Yisrael and sisters Chaya Sarale, and Musia were among the founders of Young Zion and Hechalutz. Our home was a Zionist home, and was always open to anyone in need. The family members who remained in Volozhin perished in the Holocaust.

Standing right to left): a) Musia Topp (Rogovin), b) Yisrael Rogovin. Sitting (right to left): a) Shevach Rogovin, b) Golda Rogovin, c) Chaya Sara Widrowitz (Rogovin), d) son Efraim Widrowitz, e) Yosef Chaim Widrowitz

Musia Topp (Rogovin) Yisrael Topp, and Aryeh Topp

[Page 26]

Yisrael Rogovin, his daughter Freidel, son Yaakov, and wife Sara (nee Josefowitz)

Perpetuators: **daughters Rachel Rubinstein (Rogovin), Fruma Citrin (Rogovin), sons: Efraim and Peretz Rogovin**

* * *

Sharira Family

Yisrael Rogovin, his daughter Freidel, son Yaakov, and wife Sara (nee Josefowitz)

Our father Yitzchak Sharira and our mother Sara Esther (Antka) (she was from the family of Rabbi Chaim Hillel Fried, a scion of the splendid Volozhin dynasty), owned a medicine business.

Our father was very connected with the Etz Chaim Yeshiva of Volozhin. He would give tithes of his earnings for the benefit of the Yeshiva lads. He also gave them medicine for free.

Of the seven children, three survived, and they live in Israel.

Perpetuators: **daughters Chana Fried (Sharira), Mina Dwik (Sharira), and son Hillel Sharira**

[Page 27]

Rosenberg Family

Standing (right to left): a) Hinda Rosenberg (nee Putashnik), b) Gitel Rosenberg (nee Rappoport)
Sitting (right to left): a) Yoel Rosenberg, b) Shlomo Rosenberg, c) Mula Rosenberg, d) Reuven Rosenberg

My grandfather (see pages 500-501 regarding him) had four daughters and two sons. One daughter, Fruma, married Chatzkel Rudanski, who owned a metal and paint shop. He concerned himself with the poor, and saved many from the disgrace of hunger.

The second daughter, my mother Hinda, married Shlomo Rosenberg. My parents earned their livelihood through the pleasant attribute of hosting guests. Groups of indigents who wandered from Vishnevo to Volozhin benefited from being hosted as guests in our house that stood in the forest. My mother did a great deal of charitable deeds. "Her palm was open to the poor, and her hand was extended to the indigent." [Proverbs 31:20]

The third daughter, Sara, married Yosef Finger, a former teacher who left teaching and became involved in manufacturing enterprises. Even though Sara did not live a life of wealth, she helped poor brides, both with her own money or by collecting donations.

The fourth daughter, Rachel, married Yitzchak Mishkin, a scholarly Jew. He too was known for his good traits and efforts for those in need.

The son, Moshe Rappoport, built the flourmill and sawmill in Volozhin in partnership with my brother Reuven Rosenberg. The second son, Yehoshua Rappoport, married the dentist Sara Berkman. He was great in Torah. He had studied Torah from the greats of Minsk. He also had general education, and graduated from the gymnasja in Minsk. The only survivors of my extended family, aside from me, are my aunt Esther Rappoport and her two daughters who live in Australia.

Perpetuator: **daughter Miriam Levitan (Rosenberg)**

[Page 28]

Shif Family

Rashka Levin (nee Shif), her daughter Lea and husband Eliezer Levin

Golda Alperovich (nee Shif)

"Would it be that my head was full of water, and my eyes a source of tears, I would weep day and night over the victims…" (Jeremiah 8:23)

Perpetuator: **brother and brother-in-law Meir Shif**

[Page 29]

Volozhin Natives who Died in the State of Israel, in Volozhin, and in the United States.

Unterman, Rebbetzin Chaya Feiga. Died 26 Tevet 5725 (December 31, 1914). See her photo on page 474.

Aleksandrow, Rabbi Moshe. Died in 1968 (5728).

Baksht, Pesia

She was born in Volozhin, made *aliya* to the Land in the year 5695 (1935), and lived in Netanya. She died on 8 Tevet, 5701 (January 7, 1941), and was buried in Petach Tikva.

She came from a rabbinical family, and was married to Rabbi Eliahu in Volozhin. She was widowed while young. Despite her difficult economic situation, she made sure that her children received education and enlightenment.

She was a great righteous woman. She did not do her benevolent acts in public. She was involved in discreet giving. On Fridays toward evening, housewives would bring their pots of hot food to Pesia's oven. When she noticed that the pot of a poor person did not have enough to satiate, she would place pieces of her own meat into it so that the poor people could eat, be satisfied, and feel the pleasantness of the Sabbath.

Throughout the years of her life in Netanya, she was pained that there were no poor people in the city, and that there was nobody to whom to give charity and support.

Pesia Bakst imbued the words of Rabbi Yosi the son of Yochanan the man of Jerusalem from her father: "Let your house be open wide, and let poor people be among your household." (*Avot* 1:5). She followed this sublime humane trait all the days of her life.

[Page 30]

Baksht, Pinchas

He was born in Volozhin in the year 5660 (1900). He was the son of Pesia and Rabbi Eliahu. He made *aliya* to the Land of Israel with his family in the year 5693 (1933). He died on 24 Elul 5721 (1961) and was buried in Netanya.

He bore the yoke of the family at a young age in order to enable his younger brother to acquire education. He built his home in Netanya. He was among the first ones of that city. His soul knew much difficulty in those days – the first days of Netanya. Despite his tribulations, he gave good education to his three sons. He was like a brother to all his many family members, acquaintances, and friends. He was involved in communal affairs in Netanya. Similarly, he served as the address for those who made *aliya* from Volohin, who turned to him when they had difficulties.

When he became established there and his economic situation improved – he became ill. He died after difficult suffering.

Bunimowitz, Eliahu. Died in 1962 (5729).

Bunimowitz, Shlomo. Born in 1903 (5663). Died on 24 Elul 5629 (September 7, 1969) and was buried in Karkur.

Baksht, Meir

He was born in Volozhin in the year 5665 (1905). He was the son of Pesia and Rabbi Eliahu. He made *aliya* to the Land of Israel in the year 5691 (1931). He died in the United States and was buried in Petach Tikva on 27 Tishrei 5730 (October 9, 1969). He was buried next to his mother, Pesia Baksht.

Botwinik, Musia

She was born in 1887 (5647), and died on 4 Eul 5624 (August 12, 1964). She was buried in Holon.

[Page 31]

Bunimovich, Mendel Bunimovich (Abt) Batya   Abt Alter

My grandfather, Mendel Bunimovich, died in Volozhin in 1914 at the age of 76.

He came from a "high family." He was a relative of "The household of the Rabbi" in Volozhin. Although stringently Orthodox, he had a worldly education, thanks to the fact that in his young years, he was employed as a bookkeeper in the cabinet of Count Tyszkiewicz.

He was an intelligent and active man. He had was very involved in communal life in Volozhin. There he established the post, and he was coronated with the name "Mendel the postman."

My father, Alter (Yekutiel) Abt was born in Ashmyany, where he lived until his marriage. He came to America at the end of 1921 with his wife and children. He died there in 1941 at the age of 83.

His father, Leibe Abt, was a scholarly Jew. His mother (Grandmother Feiga) looked after her father, Reb Asher Hutner, who was renowned for his wisdom, and who occupied the "seat of judgment" in the Volozhiner Yeshiva.

Father had a strong sense of justice. He was respected in the Chevra Mishnayos [Mishna study society] for his words of wisdom. He loved quoting from our ancient treasuries. His witty parables circulate in our area to this day.

My mother Batya Abt (Basha Mendel) died in New York at the end of 1964 at the age of 90. She knew the Bible very well, and she spoke and wrote Hebrew, Russian, Polish, and later on, English. She always found time to read a book. On the fine summer Sabbath afternoons, she would gather together several women in "Petruche's Orchard" and read to them the works of Sholom Aleichem and other

Yiddish classics. She was blessed with writing talent and maintained a wide-ranging correspondence until the end of her life.

She exemplified the noble character of a Jewish mother who drew her inspiration and belief from our rich religious tradition.

Perpetuators: **Tamara Abt (Gross), Asher Abt, Feivel Abt, and Chana Golda Abt**

(Gottleib) (America)

[Page 32]

Zeev Bloch and his wife Chava Rachel

My father was a cantor and *shochet* in Volozhin for 40 years. He was great at hosting guests. My mother supported the Yeshiva lads and concerned herself about them. Woe for those who are no longer alive, but are not forgotten.

Perpetuated by: **Zelda, the cantor's daughter – America**

Ben-Sasson (Luntz), Moshe Zalman. Murdered on 2 Nissan 5697 (March 14, 1937). Buried in Yavne'el. See his photo on page 243.

Bar-Ilan (Berlin), Rabbi Meir. He was born in Volozhin on 29 Nissan 5640 (April 10, 1880). He died in Jerusalem on 11 Nissan 5609 (April 18, 1949). See his photo on page 233.

Berlin, Rebbetzin Batya Miriam (wife of the Netzi'v). Died in Jerusalem at the beginning of the year 5693 (1933). See her photo page 476.

Berman, Eliahu. Born in Volozhin in 5665 (1905). Died in 5712 (1942). Buried in the Kiryat Shaul cemetery.

Berger, Shlomo

Born in Volozhin in 1908 (5678). Died in 5697 (1937). Buried in Petach Tikva.

[Page 33]

Berman Avraham

He was the son of Rivka and Yitzchak Meir. He was born in Volozhin in the year 5673 (1913), and made *aliya* to the Land in the year 5693 (1933).

He fell on guard duty in the orchard of Moshav Herut on 2 Tevet 5717 (December 17, 1955), and was buried in Moshav Herut.

Berman, Mina

She was the daughter of Rivka and Yitzchak Meir. She was born in Volozhin in the year 5676 (1916), and graduated from the Dr. Tsharno Seminary in Vilna. She served as a Hebrew teacher in Vishnyeva and Kozhan. She died in Vilna in 5698 (1938).

Derechinski (Ben-Sasson), Rebbetzin Freidel. She died on 2 Shvat 5711 (January 27, 1951). See her photo on page 242.

Derechinski, Rabbi Shmuel Avigdor. Died on 12 Shvat 5720 (January 10, 1960). See his photo on page 239.

Wand-Polak, Michael

He was born in Piesk, Volkovisk district, in 5644 (1884). He was a known and accepted personality in Volozhin and the entire region, even though he was always occupied with his many businesses. Nevertheless, he devoted some of his time to communal work, both in the social realm (obtaining assistance for the needy), as well as the Zionist realm, especially in employing pioneers [*chalutzim*] in his enterprises. His name went forth with praise and honor.

He was a man with national pride. During the First World War, when Volozhin remained without a governor and without a regime – he stood in the breach. He organized a defense and stood at its head. He obtained weapons and distributed them to the defenders. He protected the lives and property of the Jews of Volozhin with hand weapons, along with the other members of the defense.

The Second World War forced him to go to Siberia. Full of tribulations and suffering, he succeeded in arrived in the Land of Israel on the eve of the end of the British Mandate, as the English were leaving the Land

He died in Jerusalem on 1 Marcheshvan 5727 (October 15, 1966).

Perpetuators: **His wife Riva Wand-Polak; Yosef and Bat-Sheva Schwartzberg (nee Polak); Son Shmuel and his wife Rachel; daughter Roza**

Kaminer (nee Polak); son Bernard Wand-Polak (Argentina); daughter Rachel Meshorer (nee Polak), and her husband Asher

[Page 34]

Kahanovich, Chaim Binia

He was born in Volozhin in 5666 (1906). He made *aliya* in 5684 (1924). He was one of the founders of Kfar Vitkin. He died in 5725 (1965), and was buried in Kfar Vitkin.

Levitzki, Moshe

He was born on 11 Elul 5691 (August 24, 1931), and died on 30 Av 5716 (August 7, 1956). He was buried in Rechovot.

Meltzer, Eliezer Moshe

Meltzer, Chaia Reitza

Meir Yeshayahu Meltzer and his wife Yafa (Sheina)

Meir Yeshayahu Meltzer was born in Volozhin and lived there for many years. He made *aliya* to the Land in 5695 (1935). He lived from the labor of his hands until the day of his death. He was known for his uprightness, modesty, and love of his fellow. He died on 5 Iyar 5606 (May 6, 1946).

His wife Yafa (Sheina) was a native of Vilna. She was the daughter of an honorable family. She was a faithful wife to her husband, and bore the burden of the family after his death. She died on 21 Kislev 5620 (December 22, 1959), and was buried on the Mount of Olives.

Volozhin Natives who Died in the State of Israel, in Volozhin, and in the United States {cont.}

[Page 35]

Nachshon, Rachel (Ruchele)

She was the daughter of Shlomo and Lea Nachshon (nee Shif). She was born in Tel Aviv on 23 Elul 5711 (September 24, 1951), and died on 30 Shvat 5625 (February 29, 1968).

An Elegy for Ruchele Nachshon

by Sara and Pesach Berman

Tender in years you were
And your future who could imagine?

Your image was like a beautiful flower in the eyes of everyone who saw you
And your mannerisms, like a hind in the field, a charming mountain goat.
To your parents, you were like a joyous, pleasant wing.
Your face – the face of an angel, and the goodness of your heart
Knew no bounds.

Your faithfulness to your family –
Who can estimate?

To your brother – you were a tender mother,
Protecting him from all dangers,
Lest, Heaven forbid, something bad happen to him.

To your parents, a source of pride
And of sublimity of soul,
With their mouths they gave thanks to the good, benevolent, G-d,
Day by day, and hour by hour,
That he bestowed you upon them.
Fortunate is the ear that heard the words of your mouth.

And to your grandparents –
Who can count the hours
Blessed ones, in your company,
And the reparations that the Creator of Humanity bestowed upon them,
For their suffering during the war of annihilation.

We have all been bereaved, our souls mourn.
Even if we speak, we are not calmed.
Is there any comfort over the death of a daughter-sister-granddaughter?
Is there any comfort that in the prime of your innocence,
Your mouth licks the dust.[1]

Is there any comfort,
Given that you will not return,
To bask in the light of life!

You were a sixteen-year-old girl, 16
And before you knew what life was,
You were cut off in the spring of your days.
How can we not scream out over the injustice of the cruel fate,
That stole your rights to life,

To love, and to happiness,
In our liberated land.

Holy ground, the ground in which you are buried
Shall cry out and scream
And the clods of earth shall weep.

And the heart will weep secretly
And will refuse to be comforted,
For the candle has been extinguished – the candle of Ruchele.

With bowed heads and anguished heart, we pray:
Would it be that your soul be bound in the bonds of life.
May your clods of earth be sweet to you.
Your memory will not depart from the hearts of all of us.

[Page 36]

Potashnik, Chaya Esther. She was born in Volozhin. She made *aliya* to the Land of Israel in 5699 (1939) during Aliya Bet. She was a member of Kibbutz Naan for a certain period of time, and then lived in Netanya.

She contracted a malignant illness and returned her soul to her Creator in purity after difficult suffering in the year 5706 (1946). She was buried in Petach Tikva.

Chaya Esther's lot in life was an uninterrupted chain of suffering, of agony, of pain, and of loneliness. During her final years, the years of her illness, she drunk from the cup of agony and suffering in a full measure. One can say about her: "She cried out from the depth of hear heart – – – but no ear from Above heard any more, the Throne of Honor saw no more, as such a soul was enwrapped in its agony." (Ch. N. Bialik, "My mother, may her memory be a blessing")

Potashnik, Yehuda Yosef

He was born in Volozhin in 5665 (1905), and died on 25 Iyar 5625 (May 27, 1965). He was buried in Holon.

Potashnik, Menachem Yoel

He was born in Volozhin in 5616 (1855), and was killed in Volozhin during Chanukah, 5690 (1930).

Potashnik (Eshlagi), Bracha

Potashnik (Eshlagi), Mordechai

[Page 37]

Perski, Galia

She was born in 5645 (1885), and died on 9 Shvat 5721 (December 16, 1961). She was buried in Bnei Brak.

Tzubner, Avraham

He died on 13 Sivan 5722 (June 15, 1962), and was buried in Kiryat Shaul, Tel Aviv.

Tsiberski, Tzvi Hirsch

He was born in Volozhin in 5646 (1886). He studied in Yeshivas in Minsk, Krynki, and the Etz Chaim Yeshiva of Volozhin, where he was ordained as a rabbi by the Yeshiva head, the Gaon Rabbi Rafael Shapira. He was among those who frequented the home of Rabbi Rafael Shapira. He stood out with his jolliness during celebrations of the Household of the Rabbi, and was very beloved by those present.

He died in Israel on 20 Cheshvan 5722 (October 30, 1961).

Perpetuatators: **His wife Mina (a native of Lopets, the granddaughter of the** *shochet* **Yehuda Avraham, and a relative of the writer Daniel Perski), and his descendants in Israel**

Kaminer, Alexander. Died 2 Tevet 5719 (December 13, 1958).

Kivilovich, Sima (nee Sharira)

She was born in Molodchina, and died in Volozhin on the eve of Passover, 5699 (1939).

Kleinbord, Moshe

He was born in 5670 (1910), and died in 5625 (1965). He was buried in Haifa.

[Page 38]

Kaplan, Chaya Yehudit

She was born in 5627 (1867) and died on 17 Adar II 5625 (March 21, 1965).

Kaplan, Eliezer

He was born in 5669 (1909), and died on 1 Tevet 5719 (December 12, 1958).

Kaplan, Tikva

She was the daughter of Eliezer Kaplan. She was born in 15 Tishrei, 5696 (October 12, 1935). She was killed during the Egyptian bombardment of Tel Aviv on 3 Tammuz 5705 (July 10, 1948).

Rubinstein, Yisrael. He was born in Volozhin. He was a straightforward, upright man, G-d fearing and turning away from evil. About him, one can say the following section of Psalms: He that walketh uprightly, and worketh righteousness, and speaketh truth in his heart; That hath no slander upon his tongue, nor doeth evil to his fellow, nor taketh up a reproach against his neighbour; He that putteth not out his money on interest, nor taketh a bribe against the innocent. (Psalms 15:2-3 and 5).[2]

Rogovin, Batya Malka (nee Schwartz)

She was born in Volozhin in 5644 (1884) and died in Israel in 5724 (1964).

Rudanski, Avraham Yaakov

(Avrahamel Yankel Yochanan's). He was one of the great scholars of Volozhin. He would conclude the study of the Talmud every seven months. He died in Volozhin.

[Page 39]

Rosenberg, Hinda. She was born in 5646 (1886), and died on 12 Kislev 5721 (December 1, 1960).

Sholman, Aharon

He was one of the first of Hechalutz in Volozhin. He was buried in Petach Tikva.

Shulman, Baruch Leib

He was tall, modest, and observant of the commandments – such was our grandfather, Baruch Leib Shulman. He died at the beginning of the 20th century.

Perpetuators: **P. and her husband Chaim Deitsh, Los Angeles, and other grandsons and granddaughters in Israel and the United States: Yitzchak Fruma Freda, and Shoshana**

Shif, Avraham MosheShif Leah

He was born in 5619 (1859), and died in Volozhin in 5700 (1940).

She was born in 5625 (1865), and died in Volozhin in 5681 (1921).

[Page 40]

Shani, Eliahu

He was born in Volozhin in 5665 (1905), and made *aliya* to the Land in 5684 (1924). He was one of the first of Hechalutz in Volozhin. He lived in Kfar Sava for all of his time in the Land. He died in 5726 (1966), and was buried in Kfar Saba.

Shapira, Rabbi Aryeh

He was born to his father, the Gaon Rabbi Rafael Shapiro, in the city of Novo-Aleksandrovsk (Kovno Region) in 5640 (1880). When Rabbi Rafael was appointed as the Yeshiva head of the Etz Chaim Yeshiva of Volozhin in 5659 (1899), Rabbi Aryeh came to Volozhin with his father. In 5666 (1906) he married Mina Gola, the daughter or Rabbi Chaim Naftali Hertz Halperin of Białystok. He served as a rabbi in Lebedevo and Białystok. He escaped from Białystok with the stream of refugees to Vilna during the Second World War. He made *aliya* to the Land in 5701 (1941). He died on 28 Nissan 5721 (April 14, 1961), and is buried in the cemetery of Bnei Brak.

Shapira, Rabbi Yehoshua

He was the son of Rabbi Shlomo Tzvi HaKohen Shapira. He died in Cleveland on 24 Kislev 5698 (November 26, 1937).

He was the father of Mr. Ezra Shapira of Cleveland United States.

[Page 41]

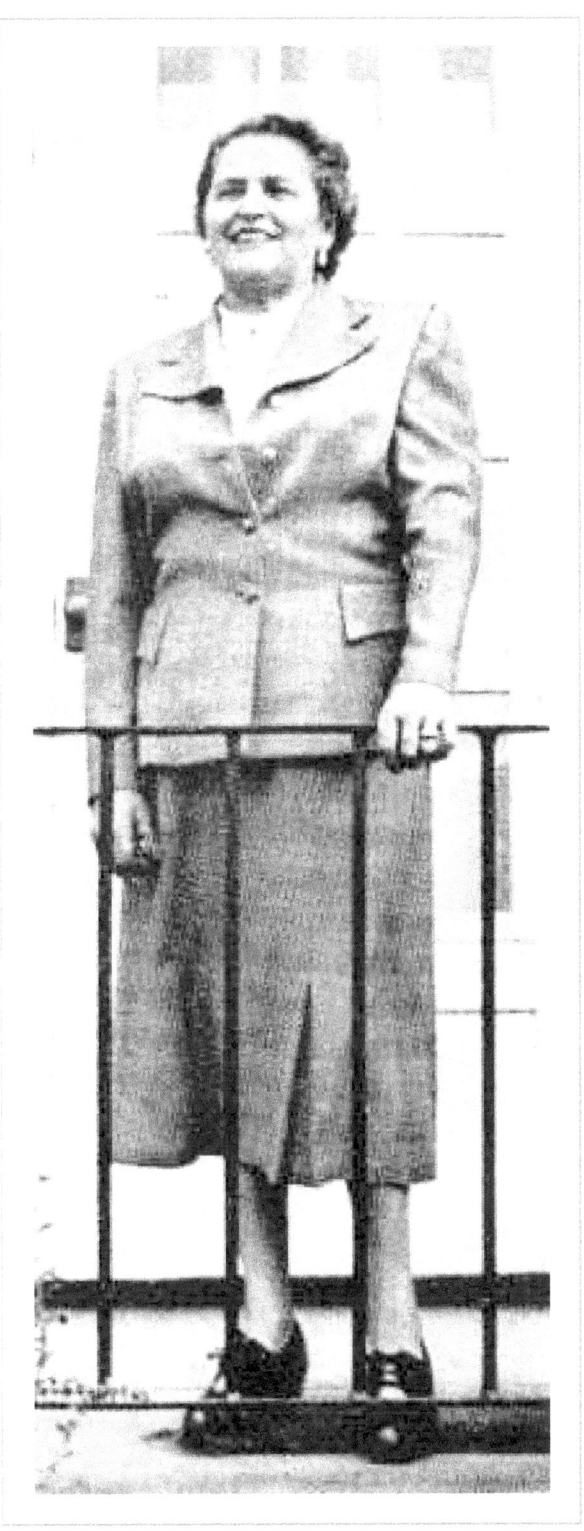

Shepsenwol, Rikla

In eternal memory of our dear mother Rikla. She was born in 5656 (1896), and died in 5724 (1964).

Perpetuators: **Tzipora and Shmuel Eidelman, Lynne Eidelmn, Chaya-Liba and Max Camhi, Sonya and Robin Camhi**

Rikla Shepsenwol

Born 1896- Died 1965

Frances and Shmuel Eidelman, Lynne Eidelman, Lucille and Max Camhi, Sonya and Robin Cahmi.

Translator's footnotes:

1. This phrase is taken from the Ten Martyrs elegy of Yom Kippur Musaf.
2. Translation from Mechon Mamre: https://mechon-mamre.org/p/pt/pt2615.htm

Supplemental Material

(Not included in the Yizkor book)

Volozhin & Volozhiners after World War Two

Volozhin now (Year 2000)

by Moshe Porat

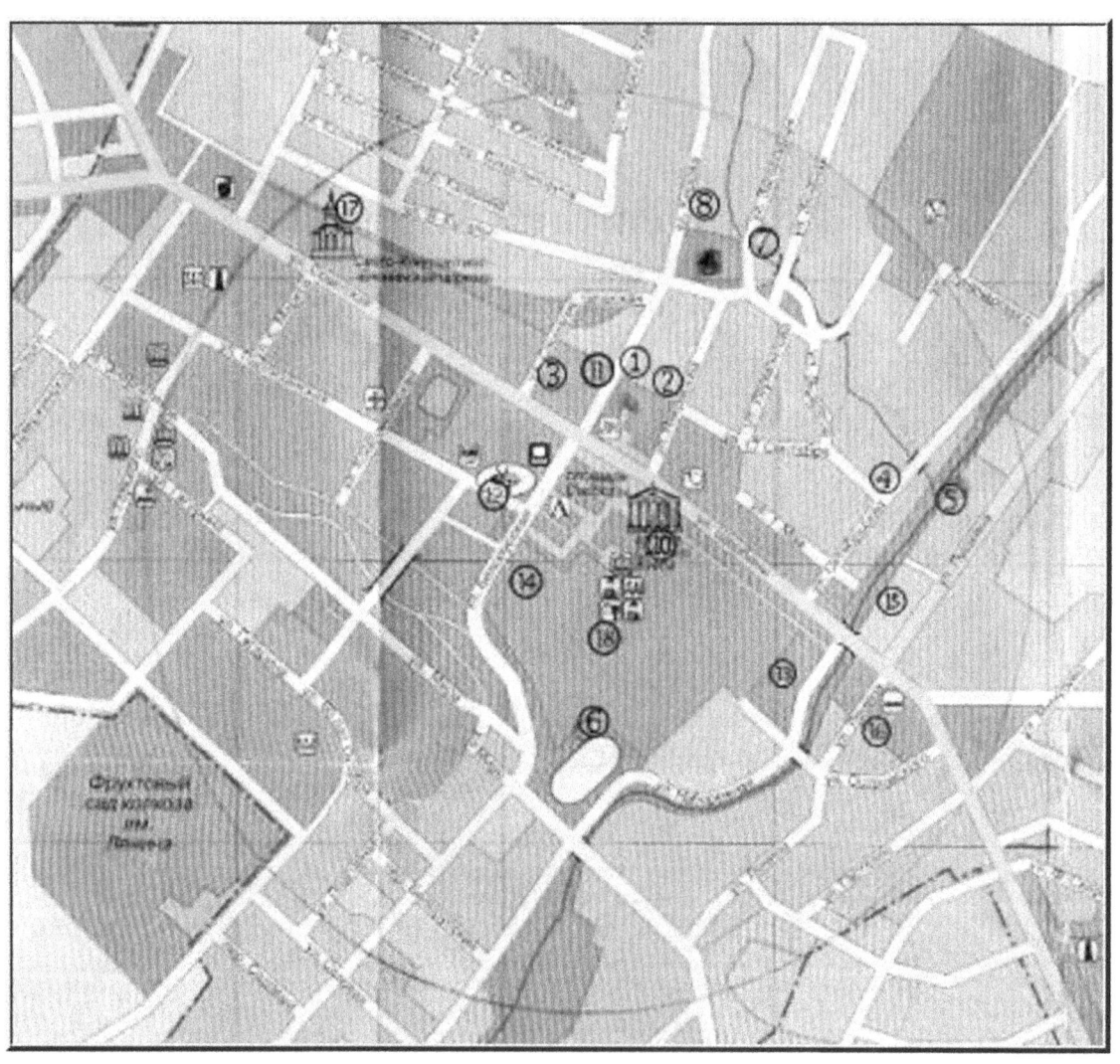

1	Etz Haym Yeshiva	
2, 3, 4	3 locations of destroyed Synagogue	
5	Aug 1942-200/300 Jews slaughtered	
6	Oct' 28, 41- 200/300 Jews slaughtered	
7	May 10, 42-2000 Jews slaughtered	
8	Graveyard with 6 mass graves	
9	Rabbi Haym-house, drugstore now	
10	Catholic Kostiol	
11	Destroyed Tarbut school house	
12, 13	Polish, now Belarus, schools	
14	Town Authorities Offices	
15, 16	Floor grind & wood saw mills	
17	Russian Tserkov	
18	The Graph Tyshkevitsh's estate	
19	Water pond "Sazhelka"	

Shtetl Plan – The town center

Volozhiners began to visit the shtetl after the Soviet Union has been dissolved. During the thirties among the 6000 Volozhin residents, 3000 were Jews. Now the shtetl was found completely "judenrein".

The town, now populated by 12000 inhabitants expands on 2000 by 2500 meters area. The town center might be enclosed inside a small circle of 900 meters in diameter.

The center includes the town authorities offices, the graph's estate and its palace, the Catholic (Polish) and orthodox (Russian) churches, the Belarus town schools and all the places where the Volozhin Jews used to live.

Inside this small center circle the visitor will find the Kulinaria restaurant installed inside the famous Volozhin Yeshiva, the ancient graveyard and the old houses abandoned by the expelled Jews. In the same small circle he might visit the places of the three destroyed synagogues, the Streets where the Ghetto concentration camp was situated and the three mass slaughter sites.

Volozhin map in the thirties

(VYB page 8-9)

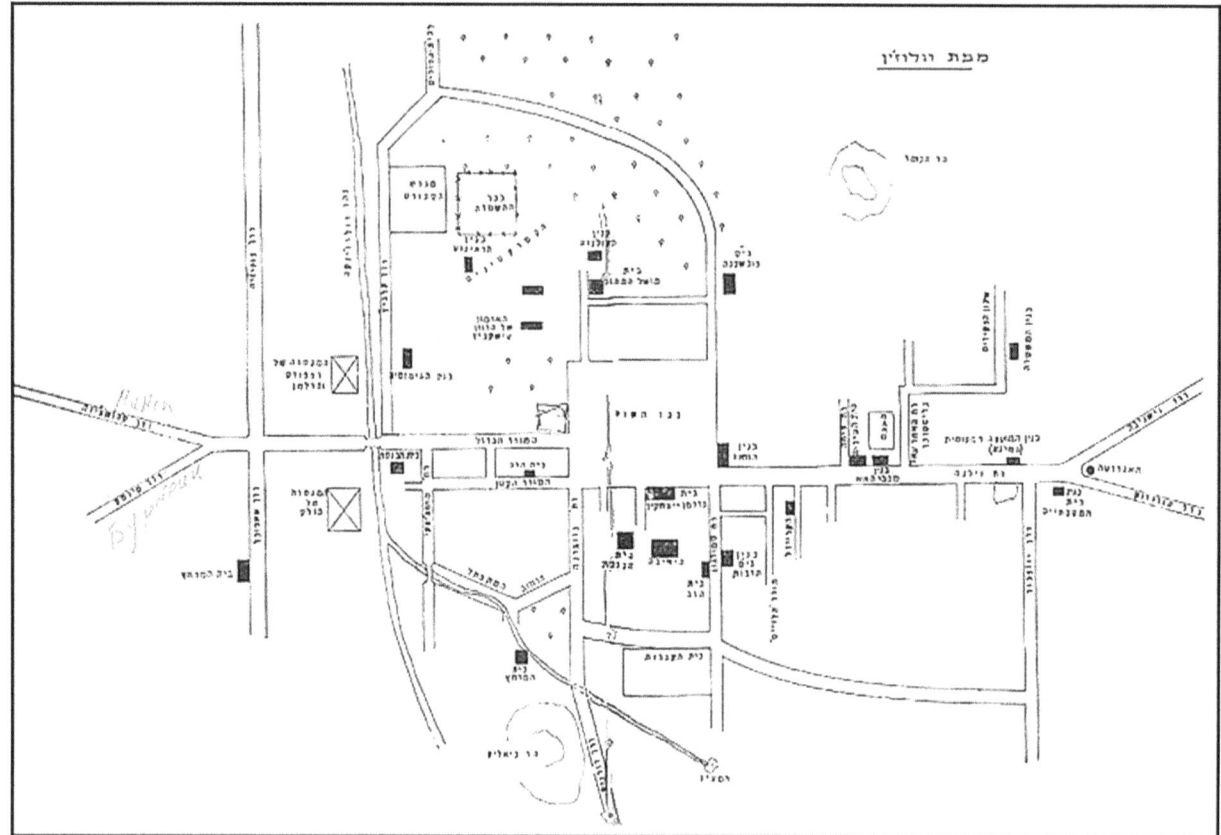

The Volozhin Yeshiva

(code 902)

The famous old Yeshiva structure, built at the 19th century's start, survived the war. It is very solid and strong. The walls are 4 (four) feet thick. The building is badly maintained with a leaking roof and outside peeled of walls. A snack bar is functioning inside and a big sign "Culinary" was fixed on its entry. During our visit in Volozhin we asked and obtained from the local authorities their permission to fix a memorial plaque on the Yeshiva entry. In Tel Aviv, we produced a large metal plaque with a three-language text engraved on it. It was sent to Volozhin and was installed in May 1999 above the Yeshiva staircase, in presence of the town mayor, the Israeli ambassador to Belarus, and a big audience. The "Culinary" sign was removed. Every one who's passing near the Yeshiva door may read and learn about its glorious past in Hebrew, Russian or English.

The Yeshiva in the thirties

(Volozhin Yizkor Book - page 116)

Volozhyn Yeshiva, East-south corner, September 1998. Above the entrance KULINARIA Signboard still installed.

The Yeshiva building
photographed from its southeast side in September 1998.

Some meters eastward a tiny grass covered hill remains as the sole sign of the Great Volozhin Synagogue.

Volozhin Yeshiva – south staircase
The memorial plaque above the southern entry staircase has been installed on May 24th 1999, after throwing away the "Kulinaria" sign.

The text in English:

The Volozhin Yeshiva **"Etz Chaim"** – **"Tree of Life"** Founded in 1803 by the prodigious **Rabbi Chaim Volozhiner**. Within these walls were educated the best young Jewish men of the 19th century. **"Mother of Yeshivot"**, it became a model for all religious schools. Because of its world renown educational methodology, great prodigious teachers and high level of scholastic students, who became religious leaders, great rabbis, poets and writers

**The Yeshiva Memorial plaque,
with text engraved in Russian, Hebrew & English
The mass slaughter sites**

The Mass Slaughter Sites

The First Action

The Soviet memorial (woman)

The Soviet memorial (text)

Monument erected in the fifties by the Soviet authority on the sport stadium. Here 200-300 Jews were executed in 1941 October 28th (among them Yani Garber the Judenrat head). The text in Russian only:

*"**HERE** are buried Soviet citizens bestially murdered by the German occupants in the years of the great patriotic war 1941-1945".*

Not a Hebrew word, not a Jewish sign, not a memorial of the Jewish genocide (Articles codes: 62, 84, 86, 87, 88, 89.1, 103.3).

The Second Action

Memorial to Volozhin Jews

Memorial to Volozhin Jews

ПАМЯТЬ

ТЫСЯЧАМ ЕВРЕЯМ
ВОЛОЖИА и окрестностей
убитым фашистами в
пределах города в 1941-3 г.
Их останки погребённы здесь
в шести братских могилах

Вечный Им Покой

זיכרון

לקדושי וולוז'ין והסביבה
לאלפי יקירינו הי"ד
שנרצחו ע"י הפשיסטים
בתחומי העיר
בשנים 1941/3
שרידיהם טמונים כאן
בשישה קברי אחים

ת נ צ ב "ה

MEMORY

to thosands of
VOLOZHYN JEWS
murdered by the fascists
during 1941-43 years
inside the town
Their remnants are buried
here in six brother graves

Peace to Their Soul

Three-language text

The Memorial to Volozhin Jews was erected on the Volozhin Graveyard hill in September 2000; The Volozhiners Organization in Israel "Irgun Yotsey Volozhin" accomplished this. The memorial overlooks the ancient ruined cemetery, the six common mass graves and the May 10, 1942 slaughter site (the second action), where the Germans and their accomplices executed 2000 Volozhin Jews. The text in Hebrew, Russian & English reads:

"Memory to thousands of Volozhin Jews murdered by the Fascists inside the town borders in the Years 1941-1943. Their remnants are buried here in six mass graves. Peace to their soul".

(Articles codes: 62, 84, 86, 87, 88, 89.1, 103.3)

The Third Action

Memorial to Volozhin Jews

The Volozhinka Streambed

This Memorial to Volozhin Jews was erected in 1987 on the Site of the third Volozhin Jews slaughter, on Volozhinka left shore, inside the streambed by Miriam and Max Cuker with the help of Sane Lavit. In the third action, in August 1942 the last 200-300 Volozhin Jews have been murdered. The text reads:

"In memory of 3000 Volozhin Jews, bestially murdered By the German Nazis and their assistants in 1941-1944 years, peace to their soul"

The Volozhin ancient cemetery

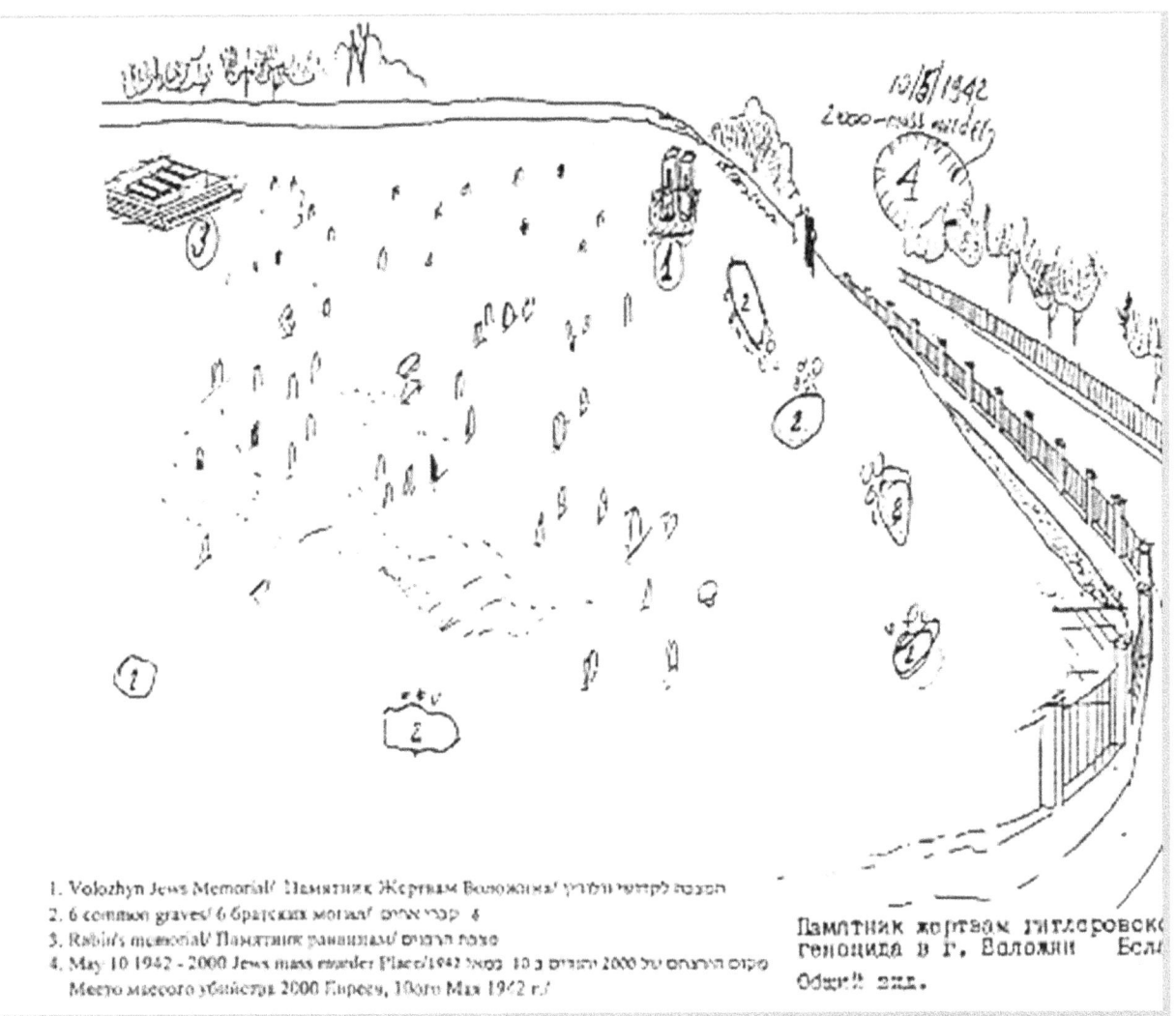

Ancient Grave Yard (Schema)

A   Memorial to the Volozhin Jews - erected in 2000
B   Six common brother graves
C   May 10,1941- 2000 Jews slaughter site
D   Rabbi Chaims' Memorial - erected in 1991

הדרך לבית־הקברות

The Graveyard Way – Thirties

The cemetery – Sheep pasture, 1988

The cemetery

Volozhiners at the tombstones, 1998

To Haye Gitls' Memory
Aron Yakov Perlman's spouse,
Daughter of Rafael Bunimovitsh

Volozhin-Graveyard וולוז'ין-בית עלמין
Tsart-tombstone מצבה לצרט
Воложин-кладбище Памятник Цартам

Memory to Sonia Perski,
Welvl's spouse, Yakov Tabakhovitsh's daughter

The cemetery – mass graves
Murdered – buried 41-42; photographed 1988

Sept. 98, Common grave at the Volozhin cemetery, one of 5 hills covering the victims remnants. 2000 Jews were murdered near the fence, 10/5/42

The cemetery – Volozhin Memorial over looking the six mass graves and the May 10th 1942 slaughter site of 2000 Jews

The cemetery – Rabbi Chaim Volozhiner Memorial,
raised in 1991 overlooking the destroyed Volozhin Grave Yard.

Rabbi Chaim was buried here. Nothing remains of his Tomb-tent *(shtibl)*

Red Cross activity

Moshe Porat

Bela Saliternik (see "In the Holocaust Shadow,", page 525) sent me two documents.

The first one is an enquiry she had submitted to The Red Cross in Jerusalem on December 11, 1941. Printed in Polish on a Red Cross official form , the translation reads: "Salitenik Bela, from Tel Aviv, 7 Nezah Israel St., Palestine, is asking the Red Cross to find out and to let her know the whereabouts of her mother, Freyda Kramnik, and family, from Volozhin, Market Square 7, Novogrudek District, Occupied Poland - Belarus." The enquiry bears several stamps: "Jerusalem Postage office", "Palestine Censor pass", "Red Cross Committee – Geneva" and "January 9 1942".

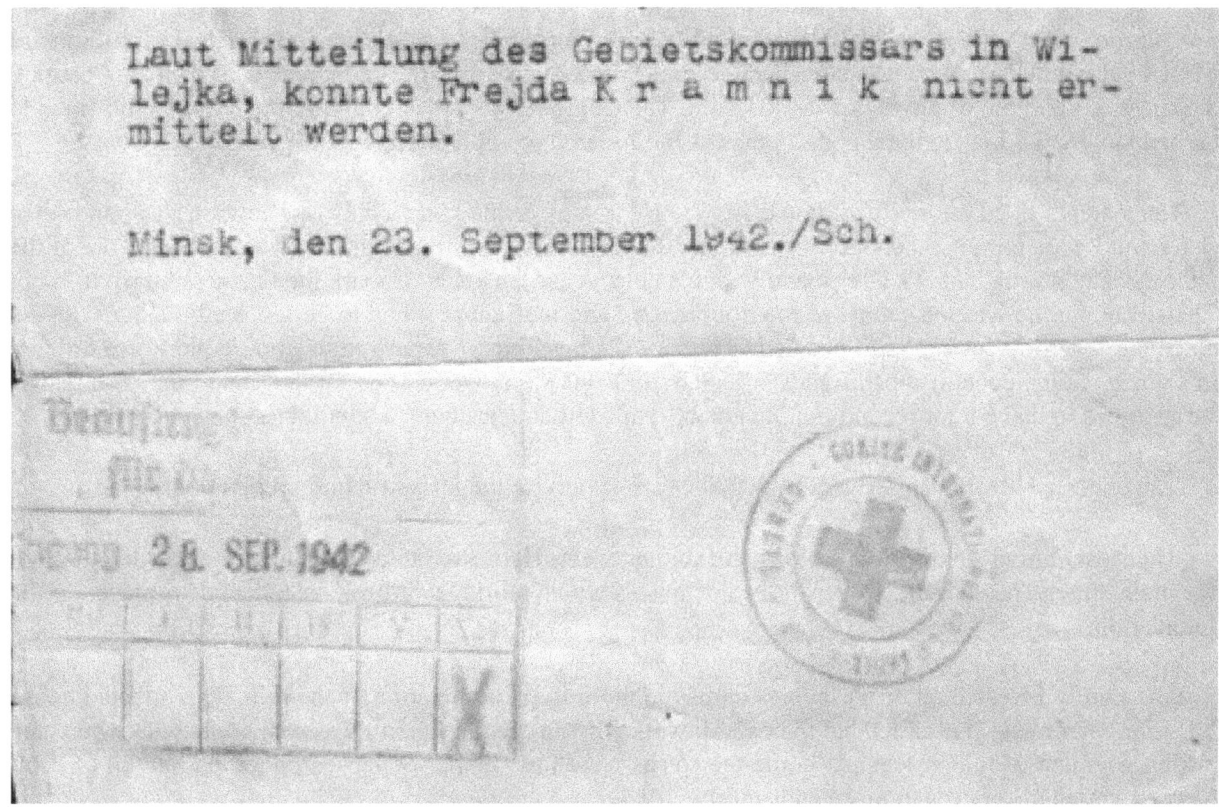

The second document is the official answer of the Red Cross in Geneva, typed in Minsk, dated September 23, 1942. Written in German, it says that the Gebits commissar in Vileyka could not find Freyda Kramnik's whereabouts.

It was all the Red Cross in Minsk agents had to tell.

It happened in the spring and summer months of 1942 when the Nazis executed hundreds of thousands of Jewish families in Belarus. The mass slaughters were accomplished in daylight, in sight of the local population, accompanied by music, dancing and ringing of church bells. The sondercomando expeditions acted at this time over the entire Belarus-Litwak Yiddish Land. Frantz Karl Hess, second lieutenant of the thirty second " Zondercommando," had completed on May 42 his bloody missions to Volozhin, Vishnievo, Dolginov and Ivia, brutally killing hundreds of Jewish children, men and women among the thousands executed by his unit and its local assistants. (See "Franz Karl Hess Trial ", page 576.)

It was done before the eyes of the entire local gentile population.

The Red Cross agents certainly knew it, but did not yell. They did not tell a word.

Our Parents' Saw and Grist Mills

By M. Perlman

Translated by Moshe Porat

Edited by Judy Montel

Our mother's father Hirsh Malkin, prior to the First World War, was the general manager of millionaire Mr. Heller's Wood Works. He established the enterprise's main office in Belokorets, near Volozhin hamlet. The peasants and the whole region came to life; The Company accorded credit to buy horses, tools. People earned money working in the woods. A decent life became possible in the Shtetl.

Our parents lived in their own house on Vilna Street near the "Sazhelke" (the town water pond). My sister and I were born in this house. Our parents established a sawmill and gristmill on the east shore of the Volozhinka on grandfather's advice and with his help. After ten years of work the business began to limp. The steam engine was the source of the trouble. Old and inefficient it had to be replaced. Father with his associate Mr. Moyshe Rapoport decided to replace the machinery. A new engine and boiler were ordered in Danzig. Coincidentally a bad fungus affected the Vilna street wood house at the same time. The family was obliged to leave it for reconditioning and to rent another apartment, a small one.

The engineer Mr. Pollak arrived from Warsaw to supervise the infrastructure preparations.

The steam boiler's transportation was an exciting event. Harnessed to a dozen horses it was led through the main streets, passed safely over the Volozhinka's wooden bridge and was installed at its place, on the foundation.

The family invested all of its savings and even more in the renovation of the mill. The infected house on Vilna Street was dismantled but the overall works did not begin. Often I was sent home with a message asking payment of tuition fees. At home the spirits were low. Father collapsed under his burden of debt. Mother stretched supplies to make ends meet.

Meanwhile the new engine was set in motion and begun to push the renovated mill forwards. The new facilities for the flourmill appeared to be profitable. And the forest business with a fresh investor flourished. The so desired good times arrived and our family moved into a more spacious place.

The horse-drawn cart made its turns. The leather sofa "*kushetka*", the wall clock, which played the hours, the big mirror which stood at an angle, flowerpots, suitcases and *peklah* were transferred over the wooden bridge and discharged into a new four-room apartment at the entrance to our saw and grist mill on the Volozhinka's left bank.

At the southern corner of Pilsudski (Minsk) Street, on the bank of the stream, which was some five meters high, a wood constructed well was situated with a tin bucket on a rope. Beside the well was the entrance to the Perlman–Rapoport mill. Farther along the street our new home was located. In that wooden house we spent the last three years in Volozhin. Here we were exposed to the events of the First World War. So it remains forged in our memory.

Behind the house was a small, fenced vegetable garden, with a rope-swing suspended from two wood poles for Sonichka and her children friends. In the window frame that faced the garden and the sun some bottles were arranged in which fruit liquors fermented, our Dad's hobby, inherited from his Father.

**Sonitshka Perlman (sitting) and Etinka (Michl Polak's granddaughter)
on the rope swing in the garden – 1938**

The mills were situated some hundred meters behind the garden, following the water stream. I would like to describe our family business in some sentences. It was an interesting one. The reader should have in mind that all I remember, I saw as a young boy, so it is likely that I'm exaggerating as to the dimensions of what I describe.

On the stream-shore, pumping water for cooling and steam producing, the engine and boiler were installed. It used saw dust and wood chips as fuel. The engine was operated by the "machine-man", Mr. Kadirka, the mechanic. His helper the "*kotshegar*" – heater - worked hard. His duty was to maintain the steam pressure, exposed in big figures on a round dial, by heating the boiler. He conveyed the wood waste to the boiler room on a hand pushed one-wheel cart and poured it into the fire spitting mouth. Besides the machine housing on the river shore, the black, tall, fuming and at some times whistling chimney had its place. A visible, locomotive like, crankshaft mechanism transferred the steam engine's linear movement to a big turning wheel. A large flat leather belt transmitted its circular movement to the long shaft under the floor, on which was mounted further transmission wheels. Flat link belts transmitted the energy in their turn to the grist and saw mills installed on the ground.

The grain-grinding heavy stones were positioned on the upper floor. The peasants used to bring their grain-sacks to the mill gate. Mr. Lieberman, the weighing-man, was at the scale. Sometimes Mother, or Ms. Rapoport our associate would replace him. After the weighing and payment in cash or in grains, the sacks were raised in a wooden lift driven by the transmission to the upper deck. The peasant's function was to empty his sacks into the big funnel above the grinding system, and to collect his flour in sacks from the exit beneath. A white dust always covered this building, and it smelled of the field, wheat grains and flour.

A bit farther over the transmission, inside a covered shed, open in two directions, the two wood saw machines were placed. The machine (*gatar*) consisted of a steel frame, inside which a set of saws moved up and down. *Vagonietka* - carts, which were mounted on narrow railways, carried the trunks to the *gatar* entry. Two iron sprocket rollers, installed inside the machine frame, rolled the trunk forcing it to pass through the sawing set. The boards were transported upon the rail carts to the other side of the sawmill plant (*tartak*). Here they were stored in rectangular towers of planks arranged in a crisscrossed form.

Gatar remnants – 1998 photo

Managing the sawmill was quite a complex business. The Volozhin landlord, Count Tyshkevitch's officials sold the live forest sections by auction. Before suggesting the price one had to carefully skillfully look over the section to estimate the timber volume and quality, the expenses involved in the forest work, transportation and boards fabrication. Father claimed that the main part of business was buying not selling. In the Russian and Polish languages a tradesman is called "*kupietz*"-buyer, not "*prodavietz*"-seller. Now, in our times, it seems to be the reverse. And maybe Father was not, or did not want to be a tradesman. I remember how in the synagogue, during chats with our neighbors, Volozhin *balabatim*; Father claimed to be proud of managing a factory instead of a merchant business.

In wintertime, the forest section trees were cut and cleaned from branches. The long trunks, each one loaded on two sledges, the first hitched to a horse and the second one attached to the first, were transferred to the sawmill. The cutting in the forest and the transporting of the trunks, an action called "*Zavoz*" was a time limited mission. It could only be done during the dry snow period. When the snow began to melt the forest road became impassable. So there was a feast when "*Zavoz*" ended on time. All the involved persons were invited, vodka with "*zakuska*" (after vodka food) was brightly and handily served, and the joy was big.

I encountered Father on workdays in the sawmill area, overseeing the functions of the machinery and the workmen, or measuring the volume of the incoming trunks.

The sawmill area provided a wide scope for our childhood games and activities. The sawdust hill, piled up to heat the steam engine, was a perfect place for all kinds of games that required tunnels, pits and hills. The rectangular towers of planks arranged in a crisscross pattern served as hiding and climbing sites.

But the best and most popular object for play was the railway cart - *vagonietka*, which moved the trunks and boards. The cart was built as a rectangular frame of wooden blocks, mounted on four iron wheels. It moved on a narrow railway by gravitation, or was pushed by hand. The real pleasure was riding on the cart frame on the downhill descent. But, the cart - *vagonietka* - rolling was not entirely legal. The quick heavy rolling could be quite dangerous. We used to do it on Sundays only, when the mill was not functioning and the area was free. Often, however, the amusement was interrupted. The mill manager used to supervise the area and when he came upon the unwanted intruders, he drove them away, shouting and yelling.

Vagonietka remnants – 1998 photo

Our plant was situated on the Volozhinka's east shore, on the south side of the Minsk road. Opposite, across the street, a similar plant operated, which belonged to Mr. Michl Polak. The rivalry between the mill owners was without compromise. In my naivete I divided the whole shtetl in two camps, the evil one – Polak's and the second one – ours. My foot did not tread on the "enemy" territory. In hard times their representatives and ours called the grain transporting peasants to bring their goods into the right mill. At our mill Mr. Polak on some occasions was called the bad man. This was the situation when our Grandpa Hirsh Malkin installed his home in Volozhin. He decided and worked hard to reconcile the parties. As a result of his efforts the positions softened and some interaction had begun.

Postscript:

All the sawmills and flourmills were nationalized soon after the Soviets occupied the region. The Perlman and Polak families were sent to Siberia. They occupied together a single room lodge in a Siberian collective farm. We became best friends, but that is a different story.

Volozhin

Edited by Judy Montel

Read at the Volozhin Memorial inauguration, at Kiryat Shaul Cemetery in Tel-Aviv, 1980 8th May, 22nd Iyar.

The ceremony was attended by many families of Volozhin descendants. The Volozhin Kehila and its Yeshiva were memorialized by Harav Goren-Israel's chief Rabbi, by Harav Zvi Neriya, Harav Dr. Grazh, by the Bar Ilan university rector and by others.

For hundreds of years we lived in Volozhin

Since the day when my Father's Great-Great Grandfather
established his home on the Graf's estate, we nurtured the Shtetl,
We loved its soil, the shallow stream, the green valleys, its bushy forests,
We enjoyed the scenery of the surrounding hills:
Snow white in winter, multicolored in summer.

We suffered countless calamities there: war, disease, plagues, water and flames
After each fire we reconstructed it, our town and its temple.
The hills landscape, its pure "educational" air enchanted us, Volozhin children
And the outlying northern shtetl turned into our home
for a dozen generations and more.

Two hundred years ago, the Rabbi's son asked to leave,
to study Torah in a remote city, abroad.
His father stopped him – a temple was built.
Placing the corner stone – Reb Chaim said:
"Like this stone, you will be held here, Itsele, my son,
Tied to my home, my town, my people and to our holy Torah."
The son did not leave and the Yeshiva was established!

Generations of Persistence and Diligence, Skill and Obstinacy,
Thinking and Initiating, Energy and Limitless Labor
did our ancestors invest in their monumental Project

And our poor shtetl turned to be the Jews' Academy of the century,
It was the "Sura" and "Pompadita" for Russia and Poland, Ukraina and Lita.
The Volozhin Yeshiva became a lighthouse of Torah and wisdom,
which spread light into the Jewish world,
from the days of Napoleon until the World Wars.

In Volozhin between the World Wars my childhood passed.
Everything related to this period I view through rose-colored glasses:

In my eyes the shtetl flourished:
Industry, labor, commerce,
Zionist youth organizations, Hashomer Hatsayir, Mizrachi and Betar,
Hachshara centers to prepare for "Aliya"
Dozens of young people went to Erets Yisra'el,
Hundreds were ready to go.

General Education: The Hebrew Tarbut School,
A "small" Yeshiva (for children),
School of commerce and a Gymnasia-High School,
Yiddish kindergarten, chord orchestra and choir.
Winter entertainments: Ice skating on the shtetl's frozen pond,
Skiing and sleighing on the snow covered hills.
Summer: promenade, excursions, bicycling and camping,

Bathing in the pure shallow stream.
a normal life – a happy childhood.

Meanwhile across the border the plot of evil intent materialized.
In June nineteen hundred forty one our town was invaded by the German hordes.
From this moment the Jews, their property, blood and body – became outlawed!
Stained by the yellow path, thrown in Ghetto, famished, beaten and humiliated-
Young and old, men and women, a whole town – sentenced to death!

The German authorities established the town Judenrat.
Yani Garber was chosen to be its head.
October 28th 1941, the S.S. ordered him to assemble three hundred people
in the cinema hall to do some work.

Only when enclosed did Yani discover the satanic plan, he understood the terrible truth:
Not to work were his town's citizens assembled. They were brought for extermination!
In exchange for diligent services he was offered his life.
But his noble soul refused the murderers' payoff,
He did not stain his people and town dignity.
Lowering his head, Yani went to his death,
And Yani Garber's blood mixed with the blood of his kehila members.
God Almighty, Bless their souls!

Close to Mount Bialik passed the dolorous path,
The poet never thought that the "BET HAMIDRASH" village, the town of
"To the Bird" and "HAMATMID," would become "The Slaughter City".

On a wonderful blue sky day,
Between our Festival of Freedom and Festival of Torah Giving,
The terrible, enormous slaughter took place.

"When God called for spring and slaughter together,
The sun was shining; the acacias were in bloom,
And the butcher murdered".

Expelled from the ghetto kennels, jammed, bleeding in the blacksmith's workshop,
Beaten, injured, murdered and burned, the Jews of Volozhin went up in flames!

The Killers were bestially satisfied, the local gentiles happy and drunk,
When our parents, sisters, brothers and children burned in fire!
And the town became Juden-rein.
The yeshiva, the glorious Volozhin Institute turned into an eatery, a "KULINARIA".
They destroyed the ancient cemetery, demolished the gravestones.
Goyim are living in our homes – they murdered and they inherited.
Not a sign, not a word upon the mass graves.
UNZER SHTETL, our beloved town no longer exists!

In black letters is Volozhin engraved on this memorial stone.
Burning words will engrave its name in our heart
And in the hearts of our descendants, forever!
We shall remember its institutions and scenery:

The Yeshiva and School, our homes and Reb Chaim's house,
the stream and pond, the hills and forest, the fields and gardens.
And like stains that never could be erased,
will be memorized: the sport stadium, the blacksmith's shop,
Bulava's courtyard and the aroptsu ghetto!

I shall remember until my last day
my classmates, Volozhin Tarbut school graduates
All of them murdered at the age of seventeen:
Berl Tsart, my best comrade, killed at seventeen,
Eyzer Finger, an excellent sportsman at the age of eighteen,
Frumke Alperovich the graceful, murdered at seventeen,
Benzike the hearts breaker, the talented Voolke Brudno,
Feygl Kleyn, Sonia Perski both young and beautiful
and many others, may they forgive me for not mentioning their names,
all of them murdered at the eve of their life, slaughtered at seventeen.
Almighty, avenge the pure innocents' river of blood!

I ask your permit to recall in some words my family members:
Rabbi Hirsh and Haya-Riva Malkin-my grandparents,
murdered and burnt in Volozhin.
My father, Yosef, great-great grandson of Reb Itsele,
perished in the Soviet gulag,
My cousins that fell on the battlefield:
Mula Malkin on the way from Krasno to his Partisan unit,
Monia Garber fighting the Germans at Monte Cassino,
Eytan Malkin at Yom Kippur war, in the Sinai desert.

Now, a sprinkle of Volozhin remnants,
We are integrated on the soil of our land,
Interwoven in all its life layers:
In industry, construction and farming,
in academy, yeshivot and in the army.

We are an obstinate people.
And as we survived Hitler,
we'll overcome his followers.
as we succeeded in remaining in the far poorer Volozhin,
for a dozen generations, to build and to glorify it
So will we build our old-new Homeland,
nurture it and make it flourish,
for generations, dozens upon dozens.

So help us God!

Babushka Khaya's letter

Translated from Russian by Moshe Porat – Perlman

Edited by Judy Montel

This letter was found among some family papers in Paris on November 2001.

It was just after the funeral of Jose, my sister Sonia's husband. We were turning the pages of the photo albums. Among the old pictures and writings we found two remarkable family documents. The first was the late Jose's father's handwritten translation from Hebrew into French of a speech he had heard at a Volozhin memorial event in Tel-Aviv. The second was a beautiful letter written in a good Russian handwriting by our babushka Khaya. We were excited to read it and the names we recalled vaguely came suddenly to life.

This is a fragment of Jewish life in our grandmother's family – loving words from the old world that no longer exists . We thought it would be interesting to others with roots in Volozhin .

Babushka Khaya-Reeva[1] wrote it in Volozhin to her children in France on April 22nd 1941, exactly two months prior to the German invasion into the Soviet Union, one year after her daughter Etia's family was expelled to Siberia and some 10 months after the Germans occupied Paris. All Grandma Khaya's sons and daughter families (Osher, Izia and Zina)[2] who lived in France had probably already left Paris at this time.

Scanned fragment of the original letter

22/IV/1941

Dear children! I received your letter-dated 22/III. I am happy to learn that you are in good health. I would like to know if you have to buy garments and underwear to replace all you had left in Paris. *Papa* (Father) was with me only a couple of days during Passover.

Malka, Yossif's mother was also with us. She spent this winter in Moscow at her daughter Fania's house. She came here to liquidate her property on the holiday eve. Soon she would return to Moscow, not to much desiring it. Poor Malka I have pity for her. Yania[3], her widowed son in law got married to Brokhke Perski, Velvl Shmuel's sister in law. As for her grand children, Yani's two sons: Monia[4] remains with him, Dania is studying in Minsk Conservatorium. He married a girl from Bobroysk recently; She's a Pianist too. That's the story of shviguer Malka and her family.

Dear Osher I'm reading your letter again and again. I'm searching a piece of hope to see all of you again. It would be for us, old people a comfort, but to our sorrow, its accomplishment seems to be very far. Until then we should be satisfied with your letters.

I'm glad that Daliusha is growing up becoming tall like Osher and that Susanochka develops very fine.

Please send us her picture. Motia, in his letter, is asking for it too.

I'm receiving letters from Etia[5]. Her children too are adding a couple of sentences. I would send you some letters, but they are written in Yiddish and they may not reach you. Monitshka[6] writes very fine letters in Russian, Polish and Yiddish. Those letters are highly praised by his comrades in Volozhin. If he had a chance to continue his studies he would certainly succeed and arrive far away, but unfortunately his fate turned otherwise. Etia writes that he's a devoted son.

Zinotshka, you're asking about what we send them. Beginning from flour, fats, sugar to the last details including money too. Poor Etia, she is so unfortunate, I have no words to describe her painful life. And add to it that she does not know from Yossif[7] anything until now. Reading her letters, the heart becomes flooded with blood, and the sole help we can offer is the posting of parcels.

We receive letters from Motia[8] and Irka. Motia is working 2 weeks on the field and 2 weeks in the kibbutz office.
Izia writes that he's satisfied with his new work He praises his son very much. Rita became pregnant. She is not like French women, and God will help her.

Dear Olinka, we received a letter from your father in Konotope. I'm writing him each year on the Passover eve asking him to go to the graveyard on the day of our daughter Ola's death. He's fulfilling my demand and I'm grateful.

Please, write often and about all. We wish you health and good luck.

Strongly embracing all of you,

Khaya, Your mother,

I'm very glad to read Suzanotshka's regards, written by her little hand. We are thanking her for making happy her Diedushka and Babushka. I kiss her strongly.

Some notes regarding the persons involved background and destiny.

Bierezno 1929: Clockwise: Babushka Khaya Reeva, Monitshka, Diedushka Eliyahu-Hirsh, Izia, Etia, Motia, Zina, Yossif

Volozhin 1935: Clockwise: Babushka Malka Perlman,
Sonitshka and Monia (Etia's Children) Dania and Monia (Yani's children)

1. The grand parents Khaya Reeva (born Marshak) and Hirsh Malkin remained in Volozhin after the Germans occupied the town. They were flung into the Ghetto and were murdered at the second mass slaughter near the Volozhin Grave Yard on May 10th 1942.

2. Osher, Zina and Izia Left Paris before the Germans invaded the town. They survived the war under faked names in the not occupied South of France territory. Their families live now in France.

3. Yani Garber was nominated as head of the Volozhin Youdenrat already after the Germans took control of Volozhin. They ordered him to assemble 200 Jews as though to work. Discovering that they had been brought to extermination he asked to be shot together with his congregation members. It was the first mass slaughter in Volozhin on October 28th 1941.

4. Monia, Yani's Son. Was arrested and sent to Goulag by the Soviets. When released, he joined the General Anders unit of the Polish Army. He arrived with his unit in Italy and fell fighting the Germans in the Monte Cassino battle in 1944. He was 22 years old.

5. Etia , The Malkins' eldest daughter with her two children were "ressetled" by the Soviets into Siberia a month after her husband Yossif was arrested.

6. Etia's son "Monitshka", was mobilized by the Soviets in Siberia, first into the work-battalions and thereafter into the Red Army as infantry soldier. He finished the war meeting the alien western forces on the Baltic coast near Rostock. Freed from the Soviet Army on May 1946, he undertook his long route to Israel where he arrived on the "Altalena" boat and joined the Israel Army on June 1948.

7. Yossif, Etia's husband was arrested by the Soviets as a "Capitalist" in Volozhin on March 1940. He was imprisoned in a Soviet Concentration Camp. He had never returned from the Soviet Goulag. His family had never had any news about him. He was 42 years old.

8. Motia, the Malkins' youngest son with his wife Irka went to Israel as a "Haluts" (pioneer) in 1937. His son Eytan participated as paratrooper officer in the Yom Kippur war. He fell on the battle camp in the Sinai desert on October 1973. He was 32 years old.

How did I survive

By Leyzer Meltser

Translated from Russian by M. Porat z"l

Edited by Judy Montel

I, Meltser Dovid-Leyzer was born in Volozhin in 1923. Meltser Shimen Itskhok son of Zvi of Vishnevo was my father; Sore Sheyne nee Rabinovitsh was my mother.

I was studying in the Volozhin Hebrew Tarbut School and in the Polish Primary Povshekhna until 1939. From 1939 until 1941, during the Soviet rule, I completed my studies in the Russian School.

The Germans occupied Volozhin in June 1941. All the Jewish inhabitants were transferred into the Ghetto a month later. 200 Jews were gathered at the town's Sport Stadium and executed by shooting in October 1941. It was the first mass slaughter in Volozhin. The second massacre occurred near the ancient graveyard on May 10, 1942, where 2000 Jews were murdered. The last mass slaughter, the third one took place in the Volozhinka streambed in August 1942.

Our family; my parents, brother and sister and I were driven away from the ghetto by the Germans and their assistants; local policemen. We were taken into the blacksmith building that was erected during the time of the Soviet rule. The building was located on the Dubinski Street (now Sovietskaya)

The Aktion took place during the second Pogrom, They put us in groups of eighty people each and transferred us group by group to the killing field.

The killings were conducted near the Jewish Graveyard The Jews were executed by shooting.

My father told me:

"Run, my son, perhaps you'll be the sole to survive of our family".

I put myself on his shoulders, removed some tiles from the roof and ran away.

One other person was able to jump and run away after me, It was Ele Mlot. I spent some days in forest, then returned to the Volozhin Ghetto where I hid in a nook.

I found out that my parents, my sister and brother were executed on May 10, 1942.

I ran back into forest after the third slaughter, then I was able to transfer to the shtetl Krevo, where a ghetto still existed. From Krevo I went to Smorgon and from there they transferred us to Lithuania and imprisoned in the Zhensistoria concentration camp.

They brought a group of us into Vilnius in December 1942, where we were ordered to build a commercial rail station.

Once in the evening, returning from work, I ran away into a nearby forest. I wandered there for some days until I met with Russian Partisans. I joined the Bagration group of the Voroshilov Brigade. I was with the partisans until the liberation of Belarus and Lithuania. After liberation I joined the Red Army. On Victory Day I was in Magdenburgh, Germany.

I was released from the army and returned to Volozhin in December 1945 and went to work. I married Sofiya (Sonia) Milikovski, daughter of Leyzer Itskhok and Hana born Berman from Horodok.

Our marriage took place in Volozhin in 1947. Our daughter Hasia was born in 1950. She was ill and passed away at age 31 to our great sorrow in the year 1981.

Our son Shimon was born in Volozhin on 1954. We made Aliya to Israel, the entire family, my wife, my son Shimon, his wife Polina, his children Asia and Yakov and me where we now live.

Leyzer Melzer (right) with Zhurkevitsh* at the Volozhin Kehila memorial in the ancient graveyard in Volozhin 2001

*Zhurkevitsh told me during my visit in 1998, that as a small boy he witnessed the 1942 May 10th mass slaughter. "I was hidden here near the cemetery fence and looked at the bloody action. Our local youngsters were involved in this job more than the Germans".

A look at the country's history

By M. Porat

Edited by Mike Kalt

Based on articles from "Volozhin Yizkor Book"(Hebrew),
"Pamiat'-Volozhin District History" (Belorussian) and "Jewish Lithuania" (French)

Volozhin is situated in a boundary zone, the ownership of which is claimed by the surrounding nations. It is populated by Slavic and Baltic inhabitants. Prior to WW I, 12% of the inhabitants were Jews.

The Lithuanian Rule: Lithuanian pagan tribes settled the Baltic Eastern shores in the early centuries of the first millennium. During the 13th-14th centuries, the tribes converted to Catholicism. They unified and formed a small kingdom, which was referred to as the Great Lithuanian Princedom.

Due to its well-organized governorship and efficient army, the Princedom succeeded to rule the 500 by 500 kilometer territory, which extended from the Baltic sea to the Dneiper river on its east, and the Pripiat' swamps on its south. This territory includes Lithuania, Leetonia, a part of northern Poland, and almost the entire Belarus.

The word "Belarus" means "**White Russia**". It's told that during the 13th century when the Mongols invaded the major part of Russia, they did not reach these big forests, lakes, and swamps located on the northwest of Russia. The territory therefore remained "pure" white — "free of the yellow-dark aggressor".

The great Prince Vytautas (Vitold), desired to develop commerce and economy, and therefore welcomed the Jews who had immigrated from Germany and other western countries. Many Jews settled there. They were allowed to form in this zone self-governed congregations- *kehila* - in which they lived in relative peace. Most of them dwelled in small towns (shtetls). They were able to preserve a traditional life style.

The Poland-Lithuania State: Yaguello, the Lithuanian Prince's son, married in 1386 the crown princess of Poland. The Zhetshpospolita - Commonwealth of the two States - was created. Yaguello was crowned as King of the joint state.

The Zhetshpospolita was active during four centuries. The Polish culture and language had dominated the Lithuanian. But the country retained the name of Lithuania ("Litwa" in Polish, "Lite" in Yiddish). Yiddish remained as the main language of the Jews.

The Jewish population was growing. Jews continued to arrive from Poland, which turned to repress them; and from Volynia where they were terrorized by the Khmelnitski Kozak gangs.

They continued to speak Yiddish with a unique Litvak dialect, which differed from the Volynia and Polish dialects. The Litvak dialect turned out to be the base of the classical Yiddish. The Jews living in this zone were named "Litwaks'". The territory's virtual Jewish name became "Litwak Yiddish Land".

The Russia Tsarist imperia, after a long conflict, invaded the Zhetshpospolita in 1797 and annexed the territory. The Russian Imperia ruled this country for 120 years. This territory was the main zone limit in Tsarist Russia permitting Jews to live in. The Jewish cultural life blossomed.

Volozhin was situated in the very heart of the Litvak Yiddish Land

The Litvak Jewry resisted the Hassidism. Reb Eliyahu, the Vilna Prodigy, founded and led here the opposing "Misnagdim" movement. The Misnagdim emphasized learning of the Holy scripts. They put the stress on study and knowledge above prayers. The "Litvaks" founded and built the great Yeshivas in order to strengthen this movement by Torah study. It began in Volozhin, which turned into a famous Jewish academy, and was spread into many other towns where Yeshivas were built (Mir, Radun, Slobodka, Ponivezh etc.)

The WW I postwar time: The German-Russian front passed near Volozhin. In the postwar peace treaties, the zone was divided between USSR, Poland, Lithuania and Leetonia. Vilna, Volozhin, Baranovitsh, and Pinsk became part of Poland. The Soviets ruled the land eastward of this line. The western part including Poniviezh, Kovno and Alitus, belonged to Baltic States.

The Haskala (Enlightenment) and Zionist movements became dominant in this period. The Jewish population during the 20 years interval between the two World Wars had changed its ideas. The Hebrew language and lessons of general education were taught in the schools. Tarbut – Zionist oriented schools -- slowly replaced the Heyder and the Yeshiva. Young people became members of Zionist organizations. Many of them made Aliya into the Land of Israel.

World War II: Volozhin became part of the Soviet Union from September 1939 until June 1941 (the day on which the Germans occupied the town). The fascists exterminated the entire Jewish population of this country during their occupation. Here practically began the Holocaust. Jews were condemned to death. The Fascists started by assassinations and humiliation of Jews, by gathering them in ghettos, and finally they were mass slaughtered inside the settlements they lived, until all the Jews living there during 1941-1943 were assassinated.

Post WWII: Volozhin is now a part of the Belarus Republic, a newborn entity which was established after the Soviet Union disintegrated into several independent states.

The "Litwak Yiddish Land" is mainly Juden Rein: without Jews.

Eastward from Volozhin (Volozhin included) is Belarus, with Minsk as its capital. Westward from Volozhin is Lithuania, with Vilnius (Vilna) as its capital.

Who am I and where am I from DILEMMA: Adam Mitskevitsh, the renowned poet, was born on the Nieman shore (between Lida and Navarodok). His major poem *Pan Tadeush*, written in Polish, begins: "*Litva, my Fatherland, you are like Health. How much to appreciate you, knows only one who lost you*". The Lithuanians claim that he was of Lithuanian origin (he wrote "Litva, my fatherland"), The Poles say he was Polish (the poet wrote in Polish only). The Belarussians believe that he was Belarussian (he was born in Belarus, and Belarussian was his family's everyday language). There is a different version that his mother… was Jewish.

As for my origins: I know definitively who I am: a Jew, an "Ost Jude"- But from where am I? From Poland, Russia, Lita, Belarus? Or maybe I come from the virtual Litvak-Yiddish-Land, a land whose people do not exist more.

Childhood In Volozhin

M. Perlman

Edited by Mike Kalt

Vilno Street

Our First Apartment

The Perelman family changed apartments four times during our Volozhin childhood. The first one was on Vilno Street. It stood near the *Sazhelka,* the shtetl water pond. The west part of the single story wood house belonged to my mother's parents, and was rented to the district court. We inhabited the east side, our parent's property.

Both of us, Sonia and I, were born in Vilno, the big city, where mother chose to bring us into this world. It was a whole day journey, by horse and by railway, one way pregnant, back with the newborn babies.

The apartment had four rooms: the sleeping room, the dining room, Papa's "cabinet," two entrances, a waste kitchen with a huge oven. The fourth room was rented. Objects I recall include the wall-mounted telephone, the leather sofa "*kushetka*", the hanging musical wall clock, and the large mirror.

Our house, undamaged remains, until now on Vilna (today Sovietskaya) Street
Four families (invaders from Ponizhe) are now living there.

The first event I am able to remember was my mother sitting on a jagged chair in the cabinet, beside the open fire of the high white stove. She sent me to get the iron rod (*kocherke)*, to arrange the glowing coals. I was running fast out of the kitchen darkness, rod in hand, to mama, near the warm firelight, and I bumped hard into the chair edge. My face was covered with a mixture of blood and tears. The child has lost his eye! Feltcher Avrom Tsart, the shtetl medical authority, was alerted. He applied bandages and iodine. The eye was "saved", but the scare and memory have been with me ever since.

In 1998, during our visit in Volozhin, we found the house. 4 families now occupied it. I recognized the oven with its original small wrought iron door, the place of my haunting first injury.

Russian was the first language I spoke. After the Russian revolution, our parents returned to Volozhin, which was under Polish rule, from Ukraine, where they both studied in Russian schools. Both of them, especially Mama, who was saturated by Russian literature, wanted her boy to speak the language of Pushkin. Polish they did not know, and as for Yiddish, "he'll manage to learn it in the *shtetl* courtyards". So the family members were named in the Russian manner, Mame Etl--*Mama Etia*, Tate Yosl--*Papa Yosif*, Mume--*Tiotia*, Feter--*Diadia*, Bobe--*Babushka*, Zeyde—*Diedushka,* etc.

As for my true *mame loshn,* eventually it became Yiddish. I succeeded in becoming skilled in the beautiful "Litvak" Yiddish. It caused me many struggles, especially the *RrrrEISH*, which I turned on my tongue softly like the *shkotzim,* instead of pronouncing it roughly, from the throat, as my court comrades did.

I'm still astonished when I think about the linguistic problems of our childhood. At home I heard Russian, we played with the court comrades in Yiddish, and the housemaid's language was Belarussian--we called it *Goyish*. The main language in my Tarbut primary school was Hebrew, and the government authorities communicated with us, Polish citizens, in Polish. It is a bit strange to require six-year-old children to hear, to speak, and to understand five languages. Nevertheless *goles is goles* (Diaspora is Diaspora).

Grandparents

Our ancestors lived in Volozhin, for at least a dozen generations. The town changed its sovereign frequently. At my father's birth (1898) the shtetl was part of Tsar Nicholas' Russia; at mine (1924) it was part of Marshal Pilsudski's Poland. We left our Volozhin home in Stalin's Soviet Union (1940). The fascists murdered our grandparents inside Volozhin, occupied by Hitler's Germany (1942). Now it is Belarus, a new entity with its own language, borders, flag, president, and history.

Jews, emigrating from Germany and other western countries, settled here starting in the 16th century. They formed self-governed congregations (*kehila)*, lived in small burghs (*shtetls*), and preserved their style of life, speaking the Yiddish-Litvak dialect. As for me, I spent 15 years in Volozhin, a typical Litvak-land shtetl, but I have never seen a true Lithuanian goy (gentile), and never heard or seen a word in this language.

Nevertheless, to my knowledge, all my ancestors during the last two to three centuries were 100 percent "Litvak" born.

Yehoshua (Eliyahoo?) Perlman, our father's grandfather, was the *Rov* (Rabbi) of Vishnevo, a small village near Volozhin. Prior to WW I he made aliya to Eretz Israel, where he served as Rabbi of the town of Rehovot, changing his name to "Margolis" (Hebrew for "Pearl"). His son, Moyshe Perlman (I bear his name), married Malka Itskhaykin, Rabbi Chaim Volozhiner's great great granddaughter. Moyshe Perlman owned a wine shop and an insurance agency. They lived in the famous Volozhin Rabonim's house (*Beys Harav*), Grandma Malka's inheritance. Their children--our father Yosef, his sisters Haya Dina, Feygl (Fania), and brother Eli--were all born in this house. At the dawn of World War I, the whole family left Volozhin as the Germans approached the area. They spent the war in Nikopol, Ukraine, on the Dneipr River. The Perelman family returned to Volozhin at the end of the war. Feygl and Eli remained in Russia (Soviet Union).

Before the German-Soviet war (1941), Grandma Malka left Volozhin, and went to live with her daughter Feygl in Moscow.

My mother Etl (Etia), her sister Zinah, and brothers Osher, Itzhok (Izia), and Mordhay (Motia), were born in Volozhin. Her father, our Grandpa Hirsh Malkin, the son of Yoel-Moyshe Malkin (from Lunna), was married to our Grandma Haya-Riva, who was the daughter of Shmuel-Osher Marshak (from Alitus).

Hirsh Malkin as the head manager of the millionaire Heller's large forest exploitation company, which established its main office in Belokoretz, a forest hamlet near Volozhin. The family fled Volozhin in World War I to Konotope in Ukraine, and returned back home in the early twenties. Our mother Etia was exiled to Siberia, where she survived the war. Her sisters and brothers survived the war:

Our grandparents, Zvi Hirsh Malkin and his wife Haya Riva, lived in Volozhin at the breakout of World War II. They were transferred to the town ghetto. The Nazis and their associates murdered both of them at the second mass slaughter action, on Sunday, May 10, 1942, inside Volozhin, near the ancient graveyard. May they rest in peace.

Zina, Izia, and Osher survived the war in France, Motia in Eretz Israel.

Our parents, Yosef and Etl Perelman, were married in 1923 and established their home in Volozhin. They lived in a wooden house on Vilna Street. In this house, my younger sister Sonia and I were born. The family's income came from the wood saw and steam driven flour-grinding mills that our parents erected and managed on the Volozhinka waterside. The Soviet authorities imprisoned our father Yosif Perelman and sent him to the Gulag. A month later they expelled his family, Mother Etia, my sister Sonia, and me, to Siberia.

Harav – House Of Our Father's Mother

(see picture page I-17)

The house of grandmother Malka, my father's mother, stood on the northern side of the market square. Graf Tyshkevitsh, the Volozhin and the district landowner, built a stone house in style of the estate mansion and offered it to Reb Chaim Volozhiner. The Yeshiva founder and his son Reb Yitsele were held in high esteem by the graph. Grandma Malka, Reb Yitsele's great-granddaughter, inherited the big house. She lived in this house together with her daughter Haya-Dina (my father's sister), her husband Yani Garber, and sons, Dania and Monia.

The main entrance from the market side led to the apartment through a broad wood staircase. On the opposite side, going down to the Yeshiva and Beys Hamidrosh Synagogue were narrow steep steps. On the bottom were the cellars in which my grandfather stored wine bottles prior to the First World War. Everything was big in this house. The rooms were large, the walls thick, the windows, through which you had a view of the yeshiva, were high.

My cousin Monia was tall. He was nicknamed *Monie der Greysser* (the big), while I was called *Monie der kleiner* (the small). And also small, to my luck, was my grandmother Malka. But the house was really big, large by our shtetl's proportions.

Babushka Malka was a gracious, beautiful woman, with totally white hair. A piano stood in the main room. Dania learned to play. My grandma's epigram was frequently repeated by the family members: "The teacher is already covered with gold and Dany never stops to play the octaves". The octaves saved Dany's life. The Soviets, arriving in 1939, invited him to play piano far inside Russia. Dania remained in Russia and escaped the shtetl's destiny.

Our cousin Monia was two years my senior. He owned a large postage stamp collection and had technical abilities. He constructed a radio receiver and he made it work 65 years ago in Volozhin. During Stalin's pre-war regime, when he was a student at the town high school, Monia jokingly erased the moustache of the Soviet leader on a wall-newspaper. The Soviets did not share his sense of humor. He was arrested and deported to Siberia. Monia had the chance to be free and to join the Polish ("Anders") army as the war started. They left Russia, then went to Iran, and than to Eretz Israel. Here he encountered our cousins from Vishnevo (Tsherna and Bluma--Rabbi Perlman-Margolis' granddaughters). Monia did not remain here, in spite of the insistence of his cousins. He continued with the Anders army to Italy. Monia "the Tall", Malka Perlman's grandson, the son of Yani Garber, the Volozhin Judenrat's head, soldier in the Polish army, fell at the Monte-Casino battle, fighting the Germans in Italy.

His father Yani was born in Ukraine. He had a perfect musical ear. When he joined the Beytar singing group taking the "second voice", the song became real, multi layered and, in my memory, wonderful. The Nazis, after occupying Volozhin, nominated him to be Judenrat head. On October 28th 1941, the SS ordered him to assemble three hundred people in the cinema hall to do some work. Yani Garber accomplished his mission. The Nazi commander told him to leave. At that point Yani realized that he was misled; the assembled Jews were not brought to work, but to be killed. He insisted that he should share the fate of his community. His demand was fulfilled. He was the first to be shot.

But let us revisit the big house during the thirties. When Sonia fell sick with a children's malady I was removed to live a while with babushka Malka. After the demise of his sister Haya Dina, our father passed the seven days mourning in this house. She was operated on for appendicitis, and died under the surgeon's knife in the tiny Volozhin hospital. I remember my aunt's covered corpse lying on the big chamber's floor with clothes covering windows and mirrors. The funeral was typically Jewish, without any flowers, with three prayers a day at the Perelman's house.

The   s were called the "Stone Skulls" *(moyer keplakh)*. The first reason was their stone habitation, the second one, not less important, was their erudition, education and behavior. The family head, Moyshe Perlman, was the sole person in Volozhin who used to receive daily and to read the magazine "*Russkoye Slovo*"--"Russian Word". Aunt Haya Dina, although she spent her time in the vine shop, was always reading a book. All the children graduated from high school and even attended universities. (Eli was a doctor; Feigl was a member of the Soviet Academy of Sciences). And among my Tarbut schoolmates, my father alone had a secular matriculation certificate.

Bierezno – Home Of Our Mother's Parents

Our grandparents Haya Riva and Eliyahu Hirsh Malkin moved during the thirties to Bierezno, a small town near Rovno. When summer was approaching, Mother used to pack suitcases and take the long, long ride to Bierezno. It was a wonderful journey to an enchanted place. I guard the memories--first the ride in a peasant's single horse cart to Horod'k rail station, thereafter the black steaming, smoking, and whistling locomotive approaching the station. Later we wondered at the fields and forests passing through the window frame; we were much impressed by the thunder-like noisy passage over the Nieman and Pripyat' bridges. I still have the taste in my mouth of the tasty excellent black bread with cold calf meat sandwiches. After the long trip, with two *pieresiadka* rail changes and a second horse cart transfer, we arrived in Bierezno at a late night hour.

If I have had to consider a place to be named Paradise, Bieriezno would be my choice. First of all the kindness of Babushka and Diedushka; then the house and garden. The large house where our grandparents lived was built from wood for a local squire *pomieshtchick*. Equipped with a large veranda, it stood inside a fruit tree garden with apples, pears, plums, cherries, round red small *poretchkes*, and yellow oval *agress*. Beautiful, tasty, delicious fruit, fresh-picked up from the tree.

The house had a built in *suke* with a convertible roof that could be raised by pulling a cord. It was filled with novelties, including a bathtub with a true water faucet to fill it up. Nevertheless, the water had to be drawn from the well in buckets and transferred by hand into the boiling kettle.

There was a real camera on a tripod, which was operated by Uncle Motia-Izia (I called each one of them in a double name). It was covered by a black sheet, and without any movement we stood long, long moments to be photographed. There was also a bicycle made in Germany by Durkopf, the "world best" bicycles producer.

But the crown of Bierezno was its river. Unlike our narrow, crossable-by-foot Volozhinka, the Sloutch was a water-full river, 20 to 30 meters wide, with a high steep shore on the village side and a sandy clean perfect plaza beach on the opposite shore.

Among the Bieriezno pleasures were the long sailings with Motia-Izia in their own rowing boat and the swimming and sunbathing with *tiotia* Zina on the sand shore of the beautiful river.

It was a shtetl, but a different one from our Litvak towns. Bieriezno was located in *Volyn'*, a Ukrainian territory dominated by Poland, mostly populated by Ukrainian goyim. The major part of *Volyn'* Jewry was Hassidic.

The Rebbe ruled his Bieriezno orthodox congregation. The Rebbe had his court of devoted Hassidim. He possessed his Tish-table, from which the Hassidim used to collect the festivities' remnants, the so-called *Shirayim*. Those habits and practices we did not see in Volozhin. The severe Yeshiva with the studious Rabonim was the Misnagdim Resistance bastion against the influence of the Hassidic movement.

Bieriezno residents spoke a different dialect than the Volozhin "Litvak" Yiddish dialect. They turned our "O" into an "OO"; our "OO" became an "EE". Our *doss* became in Bieriezno *dooss*, and our *hoon* became *heen*. Also the typical melody changed. The Bieriezno children listened with amazement to my strange speech and teased me "*Der Lootvak*".

Our grandparents lived in Bierezno (Volyn) until the mid thirties. Izia and Motia graduated from high school in Luninietz city (next to Bierezno). Izia and Zina left Poland from Bierezno to France. From there Motia with his wife, as pioneers (*Haluzim*) made their aliya to Eretz Israel.

The grandparents prepared themselves to visit the children, Zina, Osher and Izia, in France. Before the long journey they asked Motia to come and to stay at home. Motia left the *Hakhshara* in Kolomyya for some time and came home together with Irka Lilienberg, his schoolmate girlfriend. Hirsh Malkin could not leave the young couple alone. One day, just before the trip to France, he returned home accompanied by a

Rabbi, by two men as witnesses, and with a Stetson *"kapelush"* (hat). After the *huppe* had been finished and the young couple married, as it should be, the old Malkins could leave Bierezno and go peacefully to Paris.

The Small Incline – *Der Kleyner Barg*

Our second apartment

We spent the summer of 1930 in Bierezno with my newborn sister Sonitshka. We came back to another apartment. A bad fungus infected the wood house on Vilna Street. The family was obliged to leave it for reconditioning. A *Yeshuvnik*, a so-called country Jew, from Bielokorets, the village where Diedushka Malkin managed Mr. Heller's Forest Contor (office) before the First World War, built a new house. Father rented it for our family to live in.

Volozhin was positioned on the main road from Vilna to Minsk. The shtetl was composed of two parts. Vilna Street on the west with the Market Square in the center was called *Arouftsou*--uphill. On the eastern side was the downhill part--*Aroptsou*. Aroptsou was built on two parallel slopes, the small one, *Der kleiner Barg*, ending before the Volozhinka; and the big one, *Der Greysser Barg*, beginning close to the Polish *Kostiel*, crossed the Volzhynka Bridge and reached the East town exit, to Minsk and the Soviet border.

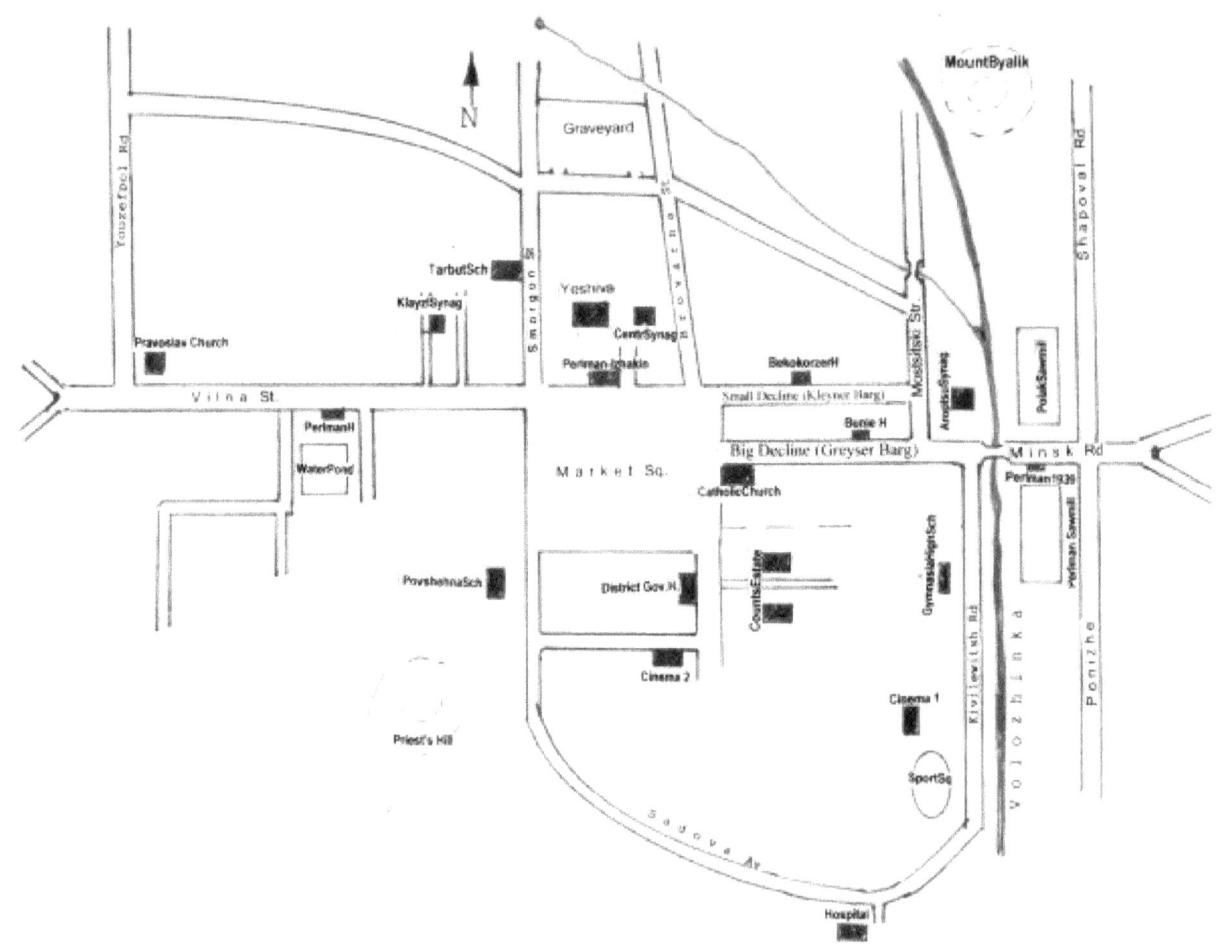

Volozhin map - 1939

(From page 8 of the Volozhin Yizkor Book)

The Bielokortser's house was located in the middle of the small incline. Mother accompanied me from this house to school. The main language was Hebrew, so we had to pass a preparation class for speaking and reading Hebrew. In the higher classes we learned Jewish history, Tanah, and Hebrew, in addition to the required-by-law general subjects like Polish history, geography, arithmetic and Polish language. We were in school the entire day, from eight in the morning until three or four in the evening, with a long pause in the middle. For lunch, we used to go home, a 5 minute run. Our way to school passed near the babushka Malka's house, beside the synagogue and the Yeshiva.

Our teachers came from surrounding shtetls. The school manager and arithmetic teacher, Yakov Lifshitz, came from Radushkevitsh. Yakov Finger, our Hebrew teacher, with his family came from Soll. Their son Benzike, my neighbor on the school bench, and I were excellent friends. Our beloved class tutor, the school choir and orchestra conductor, Mr. Baykalski from Zheludok, taught us Polish, history and geography. Mr. Taller came from Molchad' to teach the holy Bible. Ms. Rachel Melzer, our natural science schoolmaster, she alone was born in Volozhin. She married Shneur Kivilevitsh (Judenrat head in 1942). Rachel spoke to the children in Hebrew only, avoiding Yiddish, except during the pauses. We called our teachers "schoolmaster", or "schoolmistress" (Adoni, or Gvirti Hamore'a). Very polite, we stood up as they entered the class.

Across the street from our rented home, lived Freydele di Rebetsn, the rabbi Avigdor Derechinski's spouse. We were in very close relations with her. Freydele was our babushka Malka's cousin and a best friend.

Although Father was the descendant of prominent Volozhin Rabbis, he was not very religious.

Mother kept the home and food kosher. The kitchenware and cutlery were separate, one set for meat and another for milk food. A special set was reserved for Passover. *Hometz* did not pass in our home. Father conducted only the first Passover night *seder*, but never the second one, as was the Diaspora habit, and it rarely lasted after the meal to reach the *Had Gadya*. Grandfather Malkin used to conduct a real *seder* with all the rituals, sayings and melodies. He strictly guarded the *afikoman* from stealing. The boys worked hard to "steal" the well-guarded piece of *matza*. They usually arrived to perform the theft when grandpa was deeply occupied with the *kneydlah*. The meal always ended with an obstinate negotiation about the price. The demand was very high, the offer very, very low. The resulting price fell somewhere in the middle.

On the important holy days like Yom Kippur, Rosh Hashanah, Sukkoth, Passover and Shevouot, we dressed in our best clothes and went with father to the big synagogue near the Yeshiva. There, father had a reserved place at the East Wall. The most joyous holiday in Volozhin that I remember was *Simhass Toyreh*. The boys prepared themselves on the eve of the feast by borrowing small Torah rolls, called meguila, from the Yeshiva cellar, where scripts of the prophet books had been guarded.

The main Volozhin Hakofess, with multiple Torahs and meguiles in hand, took place in the Yeshiva. The Yeshiva boys were joyful, and with them the whole shtetl. They danced and sang songs such as "*Ato Bohartonu mikol Hoamim... Veytoyras emes Nota beyssoyheynu*" "You chose us from all nations... and the Torah truth did You plant in our hearts..." lasting until late in the night.

A tale was told in Volozhin that once a group of Yeshive-layt discovered that vodka is made from potatoes. It was decided to try the happy-rending-liquid fabrication. They put a kettle full of potatoes on the fire. During the boiling, the hungry boys did not cease to test the hot food. After the hunger was satiated, all of them became happy. This event taught the poor Volozhin Yeshive-boys how to become *Freylikh* without vodka, just boiling and tasting potatoes.

During Yom Kippur day all the grown family members fasted. But we never had a *Suke*. So I was very happy when Freydele di Rebetsn invited me to her Sukot rabbinical diner. It was a home built *Suke* with a convertible roof, like in Bieriezno. Freydele, I believed, was the main personality in the family, but to my astonishment, she was deprived the privilege of having her dinner together with her sons and husband. She served us a beautiful cooked gefilte fish. The Row had the head, Chayim, the eldest son, the middle. Yona the youngest received the tail, and I contained myself and was very satisfied with a tasty spicy Litvak-gefilte-fish ball.

Speaking about religion makes me recall the Sabbath skating event. Returning from his Vilna business trip, Father brought us presents. Once it was a wonderful gadget, the first scooter ever seen in Volozhin. The sloping sidewalk of our inclined street was an excellent way to ride on the one foot "*Hulay Noga*". From another journey, steel ice skates were brought. They were not made from wood like in Volozhin, and not from common steel, but from prestigious in those times and places, "pure Swedish steel". I found this gift on a Friday mid winter morning. Returning from school, we spilled water on our house courtyard until it formed a small pool. By Saturday morning we had a tiny skating area. I utilized it ardently. My pleasure was great but short. The holy Shabes desecration reached our school management. Mister Taller, our severe Bible teacher, reproved me in front of the class and the skating sacrilege stopped.

Childhood In Volozhin (cont.)

Nicknames And Child's Play

Most of Volozhin inhabitants were known by their nicknames. I recall Nahum the Hairdresser's story. Like the majority of the shtetls' much-estimated citizens he was blessed with a hernia (*kile* in Yiddish). It was a remarkable one, and the "*Nahumke der Kilun*" nickname stuck to him. The thing was growing and it became a must to be removed. After the operation had succeeded, the nickname did not match his possessor any more. A special name-giving session was called. The clever guys made a decision, and the nickname was changed to "*Nahumke der beskilnik*"--the last word is Russian and it means "The Hernia-lacking Nahumke".

My best friend and nearest neighbor on the small incline was *Hayke di Kadelihe's*. Why *Kadelihe's*? Her mother Gitl had married Kadl. After his death, the widow became *Kadelihe* and to her daughters stuck the nickname "*Hayke di Kadelihe's*, "*Merke di Kadelihe's*" and so on.

The *Kadelihe's* single-room house was situated some fifty feet uphill. Once in a winter day, sledding down to the frozen Volozhinka streambed, our sleigh fell in an ice rupture. Wet, frozen, and afraid to show my miserable appearance at home, I found a reheating and drying refuge in "*Di Kadelihe's Lezhanka*". It was the upper part of the big oven, serving as a bed for the whole family in the *Kadelihe's* single room house. All my life I'm thankful, and I remember this poor good family for the warm and dry shelter.

In another house up the small incline lived *Arke der Photograftshik's* (photographer) multiple-children family. This specialist produced during the twenties/most of the pictures that now exist of Volozhin. One of his sons was my playmate. I used to visit them. With astonishment I would follow the family's lunch. Arie's wife served her husband the whole food dish. Arie after selecting the best of it used to distribute the rest to his children.

How did we, children, play in Volozhin? Apart the classic games like "hide and seek", "classes" and "*tzizhik*" (a small stick sharpened from both sides, placed in a square mark on the ground, bounced by a racket beat and flown away by it's second hit) we had our special entertainments:

On summer days we had the Volozhinka shallow stream. On the left beach, beside a large green grazing meadow we found a suitable place. The Volozhin boys, mostly from *Aroptsu*, among them *Leyshke Shimen-Itshes, Eyzerke Finger, Chaim Lungen-Leber, Berl der Tzigayner, Itshok Hame-Leytshes* and some children from *Arooftsu* like *Avromtshe der Guiber, Voolke-Ptsholke,* The Altman brothers *Langer Shabes* and *Koortser Freytig* (Long Sabbat and short Friday), *Arke dem felcher's, Leybke Goylem,* and many others, had done the work. They would cut reeds in the long stem-grass. The reeds were spread across the riverbed. It formed a *Hadge* - a barge, which held the water. It was the best swimming pool I remember. Swimming "*corners*", header and feet jump – a true water playing paradise. But, to our great disappointment, its existence was short. As soon as the water flow to sawmill steam boiler was restricted, the angry kettle-heater arrived. In a rage, he would destroy our achievement, cutting off the joyous adventure.

Also, the sawmill area had been a place for children's games and activities. The sawdust hill, piled up to heat the steam engine, was a perfect place for all kinds of games that required tunnels, pits, and hills. The rectangular towers of crisscrossed planks served as hiding and climbing places.

But the best and most popular playing object was the railway cart-*vagonietka*, which were used to move trunks and boards. The cart was built as a rectangular wooden block frame, mounted on four iron wheels. It moved on a narrow railway by gravitation, or by hand pushing. The real pleasure had been the downhill descent riding on the cart frame. But, like the *Hadge*-barrier swimming, the cart-vagonietka rolling was not entirely legal. The quick and heavy rolling carts could be quite dangerous.

The Volozhin children took advantage of the heavy snows that covered the shtetl slopes and the hills in its vicinity in winter. They also exploited the low temperatures that covered the Volozhinka and the town–water pond (*Sazhelke*) with solid ice. Sleds, ice skates, and skis were hand-made. These transport tools were able to slide at significant speed, on the inclined, frozen, almost empty, evening streets. It was a real pleasure. But we had to be careful to avoid the enemy of our winter sports. Seizure or destruction of our sleds and skating devices was a hobby of Mr. Kasko, the Volozhin policeman.

Father, I think, understood the importance of sports. He used to tell with a shadow of pride about his traversing the Dneipr in Nikopole, swimming from shore to shore. Later I demonstrated before Sonia a similar deed, traversing the Siberian Irtish River. All of the presents that our father used to bring from his Vilna business trips were meant for sport or to physical training. Among them we received, steel ice skates, bicycles, fabricated sleds, barbells, skis etc. We used it to our wealth and pleasure.

A year after the shabbes skating fiasco, the town authorities arranged for efficient use of the small water pond. It was used in winter for ice-skating, and in summer days for kayak sailing. We made excursions on bicycle, on skis, or by foot to the forests and rivers in the vicinity.

My sister Sonia and I were far from being athletes. But we carried Father's teaching. Both of us spend a lot of time swimming, skiing, skating, bicycling, sailing and so forth, as do our children and grandchildren. I hope that our young descendants will read this story, and remember sometimes, their Grandpa, Yosif Perelman, when performing physical culture.

The Big Incline - *Der Greysser Barg*

Our third apartment

The family mill business was limping. The steam engine was the source of the trouble. Costly breakdowns occurred often. Old and inefficient, it needed to be replaced. A new engine and kettle were ordered from Danzig. The engineer, Mr. Pollak, arrived from Warsaw to supervise the infrastructure preparations. He was given the children's room. Each morning he used to stand bare-chested over a basin of cold water to bathe. This action impressed me deeply.

The family invested all of its savings and even more in the mill renovation. The infected house on Vilna Street was dismantled, but the overall work did not yet begin. Often I was sent home with a message asking for payment of tuition fees. At home the spirits were low. Father collapsed under his burden of the debts. Mother twisted to bind the edges.

Renting the big *Belokortser's* house became a heavy load. One day a horse-harnessed cart arrived to make a move, transferring furniture pieces and *peklah* down the big incline. Arriving at Bunia and Osher

Yiche-Ber's house at the Pilsudski Street (originally Minsk St.), on the west side of the Volozhinkas' bridge, all our belongings were unloaded.

Osher Yiche-Ber's house had three parts. In the front façade overlooking the street, lived Osher the landlord's family. We had to stay in the two-room apartment in the rear. Both apartments were divided in the middle by a common kitchen with a huge Russian oven. The backside of the oven formed a surface, which together with an additional corner, was the living place for both our families' housemaids. Here in Bunia and Osher Itshe-Ber's "posterior", as Mother used to say, our family found a refuge, hoping that better days would come.

In this backside apartment I made my first and serious acquaintance with the printed word. I began to read in the *Bielokortser's* house. The first pleasure book I remember was in Hebrew, the Pentateuch *"Bereishis"*. I attempted to read the holy, but exciting book prior to learning it. I used to read it at evening in bed, covering my head with a cap to respect the book's holiness.

But the heavy, serious, true juvenility reading I did in this two-room apartment. It was implemented in the Polish language. My cousin, Monia the Tall introduced me to the Volozhin district library *Biblioteka Seymikova*, which was located inside the District Governor's House, the place from which I used to draw my life pleasure. On my way to Volozhin, 60 years afterwards, one of the main sites I intended to visit was the *"Biblioteka"*. Here we borrowed and consumed the literature of our youth: *The Desert and the Jungle, Quo Vadis, By Sword and by Fire, The Three Musketeers, The Count of Monte Cristo, The Last of Mohicans, Ivanhoe, White Fang*…written by famous authors such as Sienkevich, Reymont, Dickens, Pruss, Mostovich, Mickevich, Dumas, Jack London, Sholom Ash, Tolstoy, Sholokhov, Cooper, etc., etc. It was a world of beautiful fiction, which we hungrily absorbed in our native shtetl.

**The District Governor's House was built by Graf Tishkevitsh in the 19th century
Photographed by author in 1998.
Inside on the ground floor was situated "my" library the "biblioteka Seymikova".**

When the Soviets took over the house, they could not find any ovens inside the building. After some research they found in the cellar a big incinerator and a stack of tree beams to feed it at cold weather. The heat passed to the chimneys on the roof through channels in the walls and so it was warmed. By a central heating system built in Volozhin 200 years ago.

People I know from the Polish western side of Belarus, including my relatives, preserve and love all written words said, and particularly sung in Russian. At the same time they detest and despise even the sound and tone of the Polish language. I'm not a lover of the Polish people; I did not love them when growing up under their rule in Volozhin, not after their deeds during the Shoah, and especially not after the recent publication of the Kaydany Jews Butchery, purely Polish-made. But my massive Polish language reading, when I was very young, left its footprints. During and after the war I had few opportunities to read, to hear, or to speak Polish. But when it arrives and I encounter it, I'm very much pleased.

My Bar Mitzvah was celebrated in this small backward apartment. I learned the Torah reading from my Bible teacher, Mr. Taller. The ceremony took place in the great synagogue. The Torah was read in Ashkenazic Hebrew. A table was spread inside the apartment. The *Droshe* was said in a pure Litvak Yiddish. My "big" *Ihess*, descending from the Volozhin Yeshiva founders and leaders, was much appreciated during all those ceremonies.

Father subscribed to the Jewish daily journal *"Nash Psheglond"*, printed in Polish. I participated in its reading. There was published in serial form Shneyer's novel *"Noah Pandreh"*. The novel's story was a fictional portrayal of the deportation of the whole Polish Jewish population to Madaskar, and its return, because, as per Mr. Shneyer, the Poles could not manage their country without Jews. History proved to the contrary. Father also did not agree with Mr. Shneyer. He was persuaded that the Jews must leave Poland and settle in Eretz Israel. But words and actions were two different things. Also… nobody was ready to buy that "stumbling mill business!"

On The Volozhinka Shore

Our fourth (last) apartment

On the Pilsudski (Minsk) Street southern side, on the streams, some five meters higher than the beach was situated a well constructed from wood. The entranceway to our wood sawing and flour grinding mills passed beside the well. Further up along the street was our new home. In that wooden house we spent the last three years in Volozhin.

The house had two entries. The front entry went from the street to the dining room and through a fixed stairway to the attic. The rear, the more frequently-used and more spacious entry room, was joined by a door to the kitchen, and through a staircase, the cellar. A high, tile-lined oven, located in the center of the apartment, at the corners of the four rooms, heated all of the rooms. Inside the kitchen stood a huge oven, for all kinds of cooking and baking.

Every Thursday evening Mother filled two wood receptacles (*deyze*) with dough. One, containing ordinary dough, was designated for *Hales*, the other, enriched, for cakes. Both of them were covered with blankets and were put in a warm place to ferment during the night. The next day, early in the morning, began the "Short Friday" workday. The well-arranged wood pieces burned in the huge oven. The good food was boiling, and the *Hales* (bread for shabes), *bondes* (potato bread), *Zemelah* (kind of croissant), and other tasty specialties were baking.

All four apartments, like all of the dwellings in the shtetl, lacked running water, sewer and water toilets. Water was drawn from the well, dragged home in buckets, and stored in a wood barrel. A small outside shack built over a pit, with a seat made from wood, served as the family toilet.

Our grandparents, before coming to Volozhin, had gone to France to see their children and grandchildren living abroad. They were impressed by the journey. Paris--the big town, the underground metro, the broad avenues, and the royal palaces--overwhelmed them, especially my grand mother Haya Riva. She was still disappointed, not meeting the famous elegantly dressed women on the streets of the City of Light. But fortunately she was invited to hear and to see *Carmen* at the Paris Opera, so she had also the opportunity to see the audience. Here, our Grandma Haya Riva understood, as we had been told later, the real *a la Paris* dressed "Parisiennes" moved not by foot, not in buses, and not even by metro, but were driven in luxury cars. In summer 1938 we had a guest, Aunt Zina, our mother's sister, who came from Paris to visit her family in Volozhin.

The last photo in Volozhin - 1938
From left: The author in Gymnasia uniform; Grandma Malka Perlman;
Tante Zina Dreyfuss, Sonitshka, Grandma Haya-Riva; Uncle Yani Garber;
Grandpa Hirsh Malkin; Mother Etia; Father Yossif, Cousin Moola Malkin

The school year 1937-38 was my last year in the Hebrew Tarbut School. A horse-market functioned from time to time on the other (west) Volozhinka side, opposite our mill-plant. Most of the time the yard stood empty. This year the yard changed. The active Volozhin mayor, Pan Trechinski, the former Polish Povshehna school manager, worked hard and efficiently to build and to establish on that place the first high school in Volozhin, the Polish gymnasia. Just when I finished the seventh and last tarbut class, the gymnasia opened its doors. The acceptance of students was based on two criteria: the candidate's knowledge, and his religion.

I prepared myself for the examinations very, very seriously. The examinations in written and verbal forms took place in the classrooms of the Polish public school, the "*Shkola Povshehna*", in July 1938. I was not sure as to my success. We waited outside the building to see the list. It appeared on the wall. Among the lucky one hundred, ten were Jews, exactly 10%. They knew arithmetic--the Polish *Numerus Clausus* specialists.

Among the ten, five came from our Hebrew Tarbut School, and the other five were from the *Povshehna*. (Their names are listed in "The Volozhin Gymnasia-High School" article).

Prominent among the ninety gentile students was the *Starostianka*--the Volozhin district *Starosta's* (governor) daughter. The *Starosta's* office was in the same stone building, built by count Tyshkievitsh in the 19th century, where my *Seymikova Biblioteka* was. He lived in a beautiful villa in the *Domki*--the prestigious quarter of the Polish functionaries. The high school students could choose the foreign language they wanted to study. Most of them preferred German, and some of us chose French. The Starosta's daughter and I were among this minority. Our French language teacher was a Polish nun. She came to the lessons dressed in a typical Jesuit nun's costume. She was a good teacher. I still remember the popular songs she taught—"*Freres Jacques*", "*Au Clair de la Lune*", and more. Her teaching during one year, once a week, helped me later to learn this language, passing 18 months in France.

I visited Volozhin in 1998. The Povshehna School, the Gymnasia, the Starosta's office building and villa remain as they stood 60 years ago. In the Gymnasia, I recognized my school bench in its same place. The starosta's villa was converted to contain the Volozhin Municipality museum, with a little corner for Jewish life (maybe?). The office building is well maintained but I didn't find my library, the *Seymikova Biblioteka*. The Tarbut School left no sign, nothing. Only a small green hill remained where our Synagogue stood.

As for teachers, all of them were Catholic Poles. We had to call them "Professor". Pan Konopnicki, the School director, was very liberal and bright minded. He taught mathematics, but not too much. The main part of his lesson focused on public matters, on politics, and so forth.

The Polish language teacher, Mr. Protasievitsh, a clerical school graduate, did not hide his anti-Semitic sentiments.

my Tarbut, Jewish *Kehila* school, I was accustomed to excellent grades. In the gymnasia high school an earthquake occurred. In the first half-year estimation certificate I found two E grades, in Polish language and in history. Each one was strong enough to retain me for a second school year in the first Gymnasia course. I was glum and deeply depressed. At home I was strongly reprimanded by my parents. Being a Jew was not an excuse. "You shall work hard and be smart". So I took myself to work. I made serious study in ancient Roman history. In Polish composition work--"what do I want to become in the future?" I answered "A workman". "Why?" "To strengthen and glorify Poland!" My anti-semite professor was astonished reading so strange an answer from a Jew-boy As part of this exercise, my Polish writing, also was not bad. At the end of the school year I had a few good grades, without any E-grades. Our family could breathe with relief.

My first Gymnasia 1938/1939 School Year was also my last one.
On September 1st, 1939 the World War II broke out.
This date became also the last day of my childhood.

Воложин
Жертвы Холокоста
1941 – 1943

Страницы 605 - 616 в книге:

«Воложин – Город, Люди и Святыня»

Имена на иврит списаны кирильскими буквами – Моисей Перельман

[From Volozhin - Martyrs (1275 names)]

А
Авром (Родес)
Акалчик Роза с семьёй
Акселброд Ефраим и жена его
Альперович Голда и сын Шимон
Альперович Мэндель, жена Тамара, дочь Фрума, сыновя Берл и Ёаш
Альперт Аврам, жена Хая с семьёй
Альперт Шамай и жена его Хая
Альперт Яков и жена его
Альтман Ицхок, жена Лифша, сыновья элиэзер и Иосэф
Арон-Довид и жена его
Аскинд (рав) Нафтали и жена его, Хашка
Б
Байдес, жена Фейгл, дети их Гилел и Леа,
Бакшт виниямин и жена его
Бакшт Егошуа Лейб
Бакшт Мойше и жена его
Баскин Арие и жена его
Баскин Хаим, жена Фрума, дети Сара и файвл
Басук Хезкл, жена Гита, дети Яков, Хая и Сара
Бекер Иуда, жена его Хана Рохл
Бергер Файче, его дочери Гинда и Леа

- Бергман Хаим и его жена
- БергманЕрахмиель и его жена
- Беркман Дося
- Беркман Мина
- Беркман Сима
- Беркович Аврам, жена его Кейля м сын лейб
- Беркович Исроэл, жена Бэйля
- Беркович Яков, жеа Соня
- Берман Айзик с семьёй
- Берман Алтер, жена Сара, сын Шмуэл
- Берман Арие-Лейб, жена Батья с семьёй
- Берман Арие-Лейб, жена Элька, дети Яков, Шмуэл, Этл, Хана и Фэйгл
- Берман Арие-Лейб. Жена Мира, дети Цви и Броха
- Берман Геня-Мэра с сыном Хаим-Меир
- Берман Гершон с семьёй
- Берман Голда с сыном Мэир
- Берман Егошуа с детьми
- Берман Ёсиф, жена Ципора с детьми
- Берман Ёсиф-Бер, жена его, Хая - Люба
- Берман Златка, дети Гершон, Рахмиель,
- Берман Зхария, жсна Гитл, дети Егошуа, Натан, Шрага, Файва
- Берман Ицхок, жена Малка, дети Цви, Авром и Рохл
- Берман Иче-Меир, жена Ривка, дети Роза и Нотэ
- Берман Мордхай, жена Соня-Сара, дети Моня и Моше
- Берман Моше и жена
- Берман Хая-Юдис и семья
- Берман Хона, жена Михля, дети Геня и Исроэл
- Берман Шмуэл с семьёй
- Берман Шуля с семьёй
- Берман Эли-Бер, жена Хана, дети Мира и Зэв
- Бернштейн Авром, жена Кейля, сын Арие - Лейб
- Блох Юда и его жена

Бомарш Яков, жена Гинда и дети
Борохович Хаим, жена Мирьям и дети
Ботвиник Герцл, жена Баша-Лея, дети Била, Хава, Перла Моше, Рохл и Винямин
Ботвиник Егошуа, жена Тэмка с семьёй
Ботвиник Ицхак с семьёй
Ботвиник Калман, жена Либа, дети Хана, Сара, Михля и Барух
Ботвиник Хаим
Брен Файва, жена Двоша,
Брен Файва, жена Ривка, дети Авром-Эли, Двора и Раша
Брен Яков, сын Тувия
Брудно Баша (Батия)
Брудно Икутиэль, жена, сыновья Винбямин, Гавриэль
Брудно Шлоймо-Хаим, жена Пеше-Рейзл, сыновья Михл и Вуля-Зэв
Брудно Эли-Мойше, жена Ципа
Бунимович Авром-Мойше, жена Лея
Бунимович Айзик с семьёй
Бунимович Алтер, жена Гитл
Бунимович Арон и жена его
Бунимович Борух, жена Фрума, Дети Рахиль, Риша и Сара
Бунимович Гилел, жена Дина
Бунимович Давид, жена Рахиль
Бунимович Ёсиф, жена Сара
Бунимович Исраил и жена
Бунимович Ишай и жена
Бунимович Лейб и жена
Бунимович Михаил и жена
Бунимович Мойше, жена Фрума Бейля
Бунимович Мордух и жена Гинда
Бунимович Пинхас, жена Мирелэ
Бунимович Хаим и жена
Бунимович Хана с семьёй
Бунимович Цви с семьёй

Бунимович Самуил, жена Шейна, дети Двора, Мирьям утримович Рахиль с семьёй

В

Вайнер Моше, жена Рахиль, дочь Лия и сын Мордхай

Вайсборд Илия, жена Хася

Вайсборд Михал и жена

Вайсборд Моше и жена Хая

Вайсборд Хаим-Ицхок

Вайсборд Шимон и жена

Вайсборд Яков, жена Матка

Вайсборд Яков, жена Шейна-Рива, дочери Михля и Рейзл, сын Гейнах

Велвел Лейб

Видрович Иосиф-Хаим, жена Хая-Сара, дочь Гинда и сын Эфраим

Волкин Хаим (глава Ешивы), жена Бейля, дочки Дрейзл и ХаяЛеа

Волкович Малка и дочь Шуламит

Волкович Шмуел, жена Элька-Хая, сын Моше и дочь Сара

Г

Гальперин Арон, жена Хая-Соре и пятеро детей

Гарбер Моше (Моня)

Гарбер Яков, жена Броха и дочери

Гелер Меир и сын Арие-Лейб

Гельман Айзик, жена Матка, Дочери Хайка и Леа

Гельман Борух, жена Фейгл

Гельман Иоханан, жена Зелда

Гельман Итка

Гельман Ицхак, жена Хена, дети Элиягу, Хаим и Ривка

Гельман Мерка, её сын Хаим

Гельман Мордхай, жена Рейзл, сын Элиягу, дочки Хана и Фейгеле

Гельман Элта, её дети Рахил, Елиша и Михал

ГельманХаим-Цви

Гендельман Залман с семьёй

- Герцовски Зэв, жена Ривка-Мирьям, дочь Хая-Сора
- Гинсберг Сара-Ривка, дети Бейля, Леа-Мина, Маша, Ёсиф, Ицхак и Рувен
- Гирдин Арие-Лейб и жена Итка
- Гирдин Дов-Бер и жена
- Гирзон Авром-Бер и жена
- Гирзон Арие, жена Сара и дети
- Гирзон Арон и жена
- Гирзон Егошуа, жена Доба-Люба
- Гирзон Матисъягу, жена Хана-Ита, дочь Ривка
- Гирзон Меир, жена Юдит
- Гирзон Михаил-Гавриэл, жена Роха
- Гирзон Мордхай-Эли и жена
- Гирзон Хаим-Эли, жена Сара
- Гирзон Цви, жена Малка
- Гирзон Шрага-Файвэ, жена Батья (Башке)
- Гиркус Айзик жена Сара и дети
- Гиркус Айзик, жена Дрейзл и дочь Леа
- Гиркус Арие, жена Хая-Леа
- Гиркус Меир, жена Эстер-Малка, дочь Хая-Соре
- Глазер Нахман с семьёй
- Глас Гилел и жена Мейтка
- Глик Ицхак и жена Наоми-Хана
- Гликер и жена
- Глоб Блюма
- Глоб Двора
- Глоб Ципора
- Голдшмид Бен-Сион и жена
- Голдшмид Бен-Сион и жена
- Голдшмид Дов_Бер
- Голдшмид Мордхай
- Голдшмид Рувен, жена Этл, дочери Хана, Леа и сын Шмая
- Голдшмид Яков, жена Леа и дети

Головенчиц Элиэзер, жена Бела, дочери Миреле, Фрума и сын Нахум

Гордон Шолом, жена Хаша-Леа, дочери Фейгл и Рудл

Гориён Эстер и семья

Гориян Мина

Горович Аврам, жена Соня и дочь Ципа

Гохберг Нота, жена Шейна

Гуревич Аврам, жена Соня и дочь Ципа

Гуревич Арие-Лейб (Забреже) жена Леа

Гуревич Ехезкел, жена Леа

Гуревич Иона, жена Малка, сыновья Моше и Гершон

Гуревич Иосиф-Ицхак, жена Эша, дочери Батья и Груня

Д

Давидсон Дов-Бер с женой

Давидсон Ёшуа с женой

Давидсон Мэир с женой Сарой

Давидсон Цирл с детьми

Дворецки Яфим-Лейб

Дворецки Шмуэл и жена Эстер-Рохл

Деречински Копл

Деречински Мойше, жена Шейна

Деречински Хаим с женой

Деул Иосиф-Иче, жена Злата

Деул Лейбл, жена Бат-Шева

Деул Лейзер-Ицхок и дети Нудл, Цивья, Ривка

Деул Лейзер-Ицхок, жена Рахиль и дети

Дикенштейн Гдалия, жена Этл

Дикенштейн Натан

Дикенштейн Натан

Динерштейн Натан и его жена

Долгов Ицхок, его жена Лея

Долгов Ицхок, его жена Либа

Долгов Цви-Гирш, жена Сара-Итка, сын Яков-Ицхок
Долгов Яков, его жена Лея
Дубински Герцл, жена Соре-Гитл, дети Алтер и Иосэф
Дубински Исроел-Яков, жена Рохе-Этл
Дудман Исроэл-Зисл, жена Фейке, дети: Елиша, Хася, Ривка и Сара

Ж З И

Жельза Шломо, жена Фейга, сын Михаил
Залб Иосифб жена Мэрка, сыновья Виньямин и Исраиль
Залб Исраиль, жена Ента и семья
Зарин Иосиф и жена
Зельцер Цви и жена Соня
Злотник Залман и Сара
Иоршнер Хаим, жена Соня, дочери Миндл и рейзл
Ицкович Мордохай и жена его Рахиль
Ицхайкин Ривка и семья
Йофе Аврам, жена Сара-Бейля, сын и дочь

К

Каган Иосэф, жена михал, дочь Шошка, сыноиья Хаим и Эйзер
Каган Иосэф, жена Ривка, дочки Шошана, Сара, сын Эзра
Каган Ихиел и жена Сара
Каган Малка
Каган Мойше и жена Фрума-Рохл
Каган Нахум и жена Батия
Каган Ноах, жена Гинда, сын Ицхак и дочь Рохл
Каган Файвл и жена
Каган Хая
Каган Цви-Гирш, жена Рохл и дети
Каган Яков и жена
Каганович Арие-Лейб и жена
Каганович Залман, жена Леша, дочери Хана и Лифша

Каганович Ишая, жена Геня и дочь Лея
Каганович Меир и жена
Каганович Мордхай
Каганович Моше и жена Двойре-Енте
КагановичИосиф и жена Добрушка
Калман Алтер и жена Рейна
Калман Хонэ и жена Рохл
Калманович ара
Калманович Хаим-Йошуа и жена Рохл
Каменецки Арон и жена Хая-Сара
Канторович Довид-Иче и жена
Канторович Лейба
Канторович Янкев-Цодык и жена Нехама-Лея (Хамэ-лэйце)
Каплан Довид, жена, сестра Ривка, сын Лейбл
Каплан Исроэл, жена Гейна, дети Батия, Рохл и Ицхак
Каплан Эле и жена Рива-Лея
Карпучевски Ёсэф, жена Мера и дети
Кац Лапидус с семьёй
Кац Мина
Кац Рахиль
Кацин Ицхак, жена Хейна-Ёхке, сыновья Ёна, Лейбл и Мордхай
Кивилевич Арон…Рахил, Тейбл и Крейна
Кивилевич Шнеур, жена Рахиль (учительница) и сын Игал
Кисель Хаим и жена Рашл
Кисель Элтягу и жена Матке
Клейн Аврам и жена
Клейн Гинда
Клейн Леа
Клейн Хаим и жена Хася
Клейн Ханан и жена Рахиль
Клейн Шимон, жена Фэйга, дочь Шейна, сын Моше-Чнкев
Клейн Шломо и жена Фейга-Рива

Клейн Яков, жена и сын Шломо
Клейнборд Мэер и жена Роза
Клейнборд Цви и жена Ривка
Клик Малка, дочки Итка, Юдит и Рохл
Ковальски Яков, жена Хая
Коген Яков и жена Бейля
Козакевич Цирл и Дочери Хана, Сора, Батия и Тема (Забреже)
Козловски Ицхак и жена
Козловски Леа
Козловски Пинхас и жена Рохл
Костолицки с семьёй
Котик – Ребецин
Крамник Фрейдл и дочь Фейгл
Красный Алтер и жена Сара
Кушевицки Файва и жена
Л
Лавит Алтер, жена Сара, дочери Златка, Мина, сын Исроэл
Лавит Мордхай-Юда и жена
Лавит Реувэн и жена Сима
Лавит Шимон, жена Гайна и дочь Бейля
Лавит Шломо и жена
Лавит Элиэер и жена Рада
Лавит-Натанел
Лапидус жена его и сын
Левин (Шадал) Шмуэл-Давид, жена Матля, дети: Малка, Хаим, Мордхай и Шломо
Левин Аба и жена Реля
Левин Аврам-Ицхак и жена
Левин Берл, жена Хана, дети Бейлька, Хася, Мириям и Йосиф
Левин Шмуэл и семья
Левинсон Ёна-Гинда, дети Ривка, Зэв и Яков
Левинсон Йохе, её сын Вольфка

Лейбович Борух с семьёй

Лемельман Хаим и жена его

Либерман Аншл

Либерман Арие и жена его, Хана-Гитл

Либерман Шабтай и жена его, Эстер

Либерман Шломо-Аврам и жена его, Рахиль

Лидрович Элиягу, жена Сара-Рейза, дети: Хая-рохл, Алтер, далия, Хаим, айкл и Мордхай

Липовицки Берл и жена его Сара-Рашка

Липовицки Исроэл и жена его

Лифшиц Нахман, жена Эйделе, сын Арие

Лифшиц Яков (учитель), дочери Шошаналэ и Хаялэ

Лозер, его жена, их дочери: Зелда, Нешка, Рашка и другие

Лунген Моше, жена Сара, дети: Шмуэл, Хаим, Песя и Рахиль

Лунин (равин) Исроэл, жена Шейна, дети: Нехама, Цивия, Гершон и Цви

Лурие Либа и сын её Меир (Забреже)

М

Мазэ Гдалия, жена Гинда, дочь Цивия, сыновья Элиэзер, Пейсах, И Шломо

Малкин Цви-Гирш и жена его Хая-Рива (дед и Бабушка мои - М.Перельман)

Малкин Шмуел (Муля)

Марецки Мордхай, жена Гинда и их дети

Меирсон Борух-Мордхе

Меирсон Екутиел и его жена

Меирсон Ехиел и его жена

Меирсон Ехиел и его жена

Меирсон Ицхок-Яков и его жена

Меирсон Кейля и её семья

Меирсон Файва и его жена

Мельцер Алтер, жена и дети

Мельцер Арие-Лейб и жена

Мельцер Гитл (жена Зелика), дочь Дася, сын Моня

Мельцер Гитл (жена Лейзера)
Мельцер Егошуаб, жена Маня, дочери Батия, Цивия, Эстер-Мина
Мельцер Исраил и семья
Мельцер Мендл-Лэйзер и жена
Мельцер Мойше и жена Михал
Мельцер Моше, жена Рахиль, дети Сара-Ривка и Цви (Забреже)
Мельцер Фэйгл
Мельцер Ханан, жена Сара, дочь Хая- Дина
Мельцер Хася
Мельцер Шимон-Иче, жена Сара -Шейна, дочь Леа-Рейза, сын Доня
Мельцер Шломо, жена Гитл, дочь Шпринца и сын Шимшон
Мельцер Элиягу и жена Гитл менделевич Рувен, жена Билга
Мендес Файвуш и жена Марца
Милер Давид и жена Ривка
Мескин Арие и семья
Миликовски Иуда и жена Лея
Мишкин Ицхок и жена
Млот Элиягу и жена Соня
Мовшович Моше и жена Батия
Молот Аврам и жена Фейгл
Молот Рохе-Матка
Мордухович Исар-Лейб и его жена
Мордухович Моше-Арон и его жена
Н О П
Намиёт Цви-Иуда, жена Сара, дочки Елта, Дуба и Рахиль
Нарушевич Аврам и жена Хася
Нарушевич Брайна
Нарушевич Елиягу с семьей
Нарушевич Ицхак и жена Сара
Нарушевич Ицхак Ицхак
Ошерович Ошер и жена его

- Парецки Асна-Хая и сын Иосиф
- Парецки Шахна и жена Фрума
- Пекер Ицхак
- Перельман Иосиф(Мой отец - М.Перельман)
- Перельман Малка
- Перски Аврам и жена Ривка
- Перски Аврам, жена Рася, дочь Голда, сыновья Хаим и Файвл
- Перски Алтер и жена Двора
- Перски Бейля Гиша и Фэйгл
- Перски Гецл, жена Хая-Райца и дочь Ривэлэ
- Перски Доба и дочь Геня
- Перски Довид и дочь Итка
- Перски Зисл, жена Рахиль и дети
- Перски Зэв и жена Гнеся
- Перски Иосиф, жена Цирл и сын Эли-Залман
- Перски Исроэл, жена Батия, сыновья Аврам и Шмуэл
- Перски Исроэл, жена Хая, дочь Лифша, сыновья Иосэф и Ицхок
- Перски Ицхак и жена
- Перски Лейбл
- Перски Липа, жена Геня, дети Ривка, Лея, Рахиль и Илиягу
- Перски Мсир, жсна Гитл, дочери Элка, Хайка, Соня и Рахиль
- Перски Мина и дочь Ришка
- Перски Михаэл и семья
- Перски Михаил, жена и сын Цви
- Перски Моше, жена Хана-Эшка,дочери Либа и Ривка
- Перски Натанэл и жена
- Перски Нисн и жена Ривка
- Перски Ноах и семья
- Перски Оре - Яков и сын Арон
- Перски Ошер, жена Буня, дочь Соня и сын Рувелэ
- Перски Соня и жена Ривка
- Перски Ури, жена Рахиль, дочки Була и Гретл

- Перски Файва и жена
- Перски Файвл, жена Рая, дочь Мина и сын Моше
- Перски Хаим и жена Либа
- Перски Хаим Эли
- Перски Хаим-Зэв и жена Дуня
- Перски Хася-Леа
- Перски Шимон и жена
- Перски Шломо, жена Фрейдл, дочь Ривка:сыновья Давид, Хаим и Ицхак
- Перски Этл
- Перски Юда-Хаим, жена Мерка, дети: Блюма, Рейхл, Яков и Зэв
- Перски Юдиг и дочь Бейля
- Подберески Арие-Ёсэф, жена Люба и дочь Батья
- Подберески Арие-Лейб, и жена Сара
- Подберески Ирмиягу, и жена
- Подберески Мендл, жена и сын Натан
- Подберески Мордхай, жена Рахиль и семья
- Подберески Натан и жена Душка
- Подберески Шмуэл и жена Рашл
- Подольски Михаил, жена Рейзлб, дочь Хана и сын Шмуэл
- Позняк Хаим и семья
- Позняк Яков и жена Добрушка
- Поляк Арон
- Поляк Нехама
- Полячек Ехиел и семья
- Поташник Акива и жена Этл
- Поташник Дов-Бер и жена Хана
- Поташник Марияша
- Поташник Нехемия, жена Хана, сыновья Хаим и Исроэл
- Поташник Элиэзер и семья
- Поташник Эстер и её дети
- Правидла Михаил, жена Ривка, дочери Хана и Ципора (Забреже)

Р
Рабинович Исак с семьёй
Радушевски Песах, жена Соня, дочь Геня, сыновья Моше и Рувен
Райхер Зэв, жена Фрума, дети Шуля и Ицхак
Рапопорт Мойшл
Рапопорт Ёгошуа, жена Сара и сын Исар
Рапопорт Ехезкел и жена
Рапопорт Зэв, жена Эстер, дети Гитл и Ёсэф
Рапопорт Элиэзер, жена Лея, дети: Гитл, Зелда, Фрейдка, Ёсл и Мойше
Рахмилевич Иосэф, жена Ента, сыновья Аврам, Дов и Мэйшке
Резник Зегава с семьёй
Роговин Аврам-Иче, жена Шейна и дети
Роговин Аврам-Лейб, жена Геня, дети Хана, Ида и Юда
Роговин Арон, жена Сара
Роговин Гирш, жена Шейна и сын Нехемя
Роговин Гирш-Лейб и жена
Роговин Довид и жена
Роговин Довид, жена Эшка, дети Галя и Мотл
Роговин Ёсэф и жена Ривка
Роговин Ёханан, жена Ривка-Двора и дочь Батья
Роговин Ехезксл и жена Фрума
Роговин Залман и жена Тэма
Роговин Иоханан и жена Двоша-Элка
Роговин Исроэл, жена Сара, дочь Фрейдл и сын Яков
Роговин Ицхак, жена Хана и дочь Фэйгл
Роговин Ицхок жена Батия и дочь Хана
Роговин Копл и жена
Роговин Мойше и жена Рейзл
Роговин Мордхай и жена
Роговин Нехемя
Роговин Хаим и дочки Ципора, Ривка
Роговин Ханан, жена Бейля-Ривка

- Роговин Цви, жена Гитл и сын Иосэф
- Роговин Шевах и жена Голда
- Роговин Шмуэл, жена, Хаим и дочь Ривка
- Роговин Элиэзер
- Роговин Эли-Яков и жена
- Роговин Этл
- Роговин Юда, жена Хая, дочь Элка и сын Зээв
- Розен Хаим и жена Фрейдл
- Розенберг Шломо
- Розеншейн Моше, жена Телка и дочь Беба
- Розеншейн Рувен, жена Гитл и сын Иоэл
- Розеншейн Цви, жена Иохевед и дочь Эстер
- Рубин Элка и сын
- Рубинштейн Авром-Довид и жена Хана
- Рубинштейн Файтл и жена
- Рубинштейн Файтл, жена Тамара и сын Хаим-Ёсэф
- Рубинштейн Хая
- Рубинштейн Шолом-Лейб, жена Лифша, дочки Броха и голда
- Руденски Меир и жена
- Руденски Яков и жена Рода
- Рудницки Гитл, её дочки Мэрка и Хайка
- Рудня Рахиль
- Рудхамкин Яков-Шмуэл и жена Цивъя

С

- Савицки Ашер, жена Батья, дочь Ривка, сын Ихезкел
- Савицки Элта
- Сапир Нооми
- Сегалович Алтер, жена Двося и сын Аврам
- Сегалович Моше, жена Сара и дочь Соня
- Сегалович Хаим, жена Матка
- Симерницки Довид, жена Дуба

Симерницки Михаил, жена Малка

Симерницки Хаим и жена

Симерницки Яков, жена Сара-Эстер

Склют Аврам-Ицхок, жена Шифра

Склют Алтер, жена Фейга

Склют Берл и жена

Склют Гилел с семьей

Склют Гита-Рохл

Склют Двора-Эстер

Склют Егошуа, жена Добрушка

Склют Ерахмиел и семья

Склют Злата

Склют Ицхак, жена Баша-Элка, дети Рохл, Рейзл, Яков и Шимшон

Склют Ицхак-Гецл и жена

Склют Лейб, жена Рива-Ента

Склют Лейвик и жена

Склют Лея-Баше

Склют Михаил, жена Хана и дочь Муся

Склют Угошуа, жена Хана

Склют Хаим-Довид, жена Рохл

Склют Хаим-Шоул, жена Раше-Двоше

Склют Шимон и жена

Склют Шломо, жена Шимка, дочь Песя и сын Шмуэл

Склют Шмуэл-Ицхак и жена Фейга

Склют Элиягу, жена Фейга

Склют Яков и жена

Сосински Ицхак, жена Песя

Спектор Дов-Бер, жена Эстер и дочь Цирелэ

Стекольщик иуда, жена Митал

Столяр Ехиел

Столяр Копл

Т Ф Х Ц
Табахович Иосиф и жена Бела
Табахович Яков и жена Хая
Таф Арие, жена Муся, дочь Това, сын Исроэл
Тиюф Залман, жена Леа, сыновья Аврам и Исраэл
Файгеньойм Наум, жена Блюма, дети Гинда, Герцл, Иосэф, Шмуэл
Фарб Лейб и семья
Фарбер Элия, его жена, ,дочь Поля, сын Шимон
Фингер Иосэф, жена Сора, сыновья Яков, Эйзер, Бенче
Фингер Меир, жена Хана, дочь Блюма, сын Арие
Хадаш Ита
Хадаш Мэрка
Хадаш Шмая и жена Фрума
Хадаш Яков и жена Этл
Хайклин Авром и жена
Хайклин Захар
Хайклин Идл
Хайклин Маша
Хайклин Мордух, жена Шоша и их дети
Хайтин Исроэл-Довид, жена Рудл, дети Мина, Хаим, Игошуа, Ицхок и Нисан
Хлопски Меир, жена Мера, сыновья Яков и Шмуэл
Ходош Рувен (Ольшанский Раввин)
Царт Аврам (лекарь), жена Цивья, дочь Нехама, сыновья Арон и
Цви
Царт Гдалия, жена Эстер сыновьяАрон и Шмуэл
Царт Ёсэф, жена Рохл, сын Дов-Берл и дочь Песя
Царт Тамара и семья
Цимерман Липа и жена Рейзл-Фэйга
Цимерман Нотэ и семья
Ципин Виниямин, жена Рахиль и сын Пинхас
Цирульник Хаим и жена Хайка

Ш
Шакер Аврам и жена
Шалман и жена
Шалман и жена
Шалман Хаим и жена Эстер
Шалман Цви, жена Гитл, дети Мирьям, Роза, Айзик, Лейб и Шломо
Шамир Мордхай, жена Марияша, сыновья Йосиф, Шломо и третий сын
Шварц Яков-Давид и жена Ривка
Шварцберг Алта и дочь Райна
Шварцберг Эли-Ицхак, жена Двора-Элка и сын Лейбл
Шейбл Мендл, жена Сара, дочь Либа и сын Муля
Шейнюк Цви и жена Ривка
Шепетницки Егошуа и жена
Шепетницки Моше и жена Буня
Шимкин Юда и жена
Шимшелевич Алтер и жена Хая-Леа
Шимшелевич Мойше и жена Батья
Шимшелевич Мордхай и жена Двоша
Шиф Аврам-Моше, жена Рейзл, дочь Голда и сын Шимшон
Шкляр Сара
Шкляр Элиягу, жена Рохл дочьГолда,сыновья БенЦион,Хаим, Песах и Копл
Шлосберг Арье-Лейб, жена Ёха, дети Рахиль, Гроним, Иосиф и Исак
Шмеркович Егошуа, жена Ривка и сын Исроэл
Шмуклер Элиэзер и жена Этка
Шмуэл сын Шабтая-Моты и два его сына из Забреже
Шнайдер Арие-лейб, жена Эстер, дочь Хана-Мэрка и сын Зелиг
Шнайдер Давид
Шнайдер Мойше, жена Мирл и дочь Сара-Рохл
Шнайдер Хаим и жена Нехама
Шнайдер Цви, жена Цирл и дочь Мирьям
Шпаценер Исроэл и жена Феля

Шриро Гесл, жена Ривка, дочь Дрейзл и сын Шммуэл
Шриро Ицхак, жена Анетл и дочь Авигаил (Галя)
Шулевич Шмуэл, жена Рахиль, сыновья Эли и Мордхай
Шустер Цви и жена Йона
Шустер Яков и жена

Э   Ю   Я

Элияшкевич Гирш и жена его Маша
Элияшкевич Исроэл и жена его Лифша
Элияшкевич Цви, жена его Рохл и дети
Элияшкевич Шимон и жена его Ривка
Эпштейн Элия и жена Фрейдл
Юзефович Цви-Меир, жена Сима и дочь Элька
Язгур Давид и жена Элька
Язгур Мордхай, жена Соня-Бейля, сыновья Ишая и Хаим
Якобсон Фейга с семьёй
Якобсон Шмуэл с семьёй
Янкилевич Элта

Боже Всевышний Отомсти Невинную Кровь!

Memory to Volozhin Region
(Valozhyn, Belarus)

54°05' / 26°32'

Translation of *Pamiat-Volozhinski Rayon*

Published in Minsk, 1996

Acknowledgments:

Translator

Moshe Porat z"l

Our sincere appreciation to V. I. Malishevski, Regional Executive Committee Chairman and the Region Editorial Commission for the creation of the History-Documental "Pamiat" Book Chairman, for permission to put this material on the JewishGen web site.

This is a translation from: Pamiat-Volozhinski Rayon (Memory to Volozhin Region). Minsk "Mastatskaya Literatura," 1996. Litsenzia LV No 3, 220600 Republique Belarus, Minsk, 11 Masherov Avenue

"PAMIAT" - MEMORIAL to the Volozhin Region

(*Pamiat' means Memorial)

Translated from Belarus language by M. Porat
Edited by Judy Montel

The book describes the region's history and geography. The Volozhin region (*Rayon* in Russian, *Poviat* in Polish) covers some sixty kilometers from Bogdanovo eastward through Vishnievo, Volozhin to Rakov, and also forty kilometers from Losk southward through Volozhin, Piershay to Ivianietz.

In the region's southern part between Volozhin and Ivianietz, alongside the Islotsh river is the big expanse of the Volozhin and Nalibok forest *("Pushtsha")*.

Working hard on this strange, new literary Belarus-language, we could detect among the 450 pages some material about the regional Jewish communities, which populated this area and formed the major part of its urban inhabitants.

The written material is scarce and disproportional to the terrible mass murder that was committed on the Jewish population which was completely exterminated in the Volozhin region by the bestial invaders and by their ardent supporters.

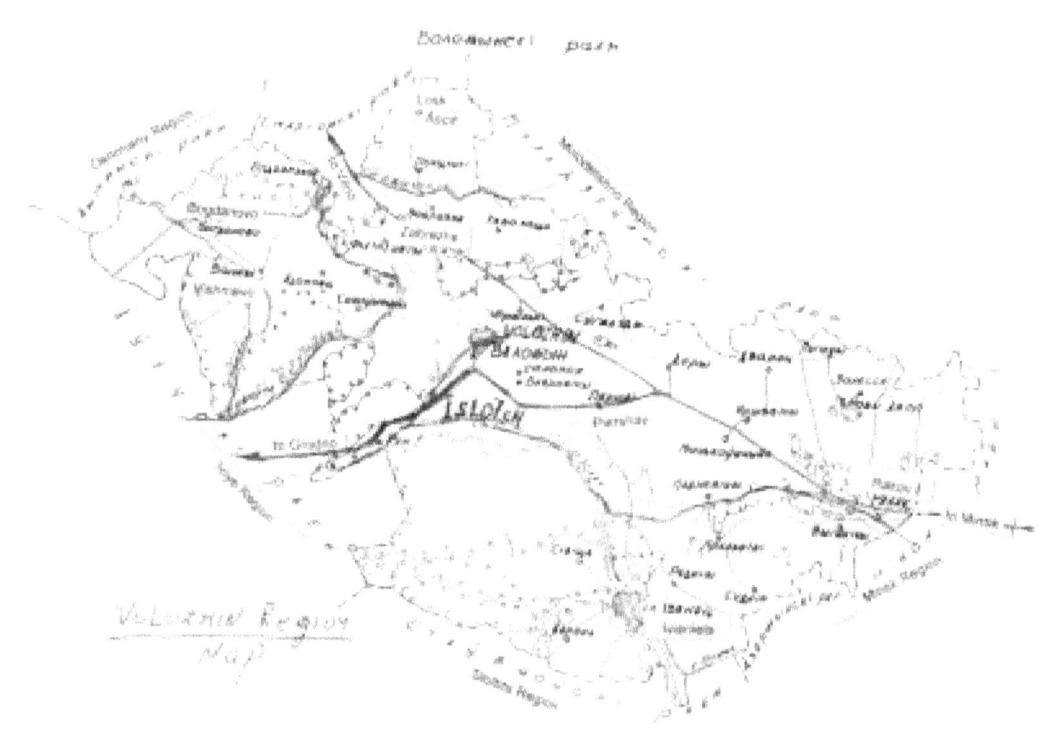

The Volozhin Region area

Islotsh – brook of the Berezina River, across a meadow in the Volozhin Forest.

New order in Vishnievo
By K. Pobal

{164}

A Red Army convoy approached Vishnievo on June 27, 1941. German aircraft bombed the convoy in the afternoon. The bombing had also set on fire seven houses on Volozhin Street. The bodies of the Red Army soldiers were buried in the Old Graves cemetery. The Germans invaded the town the same day. They established a Police center. Local people were appointed as policemen (*Politsay*) and commanders (*Komiendanty*). The policemen killed a group of Vishnievo people on their first day of operation.

Without delay they hung out written orders:

"Each Jew should put a yellow patch formed as a six pointed star (Star of David) on his breast and spine".

"Whoever shelters a Jew will be shot".

"Whoever gives bread to a Jew will be shot".

"Whoever shelters a Communist or a Soviet soldier will be shot".

The old (Polish) administrative partition was renewed. Vishnievo became a *Gmina* (Village authority) in the Volozhin *Poviat* (region), Vilna *Oblast'* (District). All inhabitants of the Gmina area were obliged to behave according to the local authorities' orders. The police imprisoned anyone who did not seem to be loyal to the German regime. **Only** an inhabitant of Polish or Belarus nationality could receive an *Ausswais*, a kind of identity card. Jews and other people had no right to carry it. Those whom they found without an *Ausswais* were shot or sent to forced labor in Germany.

The Germans with their assistants, the local "*Politsays*", established the Jewish Ghetto on the Krevo Street during the first days of occupation.

In M. Mikhaylashov's book "The Anger Storm", which was published in Minsk (1971), in the chapter "The Court Trial" on page 207 we read:

"In mid July 1942 we have gone to Volozhin town, where we shot some two thousand Jews – men, women, children. Grabe was the execution commander. In Volozhin I shot personally hundred twenty Jews. Later I arrived in the Vishnievo hamlet with our *Sondercommando* (Special Commando) unit. Here we executed one thousand five hundred Jews. The action commander was Grabe"

Today there is a memorial at the site of the execution. On it is written:

"In 1942 here were shot 2066 **Soviet** citizens".

Mr. Shimon Peres, the Israeli foreign minister visited Vishnievo in the summer of 1992. He looked for the tombs of his ancestors and visited also the big slaughter place of his relatives and friends who were so bestially annihilated in 1942. Peres was born in Vishnievo. He had gone to Israel before the war.

The destruction of Volozhin's Jews
By M. Batvinnik
{164}

We are taught by the documents from the Central archives of the Belarus Republic and from Yad Vashem in Jerusalem how the Volozhin ghetto was created and how the Volozhin Jews were destroyed during the German occupation. These documents are based on witnesses' testimonies.

In June 1941, a number of days after the Germans occupied the town, they assembled forty-five Jews and forced them to dig a pit. The pit diggers were shot where they stood. The wounded were buried alive.

The entire Jewish population was chased into the Ghetto, which had been fenced on the right shore of the Volozhinka alongside Dubinski Street.

In October 1941 the Germans assembled 220 people in the cinema building near the Polish military quarters. They were led ten by ten to the nearby sport-stadium. Here all of them were shot. After the war the local authorities raised a memorial, the statue of a woman, on which it is engraved in Russian: " **The German Fascists bestially killed here hundreds of Soviet citizens during the Fatherland War in the years 1941-1945"**

A German Sondercommando (Special Commando) unit on motorcars came from Vileyka in May 1942. They assembled 1500 men, women and children and killed them near the Volozhin graveyard. The murderers searched the ghetto for hidden Jews. They shot at sight every one that was found. The bodies were piled and set on fire, to hide and to camouflage the horrible crime.

In August 1942 the murderers assembled 300 Jews on the left shore of the Volozhinka beneath the Shapoval road into a stall, which prior to it served as a place for flax drying. They set fire on the building and the victims were burnt - most of them alive.

The last Volozhin Jews were murdered in summer 1943.

The destruction of Rakov Jews

Report written in August 1945

{165}

The committee head: Svitko I.T. - Committee members: Yatskaviets I.D., Kirzov P.M., Nissinov M.F., Garshkov, Lavrishkov, Batalin submitted this report about the crimes done by the Fascist occupants in the Radushkovits Region.

Witnesses: Rutkovska Leonida B., Gerasimovitsh, Grinholtz Vosip, Isakovitzh, Grinholtz Aron, Davidovitsh.

The witnesses reported that on June 14, 1942, the Germans had assembled forty-five Jews in Rakov, as if to work. They were led to Baruzints two kilometers from Rakov. The Germans gave them shovels and ordered to dig pits. After the pits were ready, the Germans placed the forty-five captives facing the pits and shot them with machine guns.

The same year on August 29, the Germans assembled all the Rakov-Ghetto Jews, forced them to dig pits, afterwards they counted hundred and five persons and ordered them to lie in those pits. All of them were shot at the gendarme Drobel's command.

The Jews who survived were led to Rakov. On the way they were ordered to sing and to dance. Satisfied by the concert, the murderers forced all the captives to lie down with their faces to the soil. At the gendarme Ferverg's command they were shot, each according to the killers' choice. One of the bandits cut the physician's head off with his axe because he was not satisfied with the victim's song. Also in this Action, one hundred and five persons were killed.

On, February 4, 1942, the *Politsay* commander Mikhal Ziankevitsh ordered all the Jews to assemble on the synagogue courtyard with their belongings for departure to Minsk. When the Jews assembled they were ordered to put all the valuables aside and to enter the synagogue. Some of them tried to go back, but they were beaten to death with rifle shafts. Crying children were pierced by rifle bayonets and thrown over the crowded heads. The synagogue doors and windows were blocked with nailed planks. The murderers spilled gasoline on the walls and set the building on fire. Nine hundred twenty eight Jews were burnt to death on that winter day in the Rakov synagogue.

Memories from Vishnievo Ghetto:

By Ema Mikhaylovna Murtshanka - Voroniezh (Russia)

{166}

"I witnessed and saw with my own eyes the bestial deeds of the Fascist murderers and their local cooperators in the Vishnievo Ghetto. Yes, so it was: Together with my family, friends and relatives, also with other wretched Jewish Vishnievo inhabitants, at the age of seventeen I was flung by the fascists and their assistants - local traitors - into the Vishnievo detention Ghetto-camp. Here, during 1941-42, I experienced all kinds of abuse and horrible hell treatment from the fascists and their murderous local helpers.

They enclosed the entire Vishnievo-Jewish population into the *Tserkov* (Russian church). All of them were ordered to lie on the floor and were left in this position for the whole day without any water or food. In the evening, severely guarded they were released, each one to his home to pick up the most needed things. Immediately afterwards the Jews were required to reassemble in the Krevo Street. When we arrived, we saw that a high fence with barbed wire encircled Krevo Street.

Thus the Vishnievo Concentration Ghetto Camp was created, in which were detained all the 1600 Vishnievo Jews. From this day began our painful life inside the fascists' inhuman detention camp. One thousand six hundred people had to live in a small lane. In each tiny room were crowded three or four families including men, women, elderly, sick people and children.

During the warm summer days the Ghetto dwellers would manage to live in some way, exchanging for food the objects they had managed to grab and take into the ghetto.

But when the cold arrived, the miserable inhabitants lacked food and firewood. The sole salvation was in the daily trip to work of the ghetto youngsters. They were led into the forest to prepare firewood, or to the Bogdanovo rail station. On the way they would exchange some objects, which we had still succeeded in keeping by some miracle. The *Politsays* stole the most valuable objects.

The returning workers succeeded in bringing a bundle of twigs, a bottle of milk or few potatoes. But all these goods had to be hidden in sophisticated ways. The most joyful event for the Ghetto guardians was to deprive the "smuggler" of his sprinkle of twigs at the camp gates. And when the poor, tired and terrified Ghetto worker would be able to breath with relief hoping to bring a bit of food to his little sister or to supply some heating for his old and sick grandmother, suddenly they appeared, the *Politsays* and searched him maliciously and thoroughly. When the prohibited matter had been found they took it away and beat its possessor bestially. Then they let him go home bleeding and lacerated with an empty bundle to be met empty handed by his impatiently waiting, cold and hungry relatives.

But even more frustrating was to see our previous colleagues and schoolmates among the cruel inhuman beasts, the local *Politsays* .

On our way to work we were permitted to go upon the road only. The use of sidewalks by a Jew was forbidden. We were obliged to wear on the chest the yellow-blue Star of David patch. But more than cold and hunger we feared the abuse and maltreatment of the Germans and their assistants. In particular, the children and youngsters feared it.

We were very afraid of the *Politsay* Yourovitsh and the *Komiendant* (commander) Pashkovski. I will never forget their evil faces and their cruel tortures. Until now I see in my bad dreams their bestial faces.

The *Politsays* had a dreadful hobby. They used to break into the ghetto horse riding and chasing the detained Jews from the dwellings onto the street, all of them, men and women, old and young, children and babies. They used to beat the chased Jews with horsewhips until unconsciousness. When satisfied, they looked for a baby in his mothers' hands. The child had been pierced with a rifle-mounted bayonet; the small body was lifted and then flung head down, on the stones. When the mother went crazy, they shot her in cold blood. The local murderers witnessed all that. They laughed joyfully. The bandits used to take photos of the horrible scenes.

Every day the camp awaited its liquidation. The Germans did not conceal it. The imprisoned could not sleep. Awaiting the worst, they listened to each rustle and to the wild songs and vociferations of the oppressors. Once when we were at work in Bogdanovo, Yelena Gurevitsh my friend and I, we chose a convenient moment, we ran in the forest and finally joined the Tshapayev Partisan unit.

The Vishnievo ghetto concentration camp was liquidated in August 1942. The murderers encircled the Ghetto and chased all the Jews into an empty barn at the end of Krevo Street. The shooting began immediately. Gasoline was spilled over the barn and the survivors with the dead were burnt together.

At my return in Vishnievo after the victory I found a big hill at the site of the barn. All of it was filled with black burnt human bones. Above the hill stood a horrible smell of ashes. And that was all that remained of my family, my close friends and of all of Vishnievo's Jews. After war only 10 to 15 persons of the entire Vishnievo Jewish population survived. And now there are only the two of us alive: Gurevitsh Yelena Israilovna who lives in Perm and me. "

Vishnievo Slaughter witnesses

Told by Gelanovo & vicinity peasants- inscribed by K. Pobal

{167}

Dubitski Petr Yosifovitsh (born 1914) and his wife Dubitska Stefanida Ludvikovna (born 1919) survived the German occupation inside Vishnievo. They witnessed the mass destruction of the Vishnievo Jewry. They said that the first conducted to death were the physician Doctor Padzelver, his wife the midwife and their beautiful daughter. The executioners shot at anyone who tried to run away.

Mikhaylovska Felitziya Yosifovna (born 1919) saw a pretty, five-year-old Jewish girl running away with her own eyes. The local Policemen shot at her once then a second time and the girl fell. At first groups of 20-30 Jews were led to execution under guard. Afterwards they were transported on cars. By evening all the Jews had been shot. Fumes of burned human bodies spread through the surrounding towns.

Kavetska Mariya Ivanovna (born 1927) from Vidkaushtshina hamlet remembers how the blameless Jews were shot in Gelanovo in the building that belonged to Mr. Zara. Many ran into the high rye fields. The enemy bullets reached them also in the fields. The executioners mobilized men with horses and carts in the neighboring hamlets to heap the dead bodies in a pile and to burn them. The wind blew from the east and the smell reached until Bogdanovo. The bodies burned during an entire week.

Vikentiy Matsveyitsh Gerassimovitsh from Gelanovo hamlet told us:

"It happened on Sunday in a warm summer day. The captive "Inhabitants", the genocide victims, crowded inside the ghetto fences. Policemen guarded the gates. The situation seemed to be normal. Nothing in Vishnievo indicated the oncoming disaster. Unfamiliar Germans arrived in cars at the ghetto territory. The Jewish captives had been formed into ranks, men, and women with children and old people. The Vishnievo inhabitants worried. "What is going on?" whispered the women. Nobody was permitted to approach the ghetto. After a little while some twenty to thirty people together with their families were separated from the mass of Jews. They were chased to the end of Krevo Street to Gelanovo.

The building owner, Ivan Zara was sent away. The building was encircled by machine guns. Doctor Padzelver, the most respected person in Vishnievo, with his spouse and daughter were at the head of the victims conveyed to Gelanovo.

From the Ghetto broke out screams "The German gunmen are leading the captives to death". Women from Gelanovo hamlet begged the German commander: "Pan! Let the doctor go. He did not any evil, not to us and not to you. This man saved people from death with his work. Save him, do not destroy him!"

The German refused: "He did not heal you, he infected and contaminated you". Doctor Padzelver resembled a professor. He used to heal people from various maladies. He performed surgery. The doctor drove his own car and he taught the children to speak Polish.

Five Germans stood at the building. The Jews were conducted inside five by five and here they were shot. In the house was a cellar, into which the victims were thrown dead, wounded and alive. After the first group was murdered the Germans changed the method. They ceased to chase the Jews by foot; instead they transferred the victims by cars. When they got down, the Jews were conducted five by five into the building. They were forced to climb on the bodies and were shot. Some of them were killed. Some of them were left alive among the dead bodies. By the evening the Vishnievo Jews were all executed. The Guards and their local assistants spilled gasoline on the building and set it on fire. Some survivors began to run from the building. The guards shot them. People from neighboring hamlets saw some Jews who succeeded in running away."

The Town Volozhin Martyrs of Hitler's terror

Transliterated from Cyrillic to Latin characters by M. Porat

1	Alperovitsh Haya Alperovitsh Haya, daughter of Shloyma
2	Alperovitsh Hayim, son of Shloyma
3	Alperovitsh Shloyma
4	Berman Dobka
5	Berman Leyba
6	Berman Mula, son of Leyba
7	Berman Rykla
8	Berman Feyga, daughter of Leyba
9	Berman Khaya, daughter of Leyba
10	Berman Shmuel
11	Berman Shoola
12	Berman Elka
13	Brudno Vula, son of Hayim, born: 1930
14	Brudno Mihael, son of Hayim, born: 1928

Prominent but humble woman Mrs. Beyla, daughter of Rabbi Alter
Virtuous but simple man Mr. Fayvush Shraga, son of Rabbi Naftali Herz
MEYIRSON
Peace to Their Soul

(The above text is translated from Hebrew)

15	Brudno Pesia daughter of Hayim born: 1901
16	Brudno Hayim son of Ele born: 1906
17	Bunimovitsh Vulf

18	Bunimovitsh Danie
19	Bunimovitsh Mikhla
20	Bunimovitsh Pinkus
21	Bunimovitsh Roza daughter of Pinkus born: 1890
22	Girzen Beyla daughter of Meyer born: 1932
23	Girzen Genia daughter of Itsek born: 1910
24	Girzen Itsl daughter of Mayer born: 1935
25	Girzen Meyer son of Ausey born: 1890
26	Girzen Yudess daughter of Berka born: 1899

A verse placed inside the martyrs list
(Translated from Belarus)

On the Volozhin Tombs

Upon the old tombs, not a tree.
From afar only ruins are visible.

Not a shadow upon them
Burdensome is the fate of the buried there.

A white horse, two goats and three lambs
on the scarce autumn pasture.

Like the Bible sheep, horse and goat alike,
were driven here by Shagal
to reheat the cold dungeon
to pinch the grass growing from the ashes.

The Jews of Volozhin,
Beneath the menorah and King David's Star
Buried under broken gravestones.
Would they rest in Peace!

27	Girzon Abram son of Girsh
28	Girzon Girsh, son of Mikhl
29	Girzon Malka

30	Girzon Pola, daughter of Hayim, born: 1923
31	Girzon Sora, daughter of Hersh, born: 1890
32	Girzon Hayim, son of Leyba, born: 1890
33	Girzon Yankel, son of Hayim, born: 1928
34	Gishman Hanna, daughter of Ivan
35	Gurevitsh Sayka daughter of Oysel born: 1904
36	Zissel Zhanna
37	Kovalski Raya
38	Kovalski Yudoshka
39	Kovalski Yanina
40	Kaganovitsh Dobrushka
41	Kaganovitsh Yosif
42	Kaganovitsh Sonia, daughter of Yosif
43	Kivilevitsh Shneyer, son of Mikhal, born: 1910
44	Kirzen Arye, son of Avcey, born: 1893
45	Lipovitski Rakhela, daughter of Berka, born: 1939
46	Lipovitski Sareksa, daughter of Itska, born: 1897
47	Lipovitski Sora, daughter of Berka, born: 1922
48	Lipovitski Berka, son of Efrayim, born: 1900
49	Lipovitski Yeroya, son of Berka, born: 1918
50	Lipovitski Lazar, son of Berka, born: 1928
51	Lunin Israel, son of Mora, born: 1890
52	Lunin Nakhama, daughter of Israel, born: 1915

52 names of Jews murdered in Volozhin, names recalled by some old Belarus peasants. 52 names of about 3000 killed. See the list of Volozhin Kdoshim to see a large number of the names.

Zabrezhe - Jewish Martyrs

Murdered by the Nazi Germans & local bandits
Rewritten in English letters by M. Porat

{261-2}

A	B	C	D	E	F	G	H	I	J	K	L	M
N	O	P	Q	R	S	T	U	V	W	X	Y	Z

No.	Family name	First name	Son/daughter	Father	Birth-year
1	Batsvinnik	Hayim	son	Vigdor	1890
2	Batsvinnik	Hertz	son	Vigdor	1895
3	Batsvinnik	Hertz	son	Moyshe	1941
4	Batsvinnik	Kalman	son	Vigdor	1887
5	Batsvinnik	Leyb	son	Hayim	1915
6	Batsvinnik	Liba	daughter	Ivav	1887
7	Batsvinnik	Misha	son	Vigdor	1890
8	Batsvinnik	Moyshe	son	Hertz	1910
9	Batsvinnik	Rakhel	daughter	Hersh	1918
10	Batsvinnik	Sonia	daughter	Kogan	1920
11	Berkovitsh	Issak	son	Unknown	1906
12	Berkovitsh	Mira	daughter	Issak	1935
13	Berkovitsh	Sora	son	Unknown	1908
14	Berman	Abram	son	Hayim	1895
15	Berman	Baris	son	Abrm	1930

16	Berman	Boruh	son	Hayim	1906
17	Berman	Broha	daughter	Hirsh	1875
18	Berman	Fania	daughter	Abram	1900
19	Berman	Gdaliya	son	Yosif	1925
20	Berman	Hayim	son	Shmuel	1860
21	Berman	Henia	daughter	Yosif	1928
22	Berman	Henia	daughter	Hayim	1932
23	Berman	Hirsh	son	Leyba	1932
24	Berman	Israel	son	Khone	1936
25	Berman	Izia	son	Yosel	1932
26	Berman	Leya	daughter	Leyba	1936
27	Berman	Leyba	son	Shymon	1900
28	Berman	Malka	daughter	Shymon	1908
29	Berman	Mikhla	Daug	Hayim	1900
30	Berman	Moysha	son	Hayim	1908
31	Berman	Moysha	son	Raphael	1901
32	Berman	Nota	son	Ausiey	1926
33	Berman	Riva	daughter	Abram	1928
34	Berman	Riva	daughter	Ausiey	1928
35	Berman	Sonia	daughter	Israil	1895
36	Berman	Yosl	son	Isak	1890
37	Berman	Zeharia	son	Fayvl	1830(?)

38	Bunimovitsh	Abram	son	Tamosh	1860
39	Bunimovitsh	Leya	daughter	Isak	1865
40	Daski	Yankl	son	Borukh	1904
41	Davidson	Berka	son	Shmuel	1938
42	Davidson	Moyshe	son	Hertz	1930
43	Davidson	Shmuel	son	Iot	1905
44	Davidson	Yosl	son	Shmuel	1940
45	German	Isroel	son	Sender	1939
46	German	Kasriel	son	Sender	1941
47	German	Riva	daughter	Hertz	1908
48	German	Sender	son	Yakov	1908
49	Gintzburg	Beyla	daughter	Aron	1918
50	Gintzburg	Leya	daughter	Aron	1908
51	Gintzburg	Masha	daughter	Aron	1912
52	Gintzburg	Ruvin	son	Aron	1910
53	Gintzburg	Sora	daughter	Mordkhe	1882
54	Gintzburg	Yosl	son	Aron	1904
55	Gurevitsh	Basia	daughter	Yosl	1919
56	Gurevitsh	Esia	daughter	Isak	1890
57	Gurevitsh	Gershon	son	Fayvl	1925
58	Gurevitsh	Grunia	daughter	Yosl	1917
59	Gurevitsh	Hofka	daughter	Fayvl	1938

60	Gurevitsh	Leyba	son	Yosl	1915
61	Gurevitsh	Malka	son	Moyshe	1900
62	Gurevitsh	Moyshe	son	Fayvl	1928
63	Gurevitsh	Yohka	daughter	Hirsh	1900
64	Gurevitsh	Yosl	son	Gershon	1890
65	Halperin	David	son	Hirsh	1865
66	Halperin	Sora	daughter	Shmit	1925
67	Kavetski	Alena			1908
68	Kazakevitsh	Mikhla	daughter	Abram	1922
69	Kazakevitsh	Tzima	daughter	Abram	1920
70	Kazakevitsh	Tzipa	daughter	Isak	1890
71	Kivelevitsh	Rakhila	daughter	Shloyma	1909
72	Kivelevitsh	Samueel	daughter	Shaye	1932
73	Kuzitzki	Yosif	son		1904
74	Levin	Hayim	son	Samueel	1906
75	Levin	Matzia	daughter	Abram	1892
76	Levin	Mota	son	Samueel	1910
77	Levin	Samueel	son	Hayim	1890
78	Levin	Shloyma	son	Samueel	1912
79	Liberman	Maryasha	daughter	Leyba	1934
80	Looriya	Liba	daughter	Mendl	1895
81	Looriya	Meyer	son	Hayim	1920

82	Meltser	Ausiey	son	Hirsh	1903
83	Meltser	Basia	daughter	Ausiey	1930
84	Meltser	Hirsh	son	Moysha	1932
85	Meltser	Mania	daughter	Samueel	1904
86	Meltser	Minia	daughter	Ausiey	1936
87	Meltser	Moysha	son	Hirsh	1906
88	Meltser	Rakhila	daughter	Moysha	1909
89	Meltser	Sora	daughter	Moysha	1909
90	Perski	Doba	daughter	Mendl	1900
91	Perski	Fayve	son	Hayim	1907
92	Perski	Gita	daughter	Fayve	1938
93	Perski	Khone	son	Kalman	1935
94	Perski	Mina	daughter	Kalman	1932
95	Perski	Mina	daughter	Fayve	1935
96	Perski	Osher	son	Itzke	1900
97	Perski	Raya	daughter	Moyshe	1909
98	Perski	Ryva	daughter	Shloyme	1934
99	Pravidla	Fania	daughter	Mikhael	1922
100	Pravidla	Hana	daughter	Mikhael	1920
101	Pravidla	Mihl	daughter	Yosl	1870
102	Pravidla	Ryva	daughter	Hirsh	1870
103	Rogovin	Henia	daughter	Samueel	1923

104	Rogovin	Moyshe	son	Samueel	1921
105	Rogovin	Ryva	daughter	Samueel	1928
106	Rogovin	Sonia	daughter	Moyshe	1890
107	Rybko	Minia	daughter	Borukh	1860
108	Shapira	Abram	son	Ayzik	1906
109	Shapira	Leyzer	son	Ayzik	1912
110	Shapira	Mina	son	Itska	1890
111	Shapira	Voolf	son	Ayzik	1914
112	Shmit	Esterka	daughter	Hirsh	1906
113	Shmit	Leyba	son	Leyba	1941
114	Shmit	Leyba	son	Moyshe	1906
115	Shmit	Masha	daughter	Leyba	1940
116	Sklut	Haya	daughter	Hayim	1938
117	Sklut	Sima	daughter	Hayim	1939
118	Sklut	Sora	daughter	Leybe	1906
119	Sondrak	Refoel	son	Isroel	1885
120	Sondrak	Rykla	daughter	Isroel	1890
121	Tzekinski	Hava	daughter	Hertz	1914
122	Tzekinski	Tolet	son	Hayim	1912
123	Vrubel	Basia	daughter	Hirsh	1938
124	Vrubel	Iris	son	Isak	1917
125	Vrubel	Leyba	son	Hirsh	1940

126	Vrubel	Malka	daughter	Shmuel	1913
127	Yukhis	Berka	son	Lyzer	1930
128	Yukhis	Leyba	son	Leyzer	1928
129	Yukhis	Liba	daughter	Hatzkl	1900

NAME INDEX For Volume II

A

Abramovitsh, 133
Abt, 201, 202
Agnon, 122
Aison, 149
Aleksandrow, 197
Alperovich, 66, 196, 264
Alperovitsh, 316
Alpert, 66
Altman, 66, 284
Amalek, 7
Antka, 193
Askind, 66
Avisar, 89
Avram, 66
Azbel, 12

B

Badoglio, 58
Baksht, 66, 123, 185, 197, 198, 199, 200
Bakshter, 54
Bakst, 149, 198
Banovitsh, 146, 147
Baran, 27
Baranski, 153
Bar-Ilan, 85, 86, 87, 88, 90, 92, 94, 106, 107, 146, 203
Baskin, 66
Baskind, 66
Basuk, 66
Batalin, 313
Batsvinnik, 320
Batvinnik, 312
Baydes, 66
Baykalski, 282
Begin, 41
Beikilin, 154
Beker, 66
Ben-Nachum, 115, 123, 124
Bennet, 149
Benovitz, 149
Ben-Sasson, 97, 114, 120, 123, 124, 203, 205
Berger, 66, 203
Bergman, 66
Berkman, 67, 195
Berkovich, 13, 18, 67
Berkovitsh, 320
Berkowitz, 21, 135, 161, 162, 190
Berlin, 86, 90, 143, 146, 150, 203
Berman, 13, 24, 27, 28, 30, 67, 96, 115, 123, 126, 127, 135, 142, 149, 152, 153, 158, 159, 160, 161, 188, 189, 190, 203, 204, 205, 211, 271, 316, 320, 321
Bernstein, 48, 67, 131
Bialik, 3, 52, 65, 90, 95, 103, 114, 125, 128, 212
Bialovski, 67
Biekalski, 12
Bielokortser, 282
Bielonovich, 5
Bloch, 202
Bloh, 67
Bloom, 139, 149
Bomrash, 187
Bonder, 138, 139, 149
Borohovich, 67
Botvinik, 67, 68
Botwinik, 99, 200
Bran, 88
Braun, 59, 60
Bren, 68
Brener, 174
Brodna, 8
Brodsky, 150
Brookman, 138, 139, 147
Brudna, 29, 159
Brudno, 68, 264, 316, 317
Bulava, 5, 264
Bumrash, 68
Bunim, 97, 98, 126, 127, 142, 148, 150
Bunimovich, 68, 97, 98, 99, 174, 201
Bunimovitsh, 146, 147, 249, 317, 318, 322
Bunimovitz, 144
Bunimowitz, 150, 152, 199
Burack, 146
Butrimovich, 68

C

Camhi, 232
Chadash, 8, 55
Chafetz, 144
Chaiklin, 156
Chait, 181
Charlip, 145
Chayat, 8, 55
Cheiklin, 165, 166
Churchill, 57, 58
Churgin, 85, 86, 87, 88
Citrin, 193
Cohen, 149
Cooper, 286
Cuker, 244
Cutler, 148
Cytryn, 123

D

Dameshek, 145
Daski, 322
Davidovitsh, 313
Davidson, 68, 322
Deitsh, 226
der Balegole (coachman), 44
Der Raznoshtshik (postman), 44
der Shnayder (the tailor), 44
Derechinski, 68, 69, 205, 283
Deul, 69
Dickens, 286
Dikenstein, 69
Dinerstein, 69
Dniszewdski, 33
Dodman, 55
Dolgov, 21, 69
Dönitz, 59
Drachinsky, 97
Dreyfuss, 288
Drobel, 313
Drotvitski, 9
Dubinski, 4, 13, 21, 69
Dubitska, 315
Dubitski, 315
Dudman, 69
Dumas, 286
Dunie, 54
Durkopf, 280

Dvoretski, 69
Dwik, 123, 193
Dyumin, 46
Dzik, 4

E

Eidelman, 178, 232
Eisenhower, 59
Eli the Locksmith, 40
Eliaskevitch, 55
Elishkevich, 4
Elishkovich, 178
Elishkovitz, 178
Eliyashkevitsh, 54
Elyashkevits, 69
Epstein, 69, 172
Eshlagi, 123, 214

F

Faminski, 154
Farber, 69
Faygenboym, 69
Feigenbaum, 55, 184, 185
Feivish, 101, 102
Ferverg, 313
Finger, 69, 154, 195, 264, 282, 284
Frank, 59
Frankel, 114
Frick, 59
Fried, 193
Friedeburg, 59
Frishman Gabbay, 1
Funk, 59

G

Gabčík, 58
Gabirol, 65
Gafanovich, 12
Galperin, 153
Ganz, 40
Garber, 4, 8, 70, 153, 154, 241, 263, 269, 278, 279, 288
Garellick, 146
Garshkov, 313
Gelbovich, 5
Gelman, 55, 70, 163
Genadi, 48

Gerasimovitsh, 313
German, 322
Gertsovski, 70
Ginsberg, 70, 149
Gintzburg, 322
Girkes, 40
Girkus, 27, 70
Girzen, 318
Girzon, 70, 180, 318, 319
Gishman, 319
Glas, 70
Glik, 55, 71
Gliker, 4
Glob, 71
Glücks, 57
Goldshmid, 41, 71
Golobenchich, 49, 50, 96
Golobnechitz, 174
Golovenchits, 71
Golub, 71
Golubenchich, 5
Golubnochich, 183, 184
Gordin, 71
Gordon, 21, 71, 149
Goren, 261
Göring, 58, 59
Goryan, 71
Gottleib, 202
Grabe, 35, 312
Grazh, 261
Grazovski, 97, 98
Greenberg, 187
Grinholtz, 313
Gurevitsh, 315, 319, 322, 323
Gurvich, 27, 71, 189
Gurwitz, 135
Gutterman, 149
Guzman, 169

H

Hadash, 71, 155
HaLevi, 66
Halevy, 144
Halperin, 229, 323
Hame-Leytshes, 284
Harisson, 146
Harrison, 149
Hayat, 12

Hayklin, 71
Haytin, 71
Heicklen, 139
Heicklin, 138, 149
Heiklin, 147
Heine, 3
Helckin, 147
Heler, 71
Heller, 256, 278, 281
Henkind, 146
Herbst, 149
Herzog, 87, 94
Hess, 33, 34, 35, 37, 38, 57, 59, 255
Heydrich, 58
Himmler, 59
Hitler, 22, 25, 57, 58, 59, 60, 96, 134, 264, 277, 316
Hlopski, 71
Hochman, 55, 187
Hohberg, 72
Horbatchevki, 52
Horovitz, 72
Höss, 57
Hurvitz, 144
Hutman, 189
Hutner, 201

I

Icha Tana der wasser treger, 152
Immerglick, 91
Isakovitzh, 313
Itshes, 284
Itskhaykin, 277
Itskhok, 270, 271
Izkovits, 72

J

Jablons, 125, 127, 138, 139, 141, 144, 146, 147, 148, 149, 152
Jack London, 286
Jezierski, 9
Jodl, 59
Josefowitz, 168, 169, 192, 193

K

Kadirka, 257
Kadirko, 38
Kadrov, 34

Kagan, 4, 9, 11, 16, 17, 29, 38, 41, 42, 43, 47, 54, 55, 72, 95, 96, 104, 186, 189
Kaganovich, 4, 48, 52, 72
Kaganovitsh, 319
Kahana, 114, 120
Kahanovich, 72, 207
Kahanowitz, 167
Kalman, 72
Kalmanovich, 72
Kamenetski, 4
Kamenietzki, 155
Kaminer, 165, 207, 217
Kaminietski, 72
Kantorovich, 72
Kaplan, 72, 73, 220, 221, 222
Karpuchevski, 73
Kasko, 285
Katovitz, 52
Kats, 73
Katsin, 73
Katznelson, 3, 65
Kavetska, 315
Kavetski, 323
Kazakevitsh, 323
Keitel, 59
Kelly, 149
Khadash, 6, 7
Kirshner, 139, 142, 147, 148, 149
Kirzen, 319
Kirzov, 313
Kisiel, 73
Kivelevitch, 22
Kivelevitsh, 323
Kivilevich, 4, 9, 12, 39, 73
Kivilevitch, 188, 189
Kivilevitsh, 282, 319
Kivilovich, 218
Kiwilowitz, 135
Klatzko, 145
Klein, 147, 155
Kleinbord, 28, 189, 219
Klenbord, 55
Kletzkin, 60
Kleyn, 73, 264
Kleynbord, 73
Klik, 73
Kohen, 73
Konopnicki, 289

Kook, 128, 150
Kopler, 91
Kornberg, 147
Kotik, 73
Kotler, 64, 125, 127, 142, 152, 163, 164
Kovalski, 4, 73, 319
Kowalski, 10, 11
Kozakevich, 73
Kozlovski, 73
Kramnick, 96
Kramnik, 41, 73, 190, 255
Krasny, 73
Kronenberg, 139, 147
Kubiš, 58
Kuchevitski, 74
Kuperman, 99
Kushke, 5, 29
Kuzitzki, 323

L

Lamleman, 74
Langbard, 96, 98, 100, 101, 102, 105
Langbord, 41
Lapidot, 74
Lau, 129
Lavit, 4, 28, 29, 41, 54, 74, 99, 103, 115, 123, 124, 135, 153, 155, 156, 169, 170, 171, 172, 244
Lavrishkov, 313
Lazarus, 143
Lechi, 55, 185
Leoni, 1, 57, 63, 85, 95, 113, 115, 124, 135, 136
Leveiner, 154
Leviatan, 55
Levichki, 189
Levin, 74, 195, 323
Levinson, 74, 123, 172, 173
Levitan, 195
Levitt, 96
Levitzki, 208
Levitzky, 123
Levy, 144
Liberman, 15, 41, 74, 174, 323
Lidrovich, 74
Lidski, 133
Lieberman, 258
Lifshits, 12, 18, 19, 20, 74
Lifshitz, 282
Liker, 74

Lilienberg, 280
Lipovetski, 74
Lipovitski, 319
Lipshitz, 175, 176, 188
Lipshitz-Gapanovich, 177
Lipsitz, 95
Lonim, 155, 156
Looriya, 323
Lop, 12
Lungen, 74, 183, 184
Lungen-Leber, 284
Lunin, 4, 6, 7, 9, 15, 48, 51, 74, 173, 319
Luntz, 203
Lurye, 74
Luzin, 190

M

Madan, 124
Malishevski, 309
Malkin, 75, 256, 260, 264, 269, 278, 279, 280, 281, 283, 288
Malot, 4, 40, 41, 155
Mamre, 63, 232
Maretski, 75, 189
Margolis, 277
Marshak, 269, 278
Maze, 75
Mazeh, 153
Mechanik, 184
Meir the Slovensker, 46
Meirson, 190
Meltser, 41, 75, 270, 324
Meltzer, 29, 144, 145, 149, 188, 190, 208, 209
Melzer, 272, 282
Mendel, 201
Mendel der Pochter, 152
Mendel the postman, 201
Mendelevits, 75
Mendes, 75
Meshorer, 207
Meyerson, 75
Meyirson, 317
Mezia, 190
Mickevich, 286
Mikhaylashov, 312
Mikhaylovska, 315
Miler, 75
Milikovski, 75, 271

Miller, 138, 139
Minkowitch, 153
Mintzer, 41
Mishkin, 75, 195
Mitskevitsh, 275
Mlot, 75, 271
Moka, 154
Molot, 45, 54, 75
Monya der Zeigermacher, 152
Mordchovich, 14
Morduhovich, 75, 76
Morris, 138, 139, 147, 149
Moshe der steiptzer, 152
Mostovich, 286
Movshovich, 76
Murtshanka, 313
Mussolini, 57, 58, 59

N

Nachshon, 210, 211
Nahum the Hairdresser, 284
Namiot, 115, 119
Namyot, 76
Naroshevitz, 155
Narushevich, 76
Nazatir, 149
Neria, 110
Neriya, 261
Neshri, 115, 123, 124, 135, 162
Neurath, 59
Nissinov, 313
Nul, 42

O

Olshaner, 45
Osherovits, 76

P

Padzelver, 315, 316
Palachin, 34
Paretski, 4, 76
Paretzki, 29
Partzki, 153
Pashkovski, 314
Pecker, 149
Peker, 76
Perach, 130

Perelman, 66, 76, 276, 278, 279, 285
Peres, 312
Perlman, 1, 3, 249, 256, 257, 260, 269, 276, 277, 279, 288
Perlman-Margolis, 279
Perlman–Rapoport, 256
Perski, 4, 9, 12, 15, 21, 22, 28, 29, 40, 41, 42, 45, 47, 48, 55, 76, 77, 96, 99, 123, 153, 156, 167, 179, 183, 184, 215, 217, 250, 264, 266, 324
Persky, 130, 131, 152
Petacci, 59
Pierson, 144
Pilsudski, 39, 277
Pinchas the smith, 13
Pobal, 311, 315
Podolski, 77
Podvarski, 77, 78
Polak, 8, 17, 41, 78, 165, 206, 257, 260
Pollak, 256, 285
Pomashnik, 55
Porat, 1, 12, 18, 20, 41, 44, 50, 51, 54, 64, 234, 254, 273, 320
Porat – Perlman, 265
Portnoy, 149
Potashnick, 95
Potashnik, 8, 12, 16, 17, 39, 41, 47, 78, 99, 104, 123, 124, 127, 135, 142, 148, 152, 174, 180, 181, 212, 213, 214
Pozniak, 78, 189
Pravidla, 324
Protasievitsh, 289
Providla, 78
Pruss, 286
Pucznik, 42, 43
Putashnik, 194
Puter, 21
Putshnik, 29

R

Rabinovitch, 30, 32
Rabinovitsh, 146, 270
Rabinovitz, 149
Radushevski, 78
Raeder, 59
Rahmilevich, 78
Ralbag, 145
Rapoport, 38, 78, 256, 258
Rappaport, 8, 56
Rappoport, 194, 195
Ratzkin, 14
Rayher, 78
Reches, 129
Reines, 128
Reymont, 286
Ribbentrop, 59
Riff, 149
Rivkind, 101, 124, 149
Robinson, 186
Rodinski, 102
Rogosin, 148
Rogovin, 8, 14, 15, 40, 41, 42, 43, 44, 45, 47, 48, 52, 55, 78, 79, 123, 131, 132, 133, 138, 139, 144, 147, 149, 152, 182, 190, 191, 192, 193, 223, 324, 325
Rogowin, 154, 156
Rogozin, 93, 94
Rommel, 58
Roosevelt, 58
Rosen, 153
Rosenberg, 59, 194, 195, 224
Rosenbloom, 146
Rothstein, 138, 139, 147, 149
Rotshtein, 148
Rozen, 30, 79
Rozenberg, 79
Rozensheyn, 79
Rozenstein, 164, 165
Rubin, 79, 139, 142, 148
Rubinchik, 45
Rubinshteyn, 79
Rubinstein, 44, 123, 189, 193, 222
Rudanski, 194, 224
Ruden, 149
Rudenski, 79
Rudensky, 144
Rudin, 126, 127, 146, 148
Ruditski, 146
Rudnia, 79, 187
Rudnick, 146
Rudnitski, 80
Rudnitzki, 29
Rudy, 149
Ruhamkin, 80
Rutkovska, 313
Rybko, 325

S

Sacharov, 34
Salitenik, 255
Saliternik, 41, 254
Salizh, 52
Sapir, 80
Sauckel, 59
Savitski, 80
Schirach, 59
Schmerl der Melamed, 152
Schwartz, 223
Schwartzberg, 17, 96, 99, 110, 122, 165, 179, 206
Segalovich, 80
Seligman, 149
Sepetnitski, 80
Serlin, 99
Sevez, 59
Seyss-Inquart, 59
Shabtay-Note, 80
Shadal, 74
Shafir, 96
Shaker, 14, 80
Shalman, 80
Shani, 228
Shapir, 60, 115, 120, 123, 135
Shapira, 100, 106, 111, 112, 128, 217, 229, 230, 325
Shapiro, 85, 90, 126, 127, 142, 149, 150, 229
Sharira, 193, 218
Shaybl, 80
Sheiniuk, 164
Shepsenwol, 231, 232
Shepshenwol, 96
Shertok, 90
Sheyniuk, 45, 80
Shick, 85
Shif, 80, 195, 196, 210, 227
Shiff, 55, 115, 189
Shimkin, 80
Shimshelevich, 80
Shimshelewitz, 153
Shimshilevich, 4
Shishko, 80, 96, 98, 120, 123
Shishku, 135
Shklar, 80
Shlomo der Chassid, 152
Shlosberg, 80
Shmerkovich, 80
Shmid, 80

Shmit, 325
Shmukler, 81
Shnayder, 44, 81
Shneider, 55, 149
Shneyer, 287
Shoker, 167
Sholman, 225
Sholokhov, 286
Sholom Aleichem, 201
Sholom Ash, 286
Sholomovitz, 56
Shptsiner, 81
Shriro, 81
Shulevich, 81
Shulman, 226
Shuster, 21, 29, 81
Shvarts, 81
Shvartsberg, 81
Sienkevich, 286
Silverman, 138, 139, 142, 147, 149
Simcha der Kneiper, 152
Simernitski, 45, 81
Sipkin, 149
Skaliot, 96
Skliot, 21, 28, 29, 41, 43, 51, 54
Skloot, 147, 149
Sklot, 183, 184
Sklut, 81, 82, 325
Slisternick, 96
Slitarnik, 99, 103, 115, 123, 190
Sliternick, 96
Slyovski, 29
Slyowski, 42, 43
Smith, 59
Solof, 146
Soloveichik, 150
Soloveitchik, 128, 172
Sondrak, 325
Sosenski, 82
Sosinski, 177
Spector, 82
Speer, 59
Spektor, 45
Stalin, 16, 277, 279
Staritski, 15, 49
Stark, 138, 139, 147, 149
Stauffenberg, 58
Steinman, 149

Stekolshchik, 82
Stolar, 82
Streicher, 59
Susloparov, 59

T

Tabachovich, 14
Tabachowitz, 167
Tabahovits, 82
Tabakhovitsh, 250
Taf, 82
Taller, 282, 284, 287
Teif, 189
Tishkevitsh, 286
Tiuf, 82
Tolstoy, 286
Topp, 191, 192
Torski, 153
Trechinski, 288
Trutner, 186
Tsar Nicholas, 277
Tsart, 82, 264, 277
Tsiberski, 217
Tsimerman, 82
Tsipin, 82
Tsirulnik, 82
Tyshkevitch, 259
Tyshkevitsh, 278
Tyshkievitsh, 289
Tyszkiewicz, 201
Tzart, 14, 28, 29, 183, 184
Tzekinski, 325
Tzigayner, 284
Tzubner, 216

U

Unterman, 110, 197
Untermann, 150

V

Vayner, 82
Vaysbord, 82, 83
Velvel, 83, 167
Vidrovich, 83
Vikentiy, 315
Vinogradov, 34
Vitold, 273

Vlasov, 16
Volkin, 83
Volkomich, 83
Volkovich, 4, 27, 42, 47
Volkovitch, 5, 22, 54, 55
Volokovitch, 55
Volozhiner, 150, 240, 253, 277, 278
Vosip, 313
Vrubel, 325, 326
Vytautas, 273

W

Wand-Polak, 164, 165, 206, 207
Weiner, 170, 171
Weisbord, 8, 39, 40, 168, 190
Weisman, 149
Widrowitz, 191
Wolkovich, 123
Wolkowitch, 153
Wolkowitz, 29, 30, 171
Wolper, 124, 125, 127, 138, 139, 142, 146, 147, 148, 149

Y

Yaakobi, 93
Yafa, 12
Yaguello, 273
Yankelevich, 83
Yatskaviets, 313
Yatzanin, 34
Yazgur, 83
Yiche-Ber, 286
Yoda, 39, 43
Yofe, 83
Yonah, 144
Yosef the Expeditor, 29
Youdelovitz, 145
Yourovitsh, 314
Yukhis, 326
Yurshaner, 160
Yurshner, 83
Yuzefovich, 83

Z

Zak, 112
Zalb, 83
Zara, 315

Zarin, 4, 83
Zart, 153
Zelinger, 100
Zeltser, 83
Zhale, 83
Zhurkevitsh, 272
Ziankevitsh, 313
Zigel, 189

Zimmerman, 153
Zinberg, 88
Zirolnik, 153
Ziskind, 33, 181
Zissel, 319
Zlotnik, 83
Zukerkopf, 41
Zwobner, 123, 124